D1550521

# Women, Resistance
and Revolution

# Women, Resistance and Revolution

*A History of Women and Revolution
in the Modern World*

SHEILA ROWBOTHAM

PANTHEON BOOKS

A Division of Random House, New York

First American Edition

Copyright© 1972 by Sheila Rowbotham

*Library of Congress Cataloging in Publication Data*

Rowbotham, Sheila.
Women, Resistance and Revolution.

Bibliography: p. 249
1. Woman—History and condition of women.
2. Women and socialism. I. Title.
HQ1154.R77 1973     322.4'4     72-3404
ISBN 0-394-47545-3

Manufactured in the United States of America

# Contents

# Acknowledgements

The idea of writing this book came partly out of discussions with Arielle Aberson who was killed very soon after in a car crash, and it is in her memory.

For help in finding some of the sources, thanks to Sue Finch, Christopher Hill, Thomas Hodgkin, Bessie Leigh, Betty Patterson, Penny Pollit, Alan Rooney, Marion Sedley, Wilhelmina Schroeder, Ken Weller, Barbara Winslow.

Also, for permission to consult their libraries: the Institute for Social History, Amsterdam, and the Society for Anglo-Chinese Understanding, and the T.U.C.

For laboriously reading the manuscript and telling me what they thought about it, love and gratitude to Arsenal Women's Liberation Workshop Group, Stephen Bodington, Sharon Collins, Suzie Fleming, Roberta Hunter Henderson, Vivien Lewes, Laura Mulvi, Neil Middleton, Juliet Mitchell, Jean McCrindle, Teresa Moriarty, Bob Rowthorn, Anne Scott, Amanda Sebestyen, Dorothy and Edward Thompson, Micheline Victor, Lucy Waugh and David Widgery, who also lived with it. But I didn't take notice of all their criticism and they are not responsible for the final version.

Thanks to Dr Michael Leibson, the cake stall on Ridley Road, Starcross Comprehensive, and the Workers' Education Association who gave me the employment to survive while I was writing it, and to the people in women's liberation and the socialist movement who gave me the confidence to do it.

I am grateful for permission to quote from Elizabeth Sutherland, *The Youngest Revolution*, Pitman & Sons Ltd; R. A. J. Schlesinger, *Changing Attitudes in Soviet Russia*, Routledge & Kegan Paul Ltd and Humanities Press; Chin P'ing Mei, *The Adventurous History of Hsi Men and his Six Wives*, translated by Arthur Waley, The Bodley Head; Edith Thomas, *The Women Incendiaries*, Editions Gallimard; M. Kent Geiger, *The Family in Soviet Russia*, Harvard University Press; Maxwell Bodenheim, 'To a Revolutionary Girl', in *New Masses*, an Anthology, International Publishers; Jessica Smith, *Women in Soviet Russia*, Vanguard Press Inc.; Felix Greene, description of a divorce trial in China, *The Wall has Two Sides*, Jonathan Cape; Helen Foster Snow, *Women in China*, Mouton; Keith Thomas, *Women and the Civil War Sects, Past and Present*; Francis Fytton, 'Manifestation', *Stand* magazine; Roxane Witke, 'Mao Tse-tung, Women and Suicide', *China Quarterly*; Society for Anglo-Chinese Understanding publications; Shrew Collective; London Women's Liberation Workshop; Comment; the International Institute for Social History for use of the minutes of the East London Federation of the Suffragettes; Sheffield Public Library for use of the Carpenter Collection. And to the workers of the British Museum who searched in the stacks of the B.M. to find them all for me.

# Introduction

This is not a proper history of feminism and revolution. Such a story necessarily belongs to the future and will anyway be a collective creation. Instead I have tried to trace the fortunes of an idea. It is a very simple idea, but one with which we have lost touch, that the liberation of women necessitates the liberation of all human beings. I have tried to describe the circumstances in which such a notion could come about, and indicate something of how it has manifested itself. I have tried to pursue it as a living reality as it came into and out of the lives of particular men and women, and as a political reality as they organized to act upon it. I wanted to communicate the manner in which it has changed and appeared in a different guise, assuming new shapes when it became practical. Even so there is much which I have not mentioned and much that I do not know and more that I couldn't fit in. It will be a useful book only if it is repeatedly dismantled and reconstructed as part of a continuing effort to connect feminism to socialist revolution. It contains no blueprint for what we should do in the future; it simply puts together some of the things we have already done, so that we can understand a little more clearly where we are starting from. It is a tentative first step towards correcting the masculine bias in the story we have inherited of our revolutionary past.

Women have come to revolutionary consciousness by means of ideas, actions and organizations which have been made predominantly by men. We only know ourselves in societies in which masculine power and masculine culture dominate, and can only aspire to an alternative in a revolutionary movement which is male defined. We are obscured in 'brotherhood' and the liberation of 'mankind'. The language which makes us invisible to 'history' is not coincidence, but part of our real situation in a society and in a movement which we do not control. Our subordination is so deeply internalized that it has taken women's liberation to reveal it. The pain, emotional violence, and intense rejection of the male-defined revolutionary movement, which some women have expressed as part of a specifically feminist consciousness, are inseparable from that invisibility.

There are two immediate responses to this pain. One is subservient acquiescence to the male revolutionary's definition of our role. Out of 'loyalty' or the need to preserve 'unity' we allow our daring and imagination, so briefly and recently released, to be once again restricted and held down, contenting ourselves with token acknowledgement. The other response is an angry denial that 'their' movement is anything to do with us. We decide to seek our new selves alone. While the first lets go of the explicitly female consciousness and pretends that the specific oppression of women does not exist, the second isolates female consciousness from any other movement for liberation and pretends that men are not oppressed in the world outside.

The paralysis of a male-defined revolutionary movement is as evident as the paralysis of a consciousness which can comprehend only the liberation of women. Both are caught in their own particularity. The attempt to touch, recognize and communicate the effort to go beyond this paralysis in the past is part of the task of working it through in theory and practice in the future.

Without a movement as a reference point, without the ideas expressed in that movement, and without the constant support and help of the women I know in women's liberation, I would never have written more than a fragment of this. Women's liberation brings to all of us a strength and audacity we have never before known.

I am not however speaking *for* anyone. What I write is simply a contribution to a permanent communication, which comes from me personally but only exists because of other women. An individual woman who appears as the spokeswoman for the freedom of all women is a pathetic and isolated creature. She is inevitably either crushed or contained as a sexual performer. No woman can stand alone and demand liberation *for* others because by doing so she takes away from other women the capacity to organize and speak for themselves. Also she presents no threat. An individual 'emancipated' woman is an amusing incongruity, a titillating commodity, easily consumed. It is only when women start to organize in large numbers that we become a political force, and begin to move towards the possibility of a truly democratic society in which every human being can be brave, responsible, thinking and diligent in the struggle to live at once freely and unselfishly. Such a democracy would be communism, and is beyond our present imagining.

## CHAPTER 1

# Impudent Lasses

By God, if wommen hadde written stories,
As clerkes han with-inne hir oratories,
They wolde han written of men more wickednesse
Than all the mark of Adam may redresse.

Chaucer, The Wife of Bath's Prologue,
*The Canterbury Tales*

It may be thought strange and unbecoming in our sex to show ourselves by way of petitions. . . . [But] . . . Christ has purchased us at as deare a rate as he hath done Men, and therefore requireth the like obedience for the same mercy as of men.

. . . In the free enjoying of Christ in His own laws and flourishing estate of Church and Commonwealth consisteth one happinesse of women as of men.

. . . Women are sharers in the common calamities that accompany both Church and Commonwealth, when oppression is exercised over the Church or Kingdome, wherein they live; and an unlimited power has been given to prelates to exercise over the consciences of women as well as men, witnesse Newgate, Smithfield, and other places of persecution wherein women as well as men have felt . . . their fury.

Women's petition to Parliament, 1642
– against Popery

Our desire is to shut up our kitchen doores from eight in the morning till eight at night every second Tuesday in the month unless some extraordinary business happen to keep them open; if so to enjoy an equivalent and conscientious liberty another day, but our City Dames are so nice that they will put in anything for an exception, and in case of rainy weather they may detaine us . . . therefore let it raine, haile, snow or blow never so fast; we would have leave, at our discretion, to take up our coats and steere our course as we please.

> Maid's Petition, 1647 – against the
> 'uncontrollable impositions of our surly Madams'

[Women] appear so despicable in your eyes as to be thought un-worthy to petition or represent our grievances. . . . Can you imagine us to be so sottish or stupid, as not to perceive, or not to be sensible when daily those strong defences of our Peace and Welfare are broken down and trod underfoot by force or arbitrary power? Would you have us keep at home in our houses while men . . . are fetched out of their beds and forced from their houses by souldiers, to the affrighting and undoing of themselves, and their wives, children and families. . . . Shall we sit still and keep at home.

> Petition in favour of Lilburne's release, 1647

We have for many years chattered like Cranes and mourned like Doves.

> Petition against the law on debt, 1651

> When Men unto their Wives make long beseeches
> The Women domineer who wear the Breeches
> Their tongues, their hands, their wits to work they set,
> And never leave till they the conquest get.
> . . . Nothing will serve them when their finger itches
> Until such time they have attained the Breeches.
>
> 'The Women's Fegaries shewing the great endeavour
> they have used for obtaining of the Breeches', c. 1675

If you love yourselves you must love your Wives and Children which are part of yourselves, and this suggests to you the demand they have upon your Labour and Industry in order to make a decent and comfortable Provision for them.

> Rev. Edward Whitehead,
> 'The Use and Importance of Early Industry', 1753

---

Beginnings are hard to find. People don't see themselves as beginners. How are they to know what comes ahead? They can see behind them not in front. There is no 'beginning' of feminism in the sense that there is no beginning to defiance in women. But there is a beginning of feminist possibility – even before it is conceived as such. Female resistance has taken several historical shapes.

'You have stepped out of your place,' the Calvinist church fathers in the Massachusetts Bay colony told Anne Hutchison in the mid-seventeenth century. 'You have rather been a husband than a wife, and a preacher than a hearer, and a magistrate than a subject, and so you have thought to carry all things in Church and Commonwealth as you would and have not been humbled for it.'[1]

They worked hard at humbling her. She had gathered round her a group of followers, mostly women. They met together and Anne Hutchison preached on texts, criticized some of the ministers, and became respected for her knowledge of scripture and of healing herbs. She believed every individual should aspire to direct communion with God and that God dwelt in every human being. She upset Calvinist dogma, political differentiation, and masculine superiority. She was accordingly tried by both civil and religious authority. Pregnant and ill, at one stage while she was being questioned she almost collapsed, but they wouldn't let her sit down. The governor of the colony merely noted tersely in his record of the trial: 'Her countenance disclosed some bodily infirmity.' Finally she faltered and confessed to heresy. But they were still not satisfied. 'Her repentance is not in her countenance.' She was banished from the colony. Her fearlessness, her knowledge of scripture, her eloquence infuriated them all the more because she was a woman. *They wouldn't have been angry at all if she had been a man.*

Anne Hutchison was not alone in her insubordination; Richard Hubberthorne, a Quaker, was a more tolerant man than the governor of Massachusetts Bay in the 1650s. But the most tolerant of men know where to draw the line. Travelling through England Richard drew it rather firmly when he encountered Mildred, one of the group called ranters who emphasized uncompromisingly the direct communion of true believers to God. He called her 'an impudent lass that said she was above the apostles'.[2]

It is apparent that Anne and Mildred were far from being the first women to question their place in the world and aspire to something better. However, the context and language in which they expressed their aspirations represented the beginning of completely new ways of proceeding. Ideas of insubordination fell on fertile ground in the seventeenth century. People were finding new footholds and climbing at a great pace. Puritanism could give their presumption a justification and confidence which made it much more dangerous to all those who cherished the established state of things. Time and industry appeared every day to produce new knowledge, Jonah came crying out of the belly of the whale – Nature, Reason, Justice, Rights, Liberty, Property and Freedom! There were changes in the organization of work, in the scope of trade, in the rhythm of industry. There was a protracted struggle in parliament, a civil war, a series of republican experiments. People used old principles only to find them transformed by touching this impatient reality. Anne and Mildred were just part of a much wider revolution. The growth of early capitalism, of puritanism and of new ideas of reason and science caused people to see many questions in a new light. This was true not only of religious and political ideas of order and unity, of economic ideas about poverty and idleness; it also allowed the expression of doubt about the nature of relationships between men and women, parents and children, the family and society, which the Aristotelean and Old Testament traditions had kept buried for centuries. The fact of revolution gave them a new authority. While a succession of heresies had challenged the hierarchy of clearly defined authorities – God, king, priest, husband, father, master – they had never presumed legitimacy before. They had lurked only in by-ways, murmured in taverns, whipped the crowd up at fairs, crept slyly into the universities, been defrocked, sought communion with nature, heard the music of the spheres, worshipped the sun, pursued the millennium and been hanged, drawn and quartered or burned at the stake for prophesying the possibility of heaven on earth.

Now the prophets of heaven had emerged, tempered, stern, serious and bitter, killed a king and set themselves up as the rightful government of the Commonwealth, thus upsetting the establishment and certainty of order, subordination and authority for ever. They provided the prophetesses with an amazing justification for impudence. Thus, just when the ground was being taken from under everyone's feet and a man needed a bit of peace and privacy in his own home, who should start spouting texts and interpreting God's word but the women. This seemed a preposterous and unnatural development to the man. Women's subordination was apparently part of the immutable order of things. It was well known that with a woman, a dog and a walnut tree, the more you beat 'em the better they be. Equally 'natural' was the duplicity of women. According to proverbial wisdom they were saints in the church, angels in the streets, devils in the kitchen and apes in bed. Sexual 'greediness' was a common theme in seventeenth-century drama. The preachers warned men to take heed of young women and of prophetesses. Sexuality and female theorizing combined dangerously.

There had been impudence before. The difference was that now people seemed to be acting on it. Within medieval society there had been isolated social and political rebellion, but it had proved capable always of containing discontent and absorbing the restless in the old order of things. The effect of the puritan revolution is sometimes discussed in terms of whether it made life 'better' for women. This is a confusion. It is not so much that it made it 'better' but that it made it different, and the effects of change were felt differently by women of various classes. Feudalism and Catholicism circumscribed possibility. The life of the peasant woman consumed in labour or childbearing, with few rights over her property or person, did not lend itself to free inquiry. Perhaps she might escape, but only to join the travelling flocks of whores who accompanied the medieval armies. An adventurous life, but uncertain and perilous, where her main preoccupation would be disease, and where death hung about her like a proprietor.

But even the aristocratic woman, whose life was not so close to necessity, was simply passed from father to husband, the land she brought was more important than her feelings, and her 'right' to say what she wanted went unconsidered. She came into her own a little if she was widowed, because she had property. Widows were notorious for their ambition towards independence and their lascivious delight in young husbands. But these privileged women were unlikely to make their subordination a matter for confrontation. First, there were too many retreats for them, comfortable pockets and pouches where they could lead a respected if restricted life. Second, their powerlessness was masked in elaborate ceremony and ritual which paid them court and gave them the sense of being venerated. Third, there was little in the intellectual world of the Catholic Church which could give them the means of challenging the way things had apparently always been. Rather than conflicting with masculine versions of their nature and situation, these women accepted the circumscribed dignity and security of the nunnery or the court. Sheltering behind the nun's habit, or perhaps the elaborate homage of courtly love, they evaded realization of their own powerlessness. It was as well, as they had little means of effecting material change, and the suffering would have been too great to bear. At one side there is the elevation and formalization of woman as the object of sublimated sensuality, at the other there is the constant religious malediction of the lewdness of woman. When Joan heard her voices and led an army they burned her for her pains. Christine de Pisan led no army. She simply said drily of the view of women in *Roman de la Rose*, the manifesto of courtly love, that it was not the women who had written the books. She had no army or popular following and was treated more gently.

Where could an alternative conception of women's potentiality take root? Female inferiority could be upheld within medieval Christianity by the persistent connection to animality, which Eve was held to represent, and hence with baseness. Only when she remained physically unfulfilled was the woman worthy of worship. Respect was due to the Virgin, but to man belonged the higher world of the spirit. Some medieval scholars even wondered if women had an immortal soul. Women meanwhile made their own clearings and lived as best they could. Catholicism had a way of accommodating the tortured psyche. Margery Kempe, a fourteenth-century mystic, saw devils after a difficult childbirth, communed with heaven, and subsequently '. . . never desired to commune fleshly with her husband, for the debt of matrimony was so abominable to her that she would rather have eaten or drunk the ooze and muck from the gutter than consent to any fleshly communing save only for obedience'.[3] Released from her husband, after a brief theological commotion with the local bishops, she proved her orthodoxy and became a wandering preacher, and was respected for her saintliness.

An impetus towards feminism came with the renaissance cult of the woman of poise, grace, beauty, wit and erudition. Renaissance writers envisaged a wider, more humane education for the girls of the aristocracy. This only affected the fortunate few, but it established the themes of education and emancipation, which were to be crucial demands of feminism. More explosive, and provoking more repression at the time, was the relationship of women to the numerous heresies, millenarian and otherwise. There was much confusion in the fervent imaginings of heretical doctrine on the nature and position of women. They at once denied the flesh, and demanded its fullest expression for the faithful, were deeply suspicious of women, but allowed them equal status as believers. This ambiguity, which heresy repeatedly emphasized, at source, was a dilemma within Christianity – rejection of direct experience for trust of the will in certain revealed propositions about God. The natural universe was associated with pain and peril. The church was rock and security. Defence of the church was essential. Outside was unknown, pagan, uncivilized, animal, spontaneous, dangerous. In love-making as in the extremes of religious ecstasy human beings encountered this beyond. Here individual isolation in its moment of absolute intensity broke out of itself to be at one with the self beyond. Man interpreted the world and identified woman with experience beyond the boundaries. For him she came to represent the nature he feared. She gave birth, she was fertility. But the man who was called heretic, who had to define himself in opposition to authoritatively received truth, was in a peculiarly uncertain no-man's-land. Just as homosexuality, or stepping out of 'manliness', was continually connected by opponents to doctrinal aberration, orgiastic sensuality and ascetic devotion were also associated with heresy. It was the fear of extreme emotional experience where pleasure and pain interpenetrated, and His body was commonly accessible to the unlearned, ignoble, impure. The heretic displayed a consequent nervousness towards women and found support in the Bible. However, despite the distrust of female sexuality, despite the narrow scope the sect offered them, heresy proved consistently popular with a section of medieval women. These were women in the growing towns, freed from constant labour but not admitted to the privileges of convent or court. They found in the heretical sect an important outlet, emotional, intellectual and otherwise, which they could not find elsewhere. Originally attracting many unmarried women and widows in the upper strata of urban society, they proved increasingly popular with the wives of small merchants and artisans and it was their popular character as much as their theological content that upset the orthodox powers. The two aspects of the pre-puritan religious sect appear in English Lollardy. Women drummed Lollard preachers who denounced female concupiscence out of town, but the wives and daughters of early 'protestants' were reading the newly printed English Bible for themselves and interpreting texts.

Female preachers and martyrs figured prominently in the heretical sects. Not surprisingly women messiahs appeared to claim the millennium for femininity. The 'beginnings' of feminism could perhaps be located not with Anne and Mildred but with Guillemine of Bohemia at the end of the thirteenth century, who, believing that the work of redemption had not been accomplished by Christ for women, and that Eve had yet to be saved, created round her a woman's church which attracted women of the people as well as the wives of the upper bourgeoisie and the aristocracy. The sect she left was denounced by the Inquisition in the early fourteenth century. This feminist impetus which called into question woman's part in nature, which conceived of her in direct communion with God, and gave her the authority of interpretation and the responsibility of prophecy, was to develop into another tendency in the liberation of women. Secularized later it resulted in startling conceptions which abolished God and replaced him with Love.

By the sixteenth century the traditional retreats are becoming blocked. Clearings become hard to find. Religious and secular authorities had become increasingly bureaucratic and were less able to allow for mystical eccentricity. In England the closing down of religious houses meant the convent was no longer possible. Alarm at urban growth, the insecurity of the woollen industry, fear of social upheaval and vagabondage made the lives of would-be Margery Kempes hazardous. As the pattern of industry changed men looked jealously at the traditional women's trades. The wife of Bath would have had a rough time of it competing with men in the sixteenth century. The break up of agricultural communities meant that the tolerance in the countryside of pre-marital sex, as long as a couple was later secured by the church sacrament, was replaced by a new intransigence towards women's sexuality. Unwanted children in the town meant money and trouble.

Judging by the tone of the popular literature of the bourgeoisie in the towns, their wives were by no means passive and docile creatures. There are continual complaints about the shamelessness and insubordination of women. The two were almost synonymous. Much of this can be dismissed no doubt as the product of a new market with a public that enjoyed a salacious tale with a smack of moralism. But it was also an unmistakable indication that the old mechanisms of social control were beginning to confront conditions with which they could no longer cope. It was not so much that men in the sixteenth century encountered new problems, but they encountered them on a scale and at a velocity which made them appear completely out of control. When commentators denounced unmarried mothers who were 'so little ashamed',[4] it was the lack of shame they really minded. The complaints about the companions of incorrigible rogues, 'doxies', and women pedlars or 'bawdy baskets' selling themselves along with their wares were not so much that they'd never been seen before but that the authorities didn't know what to do with them. Greater mobility and the changes in both countryside and towns presented the Tudors with a new degree of wandering poverty. Their frantic Poor Law documents express that bewilderment. As towns got bigger too it became increasingly difficult to know what everyone was doing in them. An anxious proclamation of 1547 forbade the women of London to 'meet together to babble and talk', and ordered husbands to 'keep their wives in their houses'.[5] Enforcement was another problem.

Simultaneous with the breakdown of the traditional social structures which had contained the aspirations of women, the forces which promised a new potentiality grew stronger. When in the seventeenth century the puritan revolution unleashed so many heretics, babblers and talkers upon the world, it would have been indeed surprising if some impudent lasses, like Mildred, who had been forced to keep their place, sit in silence, obey with humility, and bide their time, had not decided to join in. While impatient and radical thinkers challenged so many authorities, judged their betters, expected to be able to consent before being governed and even taught that all were equal, women tentatively started to take some of these ideas to themselves. Within the self-governing religious communities of the puritan sect they found a certain limited equality and a larger scope for self-expression. Here the Lord could pour out his spirit to all alike. The poor lace-maker could become God's handmaiden. Having got rid of the priest and proclaimed the priesthood of all believers, why confine divine inspiration to men? Anna Trapnel fasted, prophesied, and in 'The Cry of a Stone' declared that 'Whom the Son makes free, they are free indeed'.[6] If the only criterion was individual conscience why couldn't women challenge their husbands' and fathers' right to instruct them in what to believe and their power to control how they behaved. To the horror of Anglicans and Presbyterians, for whom it was anathema that those 'who lie in the same bed . . . should yet be of two churches',[7] puritan women not only chose their own beliefs but actually divorced their husbands for spiritual deviation. The notion that the authority of fathers and husbands should rest on agreement like the authority of the state, that the husband had no more right to control the wife's conscience than the magistrate had to coerce the man's, persisted. Though by no means popular with many supporters of the Protectorate it was to outlast the Commonwealth of the seventeenth century and in many legal guises find itself chased through the courts in subsequent centuries. Like the Quaker George Fox's idea that male domination belongs to sin and that in the new life men and women will be equals, it has still to be fully realized.

The implications of these notions went beyond the sects even at the time. A pamphlet called 'The Women's sharpe revenge' appeared in 1640 criticizing anti-feminist writings. Its full title was 'The Women's sharpe revenge: Or an answer to Sir Seldome Sober that writ those railing pamphlets called the Juniper and Crab-tree, lectures, etc. Being a sound Reply and full citation of those Bookes: with an Apology in this case for the defence of us women. Performed by Mary Tattle-well and Joan Hit-him-home, Spinsters. 1640.' Tattle-well and Hit-him-home protested both against the double standard of sexual morality and the restricted and confined nature of the education permitted to women. They were emphatic that all critics of women were men who had either had no success in love-making, or had been unfortunate enough to marry shrews. They quoted scripture in their defence, an old trick, pointing out that women weren't created to be slaves or vassals. After all, they didn't come out of men's heads 'thereby to command him', but neither did they come 'out of his foote to be trod upon'. With irrefutable logic they showed how women had come 'out of his side to be fellow-feeler; equal and companion'.[8] Though they undeniably demolished contemporary anti-feminists who used dubious arguments to prove that women were more prone to evil than goodness because they had been 'made of a knobby crooked rib', even such militants as Tattle-well and Hit-him-home didn't demand a say in government. The women of the puritan revolution were still incapable of expressing their claims in political terms. There was as yet no political feminist justification, though a moral one was beginning to develop. The women petitioners to the Long Parliament in 1642 apologized for petitioning against popery. 'We doe it not out of any self-conceit or pride of heart, as seeking to equall ourselves with men, either in Authority or Wisdome.'⁹

Puritanism effected a species of moral improvement in the position of women. Within a very confined sense it allowed women a certain restricted dignity. It provided an impetus for a more humane concept of relationships between the sexes, protesting against wife-beating and opposing rituals like churching which had emphasized the uncleanness and animal baseness of women. By regarding morality as an affair of the inner spirit rather than the opinion of the world or the apparatus of government, it provided a means of challenging the double standard of sexual morality. Essential to radical-puritan democracy was the idea of the individual as the independent owner of his own person and capacities, with the right to resist invasion and violation. This had obvious implications for women. Within puritan democratic thinking too was the assumption that women, as human beings, had certain inalienable rights to civil and religious liberty.

However, politically in the puritan attitude to authority there was an important ambiguity. Apart from extreme radicals and millenarians the majority would not have considered that the idea of government by consent implied any threat to the authority of the father. Ideas of liberty were soon hedged about. Popular consent was conceived as meaning the consent of heads of households. Just as the communism of the early settlers in America included only those heads of households in the covenant of the commonwealth and provoked a movement of the young men in revolt, liberty was interpreted as the liberty of fathers. It was argued that the franchise must depend on independence from the will of others. Those who were bound either by a wage contract or the wife's terms in a marriage contract had handed over part of their rights and forfeited the privilege of the franchise. Thus the idea of participation in government was restricted to those who owned property and to men. Puritan democracy spoke not for all peasants, not for apprentices, or the inferior sort of people, but for the yeomen farmers, the small master craftsmen in the towns. It certainly didn't include women, not even the more privileged women. Instead they were 'included' in the franchise of their masters.

Indeed, a combination of factors served actually to reinforce the authority of heads of households in the seventeenth century.

Politically they were now the crucial link through to the state, acting as intermediaries between the central government and their own
dependants and servants. The chain of authority was not removed;
it was changed and secularized. The father reading the Bible, instructing his family, became responsible not only for their material but for
their spiritual welfare. The worship of the Virgin, the reverence for
female saints were replaced by a stern assertion of God's fatherhood.
The economic tension of the medieval community breaking its
integument focused on the household, still an independent unit of
production but subject to the penetration of the new market relations
of early capitalism. Puritanism assumed and took for granted the
small independent concern, either farm or family business, in which
the family worked side by side and the wife could well be a partner
though still an inferior partner. But this ideal of self-sufficient
independence was rapidly ceasing to represent the new reality. The
richer yeomen's wives were already withdrawing from agricultural
labour, and in the towns, as crafts became more intensively capita-
lized, the wives of the larger tradesmen no longer worked in the
business. The roles of husband and wife were more specifically
differentiated. The external world of work became the sphere of the
man exclusively, the internal world of the family and the household
was the proper business of the woman. This was rather different
from the situation earlier amongst these middling people, when it
was customary for the young girls to do the housework while the
'housewife' attended to the family business.

At the same time changes in industrial organization affected
women's position in the structure of work. In the guilds their situation was being progressively weakened. The old protections and
privileges of widows disappeared, and as apprenticeship became
more formal the entrance of women to trades was closed. A sustained
struggle developed from the sixteenth century over the definition of
'women's work'. Some trades which had been reserved for women
were encroached upon and eventually take over by men. Brewing
was probably originally a women's trade but by the seventeenth
century brewsters (female brewers) were prohibited. In York,
despite women's resistance, men replaced them in candlemaking. As
new unprotected industries arose these became the province of
women excluded from the guilds. The textile industry was especially
suited to become 'women's work', not only by tradition but because

some of its several processes could be done at home. Though there were attempts to restrict women weavers, spinning especially was easily done by women. It had been a home industry since ancient times. The pay for this type of work was lower than the rates in regulated trades, but domestic industry was to proliferate in the eighteenth century. With every new refinement in the division of labour women found themselves allocated either a place in which they were powerless or a place in which they were more severely exploited. While their richer sisters passed out of production into leisure and domestic isolation to ape the habits of the upper classes, the women of the poor encountered merely new forms of drudgery.

Not to work, for the women of the middling people, became the mark of class superiority at the very moment when their men were establishing work as the criterion of dignity and worth. Not only was industry closed to them but their limited education made entrance into the professions impossible. The process of intellectual specialization, one of the effects of the scientific revolution, emphasized this exclusion. Here again women were confined to the lowlier, less highly paid areas of professions. This is well illustrated in medicine. As it evolved from magical art to science, requiring a more specific and theoretical learning, male doctors assumed control of the higher branches. Women surgeons finally disappear in the seventeenth century. Similarly midwifery, which had been a respected profession and for which the women who looked after the upper classes were well paid, was downgraded. The original disapproval of having a man at a birth was conveniently discarded by the rich and fashionable. Women midwives were confined to the poor. There was some resistance. Jane Sharp in *The Midwives Book* (1671) retaliated with a rejection of scientific methodology and book-learning in favour of the traditional craft lore. 'It is not hard words that perform the work, as if none understood the Art that can't understand Greek. Words are but the Shell that we oftimes break our Teeth with them to the kernel, I mean our brains to know what is the meaning of them; to have the same in our Mother-tongue would save us a great deal of needless labour.'[10] Though in 1687 Mrs Elizabeth Collier worked out a scheme for a training course for midwives it was never put into effect. In France, where similar developments had the same result, the midwives did not merely complain; they organized and formed a school of midwifery raising the status of their occupation.

This was significant of a wider difference. The persistence of Catholicism meant that the aspirations of women tended to take a secular rather than a religious form. Instead of a suspicious reaction to science, theory and the new intellectual world of emerging capitalism, feminism in France tried rather to apply reason to the advantage of women. Enlightenment has many facets. As the assumption spread that it was unwise to accept anything as true unless it could be demonstrated, and that it was possible after breaking information into several parts to proceed step by step in an orderly and rational manner to deductive knowledge of even the most complex aspect of reality, no matter how traditional and well established, new grounds for questioning the subordination of women appeared. If it could be argued that given a suitable environment and education human beings could ultimately be capable of grasping the universe, why not extend this to women. A disciple of Descartes, Mlle de Gournay, in *L'Egalité des Hommes et des Femmes* believed that the restricted education of girls accounted for their inferiority. Though this 'reasonable' feminism continuing the renaissance tradition spoke only for the more privileged women, putting their claims to compete in the opening world of the bourgeois man, politically it was to prove more effective than the religious millenarian glimpses of liberation. The demand for the access and accommodation of an upper-class intellectual elite was to meet with bitter resistance. But it had in the short term more prospect of realization than the vision of a transformed relationship between human beings and the natural environment. The demand for accommodation did not look so far ahead as the vision of liberation.

Feminist literature of this kind penetrated England during the Commonwealth and contributed to the secularization of ideas about emancipation. By the late seventeenth century, on the 'authority' of reason and 'good sense' the case that a woman was 'as good as the Man'[11] was being argued. The justification for women's rights was no longer that of being God's handmaidens or daughters of Jael but the demand to make women reasonable beings. The nature of reasonableness in a woman was still often complementary. Defoe argued they should become fit companions for their men.

In a period when a man's value was becoming the price his wits fetched him on the open market, a woman's value was harder to measure. Restrained from competing on the work market she was expected to do her business on the sex market. She could either take her wares to the exchange, protected by a marriage settlement, or she could play her stock on the kerb with Moll Flanders. Like other commodities women were subject to the flux of trade and governed by laws of supply and demand. A character in Steele's *The Tender Husband* rates a woman at her selling price. 'Ah but Brother you rate her too high. The war has fetched down the Price of Women. The whole Nation is overrun with Petticoats, our Daughters die upon our Hands ... Girls are Drugs, Sir, mere Drugs.'[12]

Just as they invested their capital in land the new accumulators put their money into women. The marriage settlement spiralled in the early eighteenth century. A family of daughters could cripple a small landowner who had made his money in the City. In the sale of daughters and the resistance which built up against it, two concepts of the family jostled one another. One came from the world of great estate where marriage was a matter of convenience; the other from the puritanism of little people now grown big and complacent. Equally contradictory notions conflicted about the worth of individual human beings. One asserted an innate value and dignity, another measured it more neatly in terms of capital, either in the form of land or stocks. But the most crucial factor in deciding the peculiar helplessness of women was the exclusion of the privileged from production. As bourgeois man justified himself through work, asserting his own industry and usefulness against the idea of aristocratic leisure, his woman's life was becoming increasingly useless. Bourgeois women did not make capitalism, they merely attached themselves to its makers and lived off their man's activity. Their dowry helped him to accumulate. Their bodies served him as ornament, toy, and mirror. Women were for relaxation.

An elaborate mythology evolved round natural feminine uselessness. The helplessness, frivolity, illogicality of female creatures was put about. A kindly paternalism cloaked women's real powerlessness. Their masters kindly protected them for their own good. They were far too weak to face the harsh, competitive world of early capitalism. In Lord Chesterfield's words, women were but 'children of a larger growth'. Confronting a world which made a mockery of kindliness men exercised their generosity on pets at home. Women's dependence provided the possibility of virtue and well-being. They became the objects of a frustrated humanity, and in the process they were deprived of the exercise of the independent human-selfness the men were claiming for themselves.

There were other aspects to this. In pornography, which in the eighteenth century expressed an unrestrained sexuality, or nature, breaking through every social convention, despising the sanctity of religion, the family, and political order, men treated women as objects in a rather different way. Pornography depends on a relationship between human beings which of necessity denies human response in the object of desire. In the eighteenth century it represented a retreat for the upper-class man from a growing self-consciousness, a search for the absolute feeling self in the absolute unfeeling thing. It was associated with a particular form of anarcho-sadistic individualism which had a curious relationship to the orderly individualism of capitalist accumulation. Its connection with nature, anarchy, energy, destruction made it apparently most threatening to bourgeois sensibility. It quite explicitly denied the concept of inviolability. It belonged to the feckless aristocrat or to the déclassé demagogue who tickled the fancy of the mob and the inferior sort of people rather than appealing to the interests of the middling people. In France there was a correlation in bourgeois intellectual groupings between opposition to *Ecole des Filles*, a seventeenth-century pornographic work, and support for the American War of Independence. Later de Sade's career is illustrative of a similar opposition. In fact though, while admitting the reality of violent human emotion, destruction and the desire to experience pain, pornography only expressed this at the level of fantasy. It challenged the hypocrisy of the bourgeois in regarding selfishness and the power to dominate others as the most essential features of manhood while taming them in the service of industry and family stability. But it never challenged selfishness or domination as the basis of sexual relations. How could it? Pornography itself would have been called into question if women had quite consciously participated. If women were explicitly and independently enjoying themselves, most of the paraphernalia of domination would dissolve. Not surprisingly, eighteenth-century pornography favours virgins. They were at an obvious disadvantage. Not surprisingly too the first recorded use of the word 'nymphomania' is in 1775. The frantic clitoris must be subdued, tamed, disciplined, taught to know its own presumption.

The vast majority of women, however, qualified for neither protection nor pornography. For them contempt went unmasked and undisguised. It was quite complacently assumed that the hardest drudgery and the lowest paid work should be reserved for the women of the poor. The 'value' of the woman was thus delicately adjusted to the 'value' of the man.

As yet nobody argued for most women. But serious and thoughtful men and women questioned morally the worthlessness of the lives of privileged women. Fénelon in France had dreamed of preparing young girls of good families to earn their living. Mary Astell in her *A Serious Proposal to the ladies* in 1694 asked them, 'How can you be content to be in the world like Tulips in a garden, to make a fine show and be good for nothing?'[13] She gathered round her a group of the most privileged women who supported her ideal for a female academy. The idea of becoming something, of having your own calling to your name, was well suited to the development of capitalism. But access to this new world of activity was barred for women of the upper classes. Education became consequently the focus of emancipation. It was the means of making a new woman. 'Had we the same literature, they would find our brains as fruitful as our bodies.'[14] This was to be a recurring theme in feminism. The exclusion from education provided an explanation of women's subordination adequate to the needs of privileged women. Access to knowledge and training was the obvious means of overcoming this. It opened the way into the closed outside world of male domination.

Because they met with resistance not only from men but from other women, the thwarted aspirations of the early feminists to compete with bourgeois man held a more generous radical impulse than the values of their men and intimated common cause with the downtrodden. Though this was still restricted to moral observation, in no sense were they equipped to emerge for practical action. A feminist *movement* at this stage would have been inconceivable. But Mary Astell's comment, 'To plead for the weak . . . seemed a generous undertaking',[15] was an early hint of the tendency in feminist thinking which later was to connect the liberation of women with the liberation of all people, and this strain in feminism was to conflict eventually with the emphasis upon absorption of a limited number of privileged women into the existing state of society.

Having confronted the fact of their exclusion the question was who was responsible for it? By the early eighteenth century another

31

current entered feminism – contempt for the male. 'Sophia' writing in 1739 used the authority of reason in an insolent manner. 'We have reason and thanks to it we can see that men are brutes.'[16] Observing bourgeois man they criticized what they saw and generalized his characteristics into a statement about men in general. Why should women take such beings as men as their criteria of what they could become? Why shouldn't they make their own criteria? Weren't men after all either fools or hypocrites? Didn't they all lie to women with their promises? Where was real feeling, real charity, real nobility, in these money grubbers with their pompous screen of morality? Many women who had acquired literacy and 'accomplishments' at the female academies, who had time on their hands, must have wondered sometimes about matters they had been taught to take for granted. Why were the terms of the contract so unequal? Why was inviolability so essential in one partner and irrelevant in the other? Who decided the forms of the contract originally? What was the relationship between woman's chastity and the security of property? Didn't the individual woman have a right to choose her husband in opposition to the ties of kin which maintained family aggrandizement by property marriage? The old puritan notion of the right to dispose of your own person as you will resurrected itself. Innocent heroines started to demand innocence in men. It was their way of claiming equality. What was right for the woman must be right for the man (though sometimes they were content simply to domesticate a rake). All these dilemmas appear in contemporary novels read avidly by literate if ill-educated women.

Richardson's book *Clarissa Harlowe* marks a further stage in this moral disaffection. Clarissa resists an arranged marriage, remains 'pure' despite being raped, and is able to extend her experience with the generalized reflection on 'one half of humanity tormenting the other and being tormented themselves in tormenting'. It was not only that woman was humiliated and oppressed; man in being compelled to act the brute lost his true manhood. Feminism becomes not just the assertion of a new hope for women, it carries hope of a new kind of world for human beings. But Clarissa can only conceive her situation as tragic irony. Women could still only lament an apparently unalterable state of affairs and hope for improvement. There is no recourse for Clarissa in the outside world, no way of challenging the basis of the alien and externally imposed 'morality'. She has only the inner voice. All she can do is transcend her situation spiritually. She is forced to fight her family and Lovelace, because they cannot allow her freedom without destroying something essential to themselves. Clarissa as yet had no way out, there was no social solution to her dilemma – though a woman corresponding with Richardson pointed out some of the radical implications of his story. Lady Bradsheigh declared the laws of society were made by men 'to justify their tyranny'[17] and argued for equality in personal relationships.

The temptation to accommodate rather than resist was strong. Some women used learning to find a privileged niche for themselves. Although some of these educated women, the original 'blue stockings', contributed to early feminist thinking, others were extremely hostile to the aspirations of other women. They enjoyed male respect and patronage in the little world of the salon. Their situation resembled that of the mulatto servant in slave society, aspiring only to be a sub-white, and thus enjoying the protection of whites. He let her into his castle but only because he could trust her not to give the key away. Mrs Barbauld, one of the blue stockings, advised women, 'Your best, your sweetest empire is to please.'[18]

For the vast majority of women there was little chance either to reason or to please to any advantage. Their history is still almost unknown. They have been regarded as static unchanging factors, as part of the background, as completely passive. They were not in fact submissive. But their resistance erupted in crime or sexual 'immorality' almost synonymous in the eyes of their betters. The revolt against 'their' world was a personal one, the attempt to shift for yourself as best you could in painfully narrow confines: stubborn women continually claiming relief from the old Poor Law, returning infected with venereal disease, coming to have their child on the parish, driven out of town to give birth under the hedges or in the removal cart. Collectively their protest is registered in the eighteenth-century food riot, the traditional manner in which the poor tried to reassert a pre-capitalist moral economy which placed need before profit, and the old community against the new state. The close connection of women to consumption meant that they figured prominently in these riots. Within this narrow necessity few had the leisure to muse on masculine superiority. Nor was this superiority evident in their men's relation to them, except in their physical strength. Their resistances were defences against new kinds of industry and

trade, they were completely unconnected with the feminist consciousness developing in a small circle of privileged women. The demands
for education or the right to be useful were nonsensical in the situation of the poor woman. More likely she would identify her interest
as the encouragement of her man in precisely the virtues capitalism
was concerned to develop amongst its labour force, sobriety, thrift,
regular work patterns, the abandonment of Saint Monday as a
'Fuddling Day'. A Sheffield cutler's wife upbraids her husband at
the end of the eighteenth century:

> Damn thee, Jack, I'll dust thy eyes up,
> Thou leads a plaguy drunken life;
> Here thou sits instead of working
> Wi' thy pitcher on thy knee;
> Curse thee, thou'd be always lurking
> And I may slave myself for thee.

Women are becoming important as consumers:

> See thee, look what stays I've gotten,
> See thee, what a pair o' shoes;
> Gown and petticoat half rotten,
> Ne'er a whole stitch in my hose . . .

But the sanctions are quite traditional:

> Thou knows I hate to broil and quarrel,
> But I've neither soap nor tea;
> Od burn thee, Jack forsake thy barrel,
> Or never more thou'st lie wi' me.[19]

There was no common experience for women of the effects of early
capitalism. Its consequences were diverse and affected different
groups of women in quite distinct ways. It tended to differentiation
of interest and expectation rather than a unifying feminist consciousness. Feminism at this stage was still aspiration and idea amongst a
small group of women; it had no possibility as movement. As for
a relationship between feminism and any conception of a completely
transformed world, this was barely visible. When it appeared it was
as mystical glimpse rather than revolutionary programme. It was
trapped in its own contradictions. The only manner of challenging
male hegemony in this life was to prophesy as the Lord's handmaiden of the next life, but the only way of seeing practical improve-

ments was to seek entrance into the barred world of men. The only way women could achieve respect and dignity was by not being women, by denying their femaleness. Virgin or blue stocking distinguished themselves as apart from other women. They were regarded not surprisingly with some suspicion by other women. The woman of the upper classes complains of her uselessness, the woman of the lower classes enjoyed no uselessness.

However, despite this conflict and the diversity of women's situation the grounds for attack were really laid in the seventeenth and eighteenth centuries. They relate closely to the values associated with early capitalism. The questioning of authority, the idea of individual responsibility and conscience as a guide for political action, the elevation of activity, the notion of control and change of the outside world, and its corollary that these changes in turn affected the characters of human beings, were as relevant for women as they were for men. The difference was in the material situation of men and women in relation to production. Indeed, the bitterness of the opposition wherever women sought to apply them to their own predicament already indicated that female impudence was even more explosive than the radical insolence of their men. In daring to invade the man's sphere the bourgeois feminist was in fact threatening the basis of the division of labour which assigned the world of reproduction and child-rearing to women and the world of production to men and thus endangered the development of that single-minded zeal to accumulate in her man. The separation of family from work had occurred before capitalism, but as industry grew in scale it appeared in its most distinct and clear form.

# CHAPTER 2

# Utopian Proposals

The education of women should always be relative to that of men. To please, to be useful to us, to make us love and esteem them, to educate us when young, to take care of us when grown up; to advise, to console us, to render our lives easy and agreeable. These are the duties of women at all times, and what they should be taught in their infancy.

J.-J. Rousseau, *Emile*

I soon noticed that the feelings I expressed were turned into jests, and that my intelligence was silenced, as if it were improper for a woman to have any. Thus I locked up in myself everything I felt. I early acquired the art of dissembling and I stifled my natural sensibility. . . . When I was caught in a lie, I never gave any excuse or explanation. I kept silent. . . . I was, and I still am convinced that women being the victim of all social institutions, are destined to misery if they make the least concession to their feelings and if in any way whatever they lose control of themselves.

Mme de Vernon in *Delphine*,
a novel by Mme de Staël

All shame is false shame. We should be a great deal better without it. Women blush because they understand. . . . Delicacy enslaves the pretty delicate dears. . . . I hate slavery: Vive la liberté. . . . I'm a Champion for the Rights of Women. . . . You may say what you will, the present system of society is radically wrong. . . . If you want to know what I would do to improve the world, I'll tell you: I'd have both sexes call things by their right name. . . . Drapery, whether wet or dry, is the most confoundly indecent thing in the world.

Harriet Freke, a caricatured revolutionary
woman in *Belinda* by Maria Edgeworth, 1808

Prostitution is the legitimate offspring of marriage and its accompanying errors. . . . Has a woman obeyed the impulse of unerring nature: so society declares war upon her, pitiless and eternal war. She must be the tamed slave, she must make no reprisals; theirs is the right of persecution, hers the duty of endurance. Society avenges herself on the criminals of her own creation.

Shelley, 'Notes on *Queen Mab*', 1813

Workers, in 1791 your fathers proclaimed the immortal Declaration of the Rights of Man, and it is thanks to that solemn Declaration that you are today free and equal men before the law. All honour to your fathers for this great achievement, but there remains for you men of 1843, a task no less great to accomplish. In your turn, free the last slaves remaining in France; proclaim the Rights of Woman, and, using the same terms as your fathers did, say: 'We, the proletariat of France, after fifty-three years' experience, acknowledge having been duly convinced that the ways in which the natural rights of women have been disregarded are the sole causes of the world's misfortunes, and we have resolved to include in our Charter woman's sacred and inalienable rights. We desire that men should give to their wives and mothers liberty and absolute equality which they enjoy themselves.'

Flora Tristan, *L'Union Ouvrière*, 1843

---

In the French Revolution the feminist aspirations of the privileged and the traditions of collective action of the unprivileged women encountered each other. They regarded each other uneasily and never really combined. But each emerged tinged with liberty, equality and fraternity and the memory of revolution. Things could never be quite the same again. Women rioting over prices in Normandy in 1789, women of the third estate in Grenoble taking action in favour of the States General, women demanding in the lists of grievances presented, better medical provision and improved education, protection of trades from male competition, women marching to Versailles to confront the baker and the baker's wife, pamphlets and petitions about divorce, prostitution, are all indications of a great acceleration of activity and consciousness.

But there was considerable ambiguity in 'liberty, equality,

fraternity' towards women. True, the thinkers of the enlightenment had questioned the immutability of apparently natural characteristics and argued for the limited access of women from the upper classes into education and professions. But there was another strain in revolutionary ideology. Rousseau's ideas of a state of nature where man was in harmony with the physical world had important liberatory implications. From this revolutionaries could oppose feeling and sensibility to authority and custom, argue for unions based on individual sex love, and support human potential against the crushing mechanical wheels of existing social institutions. But directly applied his ideas were most emphatically opposed to the intellectual and creative aspirations of women. Rousseau presents a justification for women's place in the organization of capitalist society which is at once more effective and more sophisticated than puritanism's religious homilies. He told women that 'naturally' man's world is external, woman's internal. Thus the woman had to learn that her subjection was not simply in her relationship to affairs of the spirit, to God, to politics, to production, but in her relationship with the whole external world. She is identified as part of nature. Her education should equip her to nourish and serve men, not to act of her own accord. Only in this role can she find natural fulfilment.

This version of women's 'nature' was to be expressed in certain reactionary aspects of the romantic movement. In the artistic and cultural revolt against capitalism there was considerable ambiguity about the liberation of women. In one sense romanticism demanded the freeing of human beings from repressive institutions, the realization of the true self, and thus implied a new life for women. But also men continually looked backwards seeking a golden age of naïve harmony and elevated woman as the noble primitive. With this went always an element of fear. Nature must be contained. A domesticated romanticism produced a crop of egg-faced ringleted bonneted fragile girls, which successfully internalized women's role as the helpless, emotional, hysterical angel in the house and was well suited to the division of labour in capitalist society. When she studied as much as when she prayed or worked she was still man's object, and should feel herself scrutinized by his desire. She saw herself through his eyes. She defined herself in relation to his needs, his achievements. In return she was pampered and cared for. Basking in the man's eyes, she must see in them his reflection. She only existed through him. He was her intermediary, he came before her and the cash nexus, he protected her as he protected his property, he mediated for her to his God and educated her for his delight. He made her into his idea of herself. In her he sought his lost nature. In her he located his fear of himself, by paying tribute to the instinctive intuitive sensibility he imagined she possessed. Finally he flattered her with her desire to be subdued by him, telling her that this was synonymous with womanliness.

This romantic woman cult is a complex and pervasive phenomenon which persisted in a variety of ways during the nineteenth century and is with us still. It was peculiarly effective in the early nineteenth century in teaching women to see their own subordination as 'natural' in a period when everyone else was demanding their natural rights. A dominant group is secure when it can convince the oppressed that they enjoy their actual powerlessness and give them instead a fantasy of power. John Henry dies proud in his physical strength, when the white man's money and cunning rather than his muscles are the real basis of control. Rousseauite heroines cultivate sensibility and natural freedom while their men create the economic basis for social relations in which these qualities are at once inessential, irrelevant and impossible – and are preserved as drawing-room accomplishments, hot-house plants. Women were so perfectly colonized they policed one another. The privileged women had material stakes in the world as it was. The older women broke in the younger ones and taught them to manipulate their men. At first revolutionary feminists were bewildered by resistance, naïve in the faith that liberty and equality were theirs, trustful of their men and forgetful of the warning carried in the word 'brotherhood'. They argued their case patiently and with eloquence. Petitioning the Assembly in 1789 women pointed out to the men: 'You have destroyed all the prejudices of the past, but you allow the oldest and the most pervasive to remain, which excludes from office, position and honour, and above all from the right of sitting amongst you, half the inhabitants of the kingdom.'[1]

How was it that the revolution could dissolve the subordination of the humblest and most downtrodden, including black slaves, but leave millions of women still under the yoke of their men. Carried away with enthusiasm and confidence Citoyenne Claire Lacombe declared in a revolutionary women's club in 1793 that the prejudice which relegated women into the narrow sphere of the household and made of half humanity isolated passive beings was no more. She would have been wise to grant this prejudice greater tenacity and capacity to survive. Her optimism was unfounded. Apart from a few rare individuals like Condorcet, most men including Robespierre, Marat and Hébert opposed any suggestion of an active political life for women, as unnatural. They believed women should serve the revolution in a more traditional manner as wives and mothers. These opinions Napoleon was most emphatically to endorse, though he extended the patriotic privilege of breeding to his mistresses. The feminists were only a tiny minority. The women of the First Empire flit half naked about his court or recline languidly for a portrait on a chaise longue. Their breasts are uncovered and swelling in anticipation. They moisten transparent clothes to cling to their bodies, and emphasize natural contours. They suffered from natural draughts, and shivering they fell ill. Some even died in pursuit of this unnatural idea of nature.

But a woman Napoleon disliked with a special intensity, who combined everything he most detested in revolutionary intellectual women, survived with exuberant persistence. Mme de Staël lived through the various regimes of revolution to wage a personal literary guerrilla war against Bonaparte. She glibly claimed to be non-political, but in her salons young men laughed at him, and in such novels as *Delphine* and *Corinne* women with a high opinion of their own superiority conflicted with a society that would not allow them self-expression. She twisted natural sensibility into an argument for women's rights. Mme de Staël used Rousseau just as she used everyone else – to effect. She extracted what was convenient and ignored the rest. But Napoleon's Civil Code established the rest. The emperor must have felt he'd put women firmly back in their place.

However, in the context of this same revolution a remarkable woman produced a remarkable book. Mary Wollstonecraft's *Vindication* was one of those books which provides such an intense synthesis of the past, such a brilliant condensation and expression of the experience of the moment, that it changes permanently the bases of people's thinking in the future. Written in six weeks it is frequently discursive. She advances sometimes by means of great circular detours. Sometimes you can feel almost physically the painful difficulty she had in clearing a path and seeing straight. It is not so much that the ideas had never been put before but the particular way she combines them together. This new way of seeing was made possible by a peculiar interaction of personal and political events: her own painful experience in childhood, pity and identification with her mother forced into poverty by a violent and drunken father; her rejection by her lover, the father of her child, Imlay, who left her to survive as she could; her pride despite her desperate wanting for him: 'You may render me unhappy; but you cannot make me contemptible in my own eyes.'[2] Social disgrace, a suicide attempt, yet her amazing emergence unbroken. In her writing warmth and emotional sensuality – 'I cannot live without loving, and loving leads to madness'[3] – mingle with a new kind of dignity in a woman, self-respect despite society, lack of illusion from a group surrounded by mystification. 'I long for a little peace and independence. . . . I am not fond of grovelling.'[4]

She belonged to the generation that exulted in 1789. She didn't live to share the agony of disillusionment. But she experienced an apprehension which was to become familiar for later revolutionaries, even in '93. 'I can look beyond the evils of the moment, and do not expect muddied water to become clear before it has had time to stand; yet, even for the moment, it is the most terrific of sights, to see men vicious without warmth.'[5]

Like Wordsworth she recoiled from 'the hissing factionalists', but the new language and the new consciousness were deep inside her. Revolutionary thinking was not some new authority held by, for, or on behalf of others, sitting high on the tribune, to be curtseyed to. It was a means by which the oppressed themselves broke out of the system in which they were dominated. And being a woman, Mary Wollstonecraft applied the ideas of revolutionary men to the situation of women. In the *Vindication* she asked how a woman could reasonably be expected to co-operate unless she knew why she ought to be virtuous, and observed that, if men contended for their freedom and wanted to be allowed to judge for themselves respecting their own happiness, wasn't it at once inconsistent and unjust of them to continue to subjugate women, even though they believed that they were thus acting in the women's best interest. The assumption that the subordinated must themselves be judges of their own interest was accompanied with the assertion that arguments about their inadequacy for the task were merely the superior people's justification and defence. These ideas were common currency in the radical movement. So too was the ambition for the full development and growth of each individual. Mary Wollstonecraft in claiming for women 'the virtues of humanity'[6] and protesting against a society which allowed them only 'to procreate and rot',[7] was simply extending radical ideas to the situation of women.

There is a crucial break though with earlier feminism. The French Revolution had taught her to think in terms of actual social movements. There is a new note in the *Vindication*: 'I plead for my sex – not for myself.'[8] The conscious identification with women as a group is described by Godwin:

> She considered herself as standing forth in defence of one half of the human species, labouring under a yoke which through all the records of time, had degraded them from the station of rational beings, and almost sunk them to the level of the brutes. She saw indeed that they were often attempted to be held in silken fetters, and bribed into the love of slavery; but the disguise and the treachery served only the more fully to confirm her opposition.[9]

Wollstonecraft located the origin of women's subordination in physical weakness. This was reinforced by culture and education. Men had used women 'as alluring objects for a moment'[10] and women had acquiesced in this. She understands very well the process through which women of her class became accomplices in their own subordination. Taught by their mothers to practice cunning and show 'outward obedience, and a scrupulous attention to a puerile kind of propriety',[11] their privilege rested on complicity in an oppressive system. They had no memory of any alternative. Their history disclosed only marks of inferiority. She knew how strong the silken fetter of pleasing was. But what was to become of the woman when she ceased to be a source of pleasure for man, when she found her charms were 'oblique sunbeams' and 'the summer' had 'passed and gone'.[12] She could only grow languid or look for other men. Gallantry was the man's part. Mary hated gallantry. She knew the contempt it concealed. She could see so clearly the way in which women were 'insulated' and thus contained. 'Stripped of the virtues that should clothe humanity they are decked with artificial graces that enable them to exercise a short-lived tyranny.'

Believing with other radicals that human character was mainly formed from environment, she not unreasonably extended this idea to women. The conclusion was the necessity of changing women's environment. Rousseau's ideas about the natural proclivities of little girls receive short shrift. 'I have probably had an opportunity of observing more girls in their infancy than J.-J. Rousseau – and can recollect my own feelings and I have looked steadily around me.' She concludes that the girl whose spirits 'have not been damped by inactivity, or innocence tainted by false shame, will always be a romp'.[13]

Despite this, though, Mary Wollstonecraft, like Mme de Staël, owed a debt to Rousseau. She was greatly influenced by his ideas on naturalness and simplicity in child-rearing and education of the young. She believed in coeducation, exercise, gymnastics in the open air, botany, mechanics, astronomy, natural history, philosophy, history of religion and man, politics taught by conversation in the Socratic manner. These were radical proposals in the 1790s; they are radical still. There was, however, an important reservation. She introduced a separate education for the lower classes. At nine, boys and girls were steered off. These girls would learn plainwork and millinery rather than politics in the Socratic manner. The popular revolutionary implications of her thought cannot extend beyond her own class. In fact she is demanding an education to equip the bourgeois woman for an active part in industrial capitalism.

To do everything in an orderly manner is a most important precept, which women, who, generally speaking, receive only a disorderly kind of education, seldom attend to with that degree of exactness that men, who from their infancy are broken into method, observe. This negligent kind of guess-work, for what other epithet can be used to point out the random exertions of a sort of instinctive common sense, never brought to the test of reason, prevents their generalizing matters of fact – so they do today, what they did yesterday, merely because they did it yesterday.[14]

Ironically, it is only by acquiring a bourgeois state of mind, submitting to the discipline of methodical and regular work, the exact and synchronized time-spirit, the rejection of custom, the delight in innovation, technological and intellectual, that women can cast off their traditional fetters. At this point Mary Wollstonecraft's thinking locks. There are many aspects of her radicalism which are quite hostile to the way capitalism was already breaking humanity into method. But she can only catch vague glimpses of an alternative, though she can cut right through Clarissa Harlowe's dilemma, scoffing at the hypocritical morality of the world that criticized her, as if honour meant a woman was degraded merely because she lost her chastity. But she is fastened in her own dilemma: how to shatter a whole system of domination with no social basis for a movement of the oppressed. She knew education alone could not end the oppression of women because it could not be of a really different kind until 'society be differently constituted'. She attempts an economic connection. The system of dividing property produced the corrupting dependence and tyranny of which the subjugation of women was only a part. She very tentatively claims for women a say in government. Not only is it inconceivable to her that the women of the people would demand democratic rights and emancipation, she is even cut off from women of her own kind. Mankind has claimed dignity – not woman. It is hard for Mary Wollstonecraft to feel proud of women despite her passionate longing to speak as part of a group. She mentions the occasional radical women like Catherine Macaulay who she wishes she had known. There were isolated clusters of her friends too, independent and courageous women, discussing revolutionary ideas. Again there was the circle of dissenting and progressive people who shared her hopes for a new society. But the loneliness comes through. To have an illegitimate child, to be a revolutionary, to write the *Vindication*, was in England in the 1790s to be desperately alone and cut off, socially, politically and emotionally.

Irony is frequently the weapon of isolated people facing impossible odds. Mary Wollstonecraft throws out peculiarly delicate and nonchalant ironies. From Sweden she wrote in a letter, 'At supper my host told me bluntly that I was a woman of observation for I asked him men's questions.'[15] Thus while Mary Wollstonecraft could observe so acutely the distress of bourgeois women, describing their nervous complaints, their faded wasted lives, be contemptuous of ameliorative measures, asylums and magdalens as remedies – 'It is justice not charity that is wanting in the world'[16] – she falters when she tries to find the means of effecting the social change her analysis demands. Though she felt most female 'follies' came from the tyranny of men, she cannot conceive of women becoming the agents of their own liberation. She can only hope to convince reasonable men to assist in the emancipation of their companions. 'Would men but generously snap our chains and be content with rational fellowship instead of slavish obedience.'[17]

The *Vindication*, often taken as the beginnings of feminism, was rather the important theoretical summation of bourgeois radical feminism still in the phase of moral exhortation, before there was either the possibility of a radical and socialist movement from below, to which the revolutionary feminist could relate, or a movement like that of suffragettes, of privileged women for equal rights with bourgeois man. If the man with revolutionary ideals in Britain felt painfully isolated when Mary Wollstonecraft wrote, the woman who at once loved freedom and sympathized with revolution was doubly so. Old Corruption, grown big and fat in the period of reaction following the French Revolution, hated Mary Wollstonecraft. Characteristically she was attacked sexually as well as politically. An anonymous rhyme after her death remarked on Godwin's biography of his wife:

> William has penned a wagonload of stuff
> And Mary's life at last he needs must write,
> Thinking her whoredoms were not known enough.[18]

Her son-in-law Shelley, one who sought rational fellowship most earnestly, paid her a better tribute in *Queen Mab*. 'Can man be free, if woman be a slave?' In *Prometheus Unbound* he imagined women 'changed to all they dared not be', able to 'speak the wisdom once they could not think'.[19]

In the first quarter of the nineteenth century small groups of radical men and women called into question not only political corruption but the economic basis of the society of mills, factories, steam-power, industry, competition and money-making they saw growing up around them in Britain. Their criticism was essentially moral. Society was evil because it denied the possibility of truly human social relations. It allowed only for distortion, destruction and deceit in the meetings of man with man, man with woman. Along with the ideas of freedom in government and freedom in work arose ideas of freedom in love.

Blake imagined the disappearance of:

> A Religion of Chastity, forming a Commerce to sell Loves

and with it,

A False Holiness hid within the Center.

He conceived a new kind of love,

> Embraces are cominglings from the Head even to the Feet
> And not a pompous High Priest entering by a Secret Place.[20]

Relationships, Shelley believed, should be freely contracted, and freely dissolved – 'Love withers under constraint.' To be bound by the institution of marriage was as intolerable as oppression from other institutions. Indeed, the personal and public were linked. 'Not even the intercourse of the sexes is exempt from the despotism of positive institution.'[21] It followed that you had to try to change your lives as well as political and social institutions. Not everyone tried to do this as literally as Shelley, but, once thought about, such ideas were not easily forgotten. They recur as significant radical impulses later. Despite denunciation from outside and attempts at exorcism from within, the idea of revolution and the idea of freedom in love have enjoyed a remarkably deep and long lasting relationship. The implications for women's liberation were important.

By the early nineteenth century a most practical device had been discovered and was being discussed in radical circles. A leaflet addressed 'To the Married of Both Sexes' appeared in England in 1823 with information about the vaginal sponge. It was almost certainly produced by a radical tailor from Charing Cross called Francis Place. It was disseminated in mysterious brown paper parcels throughout the industrial centres of Britain and distributed by radical workmen like William Longson, a journeyman weaver in Manchester, and young hot-headed radicals like J. S. Mill, who was arrested aged seventeen for giving them out with some friends to maid-servants scrubbing steps and to the wives and daughters of mechanics and tradesmen in markets. Mill wrote birth-control propaganda in the radical paper *The Black Dwarf*, although some radicals like the editor T. J. Wooler were opposed to contraceptives. They connected them with the ideas of Malthus and suspected they would be used as an alternative to the political and social reforms they fought for. We can't tell how many women were seduced by these stopgap measures. But from amongst the vaginal sponge radicals came a new conception of love. Instead of elevating individual sex love as the criteria of the capacity for human beings to transcend existing society, like Shelley, they attempted to reduce

46

such irrational emotion to a materialist interpretation of its origins. Shortly after 'To the Married of Both Sexes', Richard Carlile published 'What is Love?', later called 'Every Woman's Book or What is Love?' As well as giving working women information on contraception he also declared to them, 'The passion of love is nothing but the passion to secrete semen in a natural way.'[22]

Unfortunately we don't know what the women made of this. But this species of mechanical reductionism passed into the revolutionary tradition and connected to ideas about the emancipation of women. At one extreme there was a romantic search for true uninhibited feeling in liberated sexual relationships; at the other there was a matter-of-fact materialism which would take no nonsense from sensual emotion. These two strands were quite contradictory. While the latter was about more control the other wanted to make any control unnecessary. Theoretically they implied very different social arrangement. They were an awkward heritage and continued implicitly to jostle and hustle each other in the revolutionary socialist movement whenever the emancipation of women was discussed.

But by the 1820s at least one of Mary Wollstonecraft's dilemmas had been dissolved. The followers of Robert Owen were full of ideas for a cooperative society. Some disagreed with Owen's schemes and worked out others of their own. In these plans for harmony the claims of women were considered sympathetically. In John Gray's 'Lecture on Human Happiness' with articles for a London cooperative society, women are guaranteed complete equal rights within the community, and freedom from domestic drudgery. Jobs like cooking, washing and heating rooms are distributed equally. The emancipation of women was now firmly linked to concepts of an alternative non-competitive society in which the means of production were not individually owned.

One of these early anti-capitalist thinkers, William Thompson, wrote his 'Appeal of one half of the Human Race, Women, against the pretensions of the other Half, Men, to retain them in Civil and Domestic Slavery' in 1825 as a reply to a work by James Mill which denied women political rights on the grounds that men could look after women's rights for them. William Thompson had done battle with the ideas of the middle-class radicals and the new theories in political economy which were enthusiastic about the way in which Britain was becoming industrialized. He was critical of the many injustices he saw around him, from the fate of Irish peasants to the conditions in the new factory towns. He was one of the earliest economists to argue for the right of the worker to the whole produce of his labour and work out the beginnings of a theory of exploitation. He felt too that the system based on competition and domination penetrated the political and psychological areas of human life. Law and morality were 'little more than a tissue of restraints of one class over another'.[23] Affection and love were claimed by the market. 'Seldom can natural feelings display themselves . . . the mere animal part of sexual pleasure is bought by the richer of the dominant sex at the lowest price of competition.'[24]

Although his thinking inclined him by plain honest radicalism to protest against the oppression of women, he was greatly influenced by his friendship with Anna Wheeler who was part of a circle of women who despite considerable personal suffering were thinking about Mary Wollstonecraft's ideas of liberation. Thompson pays a long tribute to Mrs Wheeler at the beginning of the book. He says that although he can't feel as she would because he is a man, he can still state the facts of the case. In fact he did much more. Like Wollstonecraft he refuses to concede that the interest of one group can be entrusted to another. He points out ironically how this argument has been used by conservatives against every group struggling for liberty. Why extend the right to vote outside the narrow confines of privileged society if one section can look after the rights of another? Even if there was the possibility of being happy as a result of permission from masters, and the strong really would care for the weak, it offered little guarantee if the masters became less benevolent in the future.

Thompson located the original subjection of women in their inferior strength and the fact that they bore children. He believed that this subjection was reinforced by their exclusion from access to knowledge and by the existing system of marriage which made them legally and economically powerless.

He doesn't just argue for rights in the abstract, believing the liberation of women was impossible in a competitive system. Even if women were given completely equal political and civil rights, in existing circumstances they would not be raised to an 'equality of happiness because unequal powers under free competition must produce unequal effects'.[25] They would not only be handicapped physically but culturally. The real answer was 'to build up a new fabric of social happiness comprehending equally the interests of all existing human beings'. His alternative is a society based on 'a voluntary association, or the mutual cooperation of industry and talents in large numbers'.[26] Meanwhile he produces a programme of demands for the moment. These will secure at least the removal of restraints though not a 'positive' advance, and enable women to play a fuller part in changing society. He criticizes the nature of woman's education and the legal restraints upon her. The law marks women with 'the brand of inferiority. . . . To be a woman is to be an inferior animal, an inferiority . . . indelible like the skin of the Black.'[27] The movement against slavery very quickly led people to draw parallels with the oppression of women. Thompson was contemptuous of the justifications of slave-owners who try to impose their own definition of 'nature' on to the slave. This imposed nature was 'the mere creation of his own ignorant selfishness and injustice'.[28]

Thompson goes even further and attacks the institution of marriage and the bourgeois family. The statement, 'Each man yokes a woman to his establishment and calls it a contract',[29] cut right through not only the aristocratic property marriage but the puritan conception of a free contract for companionable domesticity in which the wife had far fewer rights than the man. At a time when the family was beginning to be elevated as a shelter from the cruel competitive world of early capitalism, in which the wife should act as comforter, Thompson exposed the hypocrisy on which this was based. 'Home . . . is the eternal prison house of the wife; the husband paints it as the abode of calm bliss, but takes care to find outside of doors, for his own use, a species of bliss not quite so calm, but of a more varied and stimulating description.'[30]

He understood the power which came from being able to decide what was right and wrong. 'He has a system of domineering hypocrisy, which he calls morals.'[31] He knew too how deeply bound women were by this system, and why they so rarely rebelled against it. The choices were too narrow. The alternatives were simply marriage, the wretched life of the spinster, or the social disgrace of sexual indiscretion. Marriage was obviously the most attractive. 'Better to be a slave and be kissed than to be a slave without kissing.'[32]

He admits frankly that the radical movement has neglected to offer women any real alternative. 'What wonder that your sex is indifferent to what man calls the progress of society, of freedom of action, of social institutions? Where amongst all their past schemes of liberty or despotism is the freedom of action for you?' He wonders at the bewilderment of radical men when women show little enthusiasm for their 'high matters of liberty', and asks 'Is their folly or their hypocrisy the greater?'[33] Still, in the thirty years between the writing of the *Vindication* and the writing of the 'Appeal' there had been significant changes. In 1825 William Thompson can appeal to women to cast off men's domination by offering them an alternative society to struggle for. Thus he raises points which were to become essential parts of socialist feminist thinking: economic independence and security for women, and communal responsibility for the upbringing of children, social support during pregnancy, the right to work. An important area of hostility would not exist. In the future society, men would be secure in their jobs and therefore wouldn't dread the economic competition of women.

Thompson argues his case for cooperative feminism with wit and eloquence. More obscurely, similar debates and discussions were going on within the cooperative movement. By offering suggestions for actually effecting a change rather than simply describing and analysing what was wrong, these cooperators and early socialists discovered a new potentiality for feminism. They transformed it from aspiration and ideas and integrated the liberation of women with a social movement which could envisage alternatives to the suffering and waste of early capitalism. From this point the conflict was explicit between the two feminisms, one seeking acceptance from the bourgeois world, the other seeking another world altogether.

Similar connections and a similar division were developing and emerging in France. Although Fourier was to modify his ideas later, his 'Théories des quatre mouvements', published in 1808, was an important contribution to socialist feminist thinking and influenced not only the early French socialists, but radicals and cooperators in England and America as well. He attempted a much more sophisticated anthropological/historical description of the development of human society. If you could show how woman's position had changed along with other changes in social relations, it was easier to imagine a different state in the future. While the details of this attempt are not particularly important now, his insight in taking the position of women as a gauge of the development of society was to have a lasting impression on revolutionary feminism. 'The change in a historical epoch can always be determined by the progress of women towards freedom, because in the relation of woman to man, of the weak to the strong, the victory of human nature over brutality is most evident. The degree of emancipation of women is the natural measure of general emancipation.'[34]

Fourier connected the economic and sexual oppression of women; he ridiculed attempts to pontificate about their 'natural duplicity' without understanding the social situation that made dissimulation necessary to them. He accused philosophers of a 'secret antipathy' towards women behind their compliments. They maintained an intellectual closed shop, excluding women from access to ideas, and then concluded that women were incapable of thinking. He thought they would be spending their time better in working out social schemes to end women's oppression.

He had a low opinion of the 'femmes savantes', French equivalents of the blue stockings. Instead of contriving the means of delivering their sex he saw them as wedded to 'philosophical egotism'.[35] They closed their eyes to the degradation of their own kind because they had managed to escape the fate of most women.

Not just in the 'Théories' but in subsequent writing, Fourier considered the claims of women to a fuller life. In his cooperative communities or phalansteries there was complete equality between the sexes. Women were economically independent of men. The upbringing of the children was the responsibility of the cooperatives not of individuals. Women's education was not simply for domesticity but for social and political participation in the community.

Behind his thinking was the conviction that the happy society was one organized to allow human beings to develop fully. He didn't want to change individuals for their own good so they would be worthy of the good society. He wanted rather to devise forms of social organization which would be the best adapted to allow everybody to do what they wanted without upsetting anyone else. He had ingenious ideas about the organization of work. Noticing that young adolescents often liked getting dirty, he allocated dirty work to them. Grown-ups who hadn't outgrown the delights of dirt could join them. These dirt-lovers organized themselves in bands or gangs called the Little Hordes. Non dirt-loving youths were given artistic work. He seemed to think the girls would prefer the latter. But if they wanted they were welcome amongst the Little Hordes.

Fourier's ideas about the position of women were not the only ones being discussed in ateliers and cafés in France in the first half of the century. 'La nouvelle femme Saint-Simonienne', an extraordinarily modern creature wearing a kind of smock over trousers, the forerunner of Amelia Bloomer, made her appearance in innumerable cartoons. Much to the disgust of many of Saint-Simon's followers, one of his disciples, Enfantin, developed the master's ideas of the need for a New Christianity and spiritual regeneration in a feminine direction. Resembling many aspects of the millenarian movements, these new heretics organized like the early Christian apostles and, sharing their goods in common, awaited the apocalypse and a new messiah. But they believed total redemption was impossible unless this time it was a Mother. The church needed the marriage of Father and Mother to symbolize the union of intellect and feeling. It was necessary to transcend the Christian denial of the flesh by its exaltation as the complement of the spirit. They shared the symbolism of the Christian fathers – woman was flesh, animality, fertility.

Enfantin and his believers, waiting for La Mère and setting off on a disastrous expedition to Egypt to find her, appear now as simply preposterous. But the fury their preaching unleashed was real enough, as was the persecution they suffered for their ideas of free unions. Their significance is rather in the effect they had upon women who had nothing else to hope with. From the interaction between the emerging labour movement and workers' associations and the extraordinary ideas of these utopian thinkers, a number of women emerged with a new conception of their own worth and dignity. It gave them the confidence to express themselves and provided them with the courage to formulate conceptions about their own possibilities, which would have been quite inconceivable to women a generation before.

George Sand's is the name that survives now but there were many much humbler women thinking about these ideas who received no adulation or acclaim. Some even have no name now. In the Club Lyonnais in 1848, 'a simple working woman, born of a poor family, the wife of a good republican'[36] stood up in the tribune and demanded that women shouldn't be slaves to men. She wanted them to be admitted into the assembly, to discuss their rights and direct their own affairs. They ought to get a decent wage for their work so they wouldn't have to depend on men. Young girls who had been seduced and abandoned ought to be able to look after their children without disgrace, and the shame should fall on the man.

It is impossible now to discover what had happened to women like her, or how they came by such ideas; impossible to retrace the slow subterranean growth of consciousness behind her words. We know a little more about other women – the ones who wrote. Susanne Voilquin, a working girl who went off to Egypt in search of La Mère, described in her 'Memories of a Girl of the People' the extraordinary effect of Enfantin's ideas upon her at a meeting. She said the discovery that the capacity for thought, feeling and independent action was within herself brought her great joy. Clair Demar produced two short books before committing suicide with her lover. She dreamed of a new social era of association, concord and harmony where there was no longer either industrial or sexual bondage.[37] She believed that the emancipation of the proletariat and of women was indissolubly linked and imagined a greater freer love between men and women. A future where there would be no longer the love of slave for master but the free proud love of equal for equal, and a revolution in sexual customs. Jeanne Deroin, a self-taught working woman, also believed that the liberation of women and the working class was inseparable. She was active in the early French labour movement and worked out an early project for the federation of unions. She produced many practical proposals to improve the domestic and working conditions of women. In her 'Cours de droit social pour les femmes' in 1848, she describes the submission of women:

Woman, still slave, remains veiled and in silence. She has lost the memory of her divine origin, she is unable to understand her noble social mission, she has neither name nor country, she is banished from the sanctuary, she seems to have accepted shameful servitude. Held down by man's yoke, she has not even the aspiration towards liberty, man must liberate her.[38]

Despite the religious language this expresses a consciousness of the internalization of women's subordination, which makes it peculiarly difficult for them to struggle against oppression.

Jeanne Deroin felt the liberation of women was not possible without a great social change but that women must play their part in effecting it. Men from long association with egoism inclined always towards despotism. With a naïve faith she believed women, previously denied responsibility for the world, would be able to organize with love.

Flora Tristan is slightly better known than Voilquin, Demar or Deroin. In her *L'Union Ouvrière*, published in 1843, she worked out one of the earliest conceptions of a world-wide Workers' International. She devoted a chapter to the rights of women, showing how important the relations between men and women in the working-class family were in creating consciousness. She thought many working-class women became soured by the contempt with which they were treated. 'I am not criticizing working-class women. It is society that is entirely to blame ... it must be admitted that there are few workers' homes that are happy. The husband is head by law and also by reason of the money he brings in. He believes himself superior to his wife, who only earns a fraction of his wage and is his very humble servant.'

The man sought refuge from his wife's bitterness and frequent quarrelling in drink. 'Taverns are the temples of working-class men.' This only worsens the effects of poverty, unemployment and bad conditions:

> She rails at him. He swears at her and hits her. And a woman has further crosses to bear, such as constant child-bearing, illness and unemployment. Misery is planted on her doorstep like Medusa's head. Add to this the yells and romping of four to five children eddying round her in one small cramped room, and one would have to be an angel not to be brutalized by it all.[39]

She saw the need for the workers' movement to create an alternative culture, and planned workers' palaces in every town to act as a focal point for organizing and education. One of their tasks would be the 'education, moral, intellectual and technical'[40] of the women of the people. She hoped this would act as an improving influence on the men of the people.

Flora Tristan's own life followed the dramatic and tragic course which seemed to be the inevitable fate of the feminist socialist. She worked as a colourist in a workshop. Her master, impressed by her beauty, married her. She was unhappy with him, and, becoming pregnant for the third time, ran away. Divorce was illegal. She travelled to South America in a vain attempt to secure an inheritance from her father's brother. After long struggles with her husband for custody of her daughter, he pursued her and shot her. Legally she was in a weak position, socially she was an outcast. But by this time, reading Fourier and Saint-Simonian literature and talking to workers interested in their ideas, she discovered that she was not alone in her unhappiness and helplessness. She visited England and met radicals and chartists including Anna Wheeler, Owen, O'Brien. She also met a madman in Bedlam whilst she was in England who disturbed her greatly. He told her he wanted to end all bondage, free the woman from slavery to the man, the poor from the power of the rich, and the soul from its bondage to sin. Flora wondered 'Was the man mad? All he had said to me revealed a man in revolt against the corruption and the hypocrisy of those who ruled the world, and who found himself unable to control his anger.'[41] The similarity to her own situation was inescapable. Just before she died in 1844, on a speaking tour to convince workers of the need to establish an International, Flora Tristan wrote to Considerant: 'I have nearly the whole world against me. Men because I demand the emancipation of women, the owners because I demand the emancipation of wage-earners.'[42]

On her tour she encountered a mixed reception. In some cases workers listened and bought her *L'Union Ouvrière*. But in other towns she found apathy, sectional conflict between trades, and inter-union hostility. Amazingly she persisted trudging from town to town, meeting to meeting, selling her book. She was often attacked in the press and harassed by the police and local officials. She became feverish and ill, driving herself to speak in torrential rain regardless of exhaustion. When she finally collapsed she was cared for by her friend Eleanore Blanc, a laundress who shared her ideas, and by the Lemonniers, a middle-class couple who also supported her. At her funeral workmen carried her coffin because they did not want paid men to do the work, and a subscription was raised for a monument at her grave. Flora left an unfinished book, *L'Emancipation de la Femme ou le Testament de la Paria* – an appropriate title. She also left a memory in the revolutionary movement. On 23 October 1848 several thousand people gathered to pay tribute round her grave. Workers returned home singing 'Flora Tristan needs a grave', and the song persisted in the ateliers for many years.

Thus despite intense opposition and repression the connection

55

between the emancipation of women and the idea of a new, more just society for the poor continued to be discussed, argued and contested in the utopian underground in the first part of the century. Women influenced by Saint-Simonian theories worked in Owenite cooperatives and returned to France with ideas of association; Owen and his followers established communities in the U.S.A. and visited France to argue with the Fourierists; Fourier's ideas were popularized in England by Hugh Doherty. Causes combined and borrowed arguments from one another. In America Frances Wright, struggling for the emancipation of the slaves, horrified everyone by taking up free love in a community in Tennessee. The transcendentalist feminist and republican Margaret Fuller shows, both in her life and writing, the manner in which radical ideas were being communicated, not only across national boundaries but across boundaries of colour, class and sex. She had links with the community based on plain living and high thinking at Brook Farm, which was converted into a Fourierist 'phalanx' in 1844. She visited France in 1847, meeting George Sand, was swept away with enthusiasm for the revolution of 1848, and took an active part in the movement for Italian liberation. Her *Woman in the Nineteenth Century* is a remarkably perceptive account of the psychological and cultural effects of women's oppression. She was really primarily concerned with consciousness which she expresses in religious terms, rather like the Saint-Simonian women. But she had different arguments. Margaret Fuller strikes straight at one of the most pervasive of anti-feminist notions. As women pressed their claims their opponents changed their tack. Instead of declaring them outright inferiors they granted them affairs relating to the heart. Women were allowed to occupy themselves with all matters that did not concern direct power. They could control, but only indirectly, through their men. Margaret Fuller recognized this as a small advance. If he was to be the head it was better to be his heart than his hand. But it only loosened the rope. She was still his creature:

I have urged on Woman independence of Man, not that I do not think the sexes mutually needed by one another, but because in Woman this fact has led to an excessive devotion which has cooled love, degraded marriage, and prevented either sex from being what it should be to itself.[43]

The struggle to find an independent self, rather than finding a self through the activity of the man, was to be a crucial theme in feminism. Fuller conceived the problem in religious terms, of living for God's sake. But she wanted the reform to be in this world. She looked at the arguments which used women's physical weakness as a reason for keeping them from government and the professions and contrasted this ironically with complacency, which allowed '... Negresses to endure field work even during pregnancy, or for seamstresses to go through their killing labours'.[44] She agreed with Fourier's ideas on the education of little girls.

She is most specifically aware of the cultural manifestations of women's inferior position. She noted amongst men a profound contempt for women. She mentions common phrases like 'Tell that to women and children'.[45] Submission was so deeply embedded, even in language. Energy and creation are synonymous with masculinity, and nobility with manliness. Whenever a woman appeared to be particularly gifted she was complimented by comparisons to men. If she claimed dignity for women, she was regarded with incredulity as making the best of it – Wollstonecraft's Swede again.

Historically Fuller connects the first hope of emancipation with the French Revolution. 'As men become aware that few men have had a fair chance, they are inclined to say that no women have had a fair chance.'[46] She notes also the influence of the movement for the abolition of slavery. She hoped for the sympathy of men who loved liberty, but felt that despite their acquiescence the only hope lay in the mobilization of women.

Her own life, often compared to that of Mme de Staël, was far from happy. Emotionally they shared the longing for a man who could comprehend their ambitions, intellectually they were both profoundly influenced by romantic notions of desolate, lonely, but noble spirits, with the task of revelation to an ungrateful humanity. Margaret Fuller understood and expressed the tragic exhaustion of the French feminist socialists, who pitted themselves not only against the dominant economic and political values of early capitalism, but also against inhuman sexual relations. Like them she was battered and bruised terribly for her insolence. Nathaniel Hawthorne's Zenobia in *The Blithedale Romance* and Henry James's Verbena Tarrant in *The Bostonians* are her epitaphs. But if she submitted in fiction, in history 'Margaret-ghost' refuses to be laid to rest. 'Many women are considering within themselves what they need that they have not, and what they can have if they find they need.'[47] Unlike Flora Tristan, who still waited for man to liberate woman, Margaret Fuller believed change could come from the women themselves.

By the 1840s connection between social revolution and the liberation of women had been made. It had fixed in people's minds. But the actual basis for connection was still only vaguely worked out. An alternative feminism to that aligned with socialism was beginning to develop. It was apparent that the interests and intentions of some women who spoke of freedom for themselves had nothing to do with the emancipation of the workers, and indeed was often explicitly opposed to the rights of labour. How did women as a group relate to the movement for a free and egalitarian society? How could they act to change society in this direction? These two were amongst the great unanswered questions of revolutionary feminism.

## CHAPTER 3

# Dialectical
# Disturbances

It is a curious fact that with every great revolutionary movement the question of 'free love' comes into the foreground.

F. Engels

. . . The first class opposition that occurs in history coincides with the development of antagonism between man and woman in mono-gamous marriage, and the first class oppression coincides with that of the female sex by the male. Monogamous marriage was a great histori-cal step forward; nevertheless together with slavery and private wealth it opens the period that has lasted until today in which every step for-ward is also relatively a step backward, in which prosperity and develop-ment for some is won through the misery and frustration of others. It is the cellular form of civilized society in which the nature of the oppositions and contradictions fully acting in that society can be already studied.

F. Engels, *The Origin of the Family*

Household management lost its public character. It no longer con-cerned society. It became a private service; the wife became head servant, excluded from all participation in social production. . . . The modern individual family is founded on the open or concealed domestic slavery of the wife and modern society is a mass composed of these individual families as its molecules. In the great majority of cases today at least in the possessing classes, the husband is obliged to earn a living and support his family, and that in itself gives him a position of supremacy, without any need for special legal titles and privileges. Within the family he is the bourgeois and the wife represents the proletariat.

F. Engels, *The Origin of the Family*

[Prostitution] demoralizes men far more than women. Among women prostitution degrades only the unfortunate ones who become its victims. . . . But it degrades the whole male world.

F. Engels, *The Origin of the Family*

---

By the 1840s the tales of Adam's rib and the sighs of Clarissa had been overtaken by a body of theory in which it seemed as if the emancipation of women was an integral part of the emerging socialist movement. But as yet this socialism was still something that ought to be projected into the utopian future. There is no necessary connection worked out between the activity coming from the material situation of any social group or class and the creation of a socialist society. Far less in the writings of socialist feminism is there any concept of a way in which women as a group could act in this manner. Women's oppression is described. The position appears as intolerable. Actuality is in conflict with an assumed potentiality. There is an historical concept of perpetual spiritual development. But there is no theory of who is to effect social change or how or why. True, there are solutions. There are new models for a new world in which women's liberation will be achieved as one aspect of human liberation. But as to the means of making a new world and the part women will play in this process, there are only a few muffled theoretical mutterings combined with much experimenting in practice. It was a time when practical development broke repeatedly from old accepted formulas for action; when old ideas were caving in and the elements of new revolutionary theory beginning to emerge.

The crucial novelty of Marxism in the nineteenth-century context was to provide the monumental working out of the necessary relationship of the working class to the eventual dissolution of capitalism and the formation of a new communist society. An essential connection was already grasped by Marx in the forties philosophically, between the practical activity of the working class and the means of breaking the hold of private capital. The working class is seen as the agency for human liberation, the carrier of emancipation for all classes through its own efforts to control the external world of work. The specific oppression of women was never studied in the exhaustive manner which Marx applied to the exploitation of the worker. He looked at women's situation more tangentially. There is no sense of women's agency for revolutionary change as there is for the worker. We find instead in Marx's writings several approaches to an analysis of women's oppression and the subsequent attempts of Engels, Bebel and other nineteenth-century revolutionaries to synthesize and elaborate on these.

By the end of the century the terms in which people could discuss the nature of women's oppression and the possibility of emancipation showed a significant advance from the discussions of the 1840s. There had been valuable general developments in the relatively new areas of sex psychology and anthropology, as well as a great accumulation of historical and sociological work which had not existed in the 1840s. Even more important, there was a much more developed labour movement, as well as the strong challenge of bourgeois feminism, which inevitably affected the way in which socialist feminism was conceived. Marxist theory about women's liberation developed in this context and the problems Marx and Engels confronted were contemporary problems which arose from the particular experience of nineteenth-century capitalism and its immediate effect on women of all classes. Both Marx's and Engels's ideas came out of the earlier tradition of romantic revolution and utopian socialism. Though they made decisive breaks with these earlier ideas, they shared, nonetheless, many of the preconceptions of utopian socialism. This is as true of their writing which dealt specifically with women as with their general theory. Their ideas about the liberation of women are obviously inseparable from their thought as a whole. However, they still contributed enough to the specific study of women's oppression to change radically the bases from which revolutionaries argued and to make much of the romantic rhetoric of utopian socialism appear relevant no longer. There are many contradictions in their writings on women's liberation. Some of these can be explained by general changes of emphasis in their thought. But others come out of the sheer complexity of the issues and questions involved. They took the woman question seriously enough to change their minds when new data didn't fit old theories. They observed many developments the implications of which they could not possibly comprehend. They both went far beyond their time in grasping theoretically aspects of a reality not yet born. We inherit from them the dilemmas they were never able to answer fully. Much of what they left us has still to be worked out in history, and disentangled and understood as theory.

To take their conclusions as in any sense final would be to ignore this and to abstract them from their own space and time. Despite the depth of their historical analysis, the range of their knowledge, and the extent of the commotion their writing has helped to create, Karl Marx and Frederick Engels were still a couple of bourgeois men in the nineteenth century. They saw a particular world through particular eyes. This is not to suggest that if they had happened to be women they would have had the last word on women's liberation, but that they were bound to see women's situation through the eyes of men, and working-class women through the eyes of middle-class men. Inevitably this affected how they saw and where they looked.

In the *Economic and Philosophic Manuscripts* written in 1844 Marx developed a theme generally discussed in utopian socialist writing on women's liberation, but expressed in a well-known form by Fourier. This was the connection of the emancipation of women with the general historical development of society:

The immediate, natural and necessary relation of human being to human being is also the relation of man to woman. . . . Thus in this relation is sensuously revealed, reduced to an observable fact, the extent to which human nature has become nature for man and to which nature has become human nature to him. From this relationship man's whole level of development can be assessed. It follows from the character of this relationship how far man has become, and has understood himself as a species-being, a human being. . . . It also shows how far man's needs and consequently how far the other person, as a person, has become one of his needs, to what extent he is his individual existence [and] at the same time a social being.[1]

Marx is not using 'nature' as a mysteriously hidden essence. He saw man as at once part of nature, and a natural being. At the same time man was a human natural being – a species-being. Human nature was not therefore something implanted; man had natural appetites and propensities, but the manner in which man satisfied these was social and historical, involving both art and morality. When man relates to woman only as slave, or as the person who feeds him, part of his own capacity, of his own ability to create his own nature as a social being, is denied. Affection between the sexes is not seen as being naturally implanted. A personal consciousness of the opposite sex is an historical achievement, part of man's creation of his own nature. By perceiving the woman as another human being with a distinct consciousness, he has moved towards a need which is not simply natural but human natural. Thus the ability to transform is linked closely to the ability to appreciate, know, be conscious of. Following Fourier Marx saw women's position here rather as an historical index of the ability of human beings to be conscious of and thus control the external environment, a gauge of the movement from necessity to freedom in society. But the existing relationship between human beings was a feature of their alienation from nature and from each other. Man's human part has become animal and his animal part human. He has become a stomach and an abstract activity. His natural functions such as procreation become animal instead of human. The actual condition of women reflects this distortion.

Marx presented a means of human self-consciousness overcoming alienated social relations. A purely philosophic transcendence was not possible; the philosopher can only philosophize from his point of alienation. His idea of woman thus is only a projection of his own self-division. The ability to understand, to control and act creatively must be expressed through practical activity to change the world, or it must be forever commenting on its own inability to comment. Ultimately, only through a transformation of the way property was owned and the social relations which came from this ownership could the real appropriation of human nature, through and for man, be historically achieved. The most general expression of human alienation was in the situation of the worker. Woman's general relation to man, prostitution, was only a specific expression of the universal prostitution of the worker. Both could only be changed in a communist society.

Although 'man' is used in the generalized sense of human being, there is still no concept of an historical agency of women. Woman is still the other, part of the world outside as perceived, grasped, controlled by man. It is not clear how woman is going to act from her specific form of prostitution. She appears as an indication of the state of society, not as a social group in movement, developing consciousness in history. The female is rather a representative symbol of man in relation to nature.

This is not to say she is denied any benefit from communism. Apparently she will share 'the real appropriation of human nature' possible in a communist society. Her body will be no man's private property. Marx believed that by removing the economic dependence of woman upon man under private property, a new, truly human relationship would be possible under communism. He was emphatically opposed to the ideas of 'crude communists' who argued communism meant community in women. He argued against this as substituting private for public property. He saw that in both cases the human development of woman herself was denied. Engels repeated this idea very clearly in his *Principles of Communism*, the draft for the *Communist Manifesto*, written in 1847:

> Community of women is a condition which belongs entirely to a bourgeois society and which today finds its complete expression in prostitution. But prostitution is based on private property and falls with it. Thus communist society, instead of introducing community of women, in fact abolishes it.[2]

Of course community of women was the bogy of the bourgeoisie:

> The bourgeois sees in his wife a mere instrument of production. He hears that the instruments of production are to be exploited in common, and naturally can come to no other conclusion than that the lot of being common to all will likewise fall to the women. He has not even a suspicion that the real point aimed at is to do away with the status of women as mere instruments of production.[3]

In the *Communist Manifesto* Marx and Engels thus ridicule the fears of the bourgeoisie. They also mock their hypocrisy and double standard of morality. Bourgeois man uses all women as his objects, and regards his woman as his property.

In *The Holy Family* Marx connects the hypocrisy of bourgeois man with his inability to understand the way in which he exploits women. He comments on the manner in which the hero of Eugene Sue's *Mysteries of Paris* treats a servant girl. He is sentimental about her fate but can't go on to 'grasp the general condition of women in society as an inhuman one'.[4] The 'fall' of a particular woman is seen as the result of individual misfortune – an historical accident. Rudolph assumes women possess an abstracted moral choice, quite removed from their actual social situation. Thus he teases Fleur de

64

Marie with the need to become 'honest'. She replies literally and with realism: 'Honest! My God, what do you want me to be honest with.'[5] Similarly the priest who converts Fleur de Marie does not allow her to develop from herself, he merely provides her with a false Fleur de Marie who she can pretend to be. This false alternative fails to solve her social situation and does not connect her degradation to the inevitable prostitution of the little girls who sell matches in the streets of Paris. Both Rudolph and the priest have too great a stake in the society which exploits Fleur de Marie and the match girls to make such connections.

These arguments develop from the climate of utopian socialist thought, but they are considerably more sophisticated in the way in which they are presented. They are quite inseparable from Marx's general ideas of alienation, and his conception of a communist society. The persistent theme of prostitution is not surprising in the context of the mid-nineteenth century. All human beings in class society met as the prostitute met her client. Just as the prostitute gives the substitute of love for money, the worker hands over his work and his life for a daily wage. The existence of such commodity exchanges made a mockery of other human relations. But the prostitute herself was a living reminder of the hollowness and corruption behind social relations.

Of course the prostitute pre-dated capitalism and prostitution continued among women in the countryside, but the growth of large industrial towns and the massing of the working class in particular compartments and areas of the city meant that the nature and scale of prostitution changed. Its causes were very clearly economic. It became a necessary way of supplementing their wages for large numbers of urban working women. Morally and socially it was an unanswerable indictment of laissez-faire and the 'free market'. Just as the bourgeois responded to the industrial working class in terms of projected fears for his own position – they are the beast, the savage with horny hands, wild, primitive sensual natural man – the prostitute became the symbol of his class and sex guilt. She was the spectre haunting his comfortable parlour. She was the lie to his much boasted sanctity of the family and of religion. Her syphilis stalked his hypocritical monogamy, mocked his connubial rights and penetrated the holy fastness of the crinoline. The degradation of one group of women was inseparable from the false reverence kept for the wife of the bourgeois. Bourgeois man located in the prostitute, who was often seen as synonymous with the lower-class woman, all the sensuality denied to his own women.

'Nymphomania' was actually used in the 1840s to describe any woman who felt sexual desire, and such women were seen as necessarily abandoned, women of the streets, women of the lower classes. Just as the white slave-owner suckled by black women sought them for orgasm rather than his white wife, the nineteenth-century urban bourgeois continually pursued his wet nurse. He retained of course the noblest, most spiritual filial devotion to his own mother, as a being apart and above physical sensation. Conversely the bourgeois in revolt tended to impute an idealized 'natural' sensuality on the prostitute as upon the lower-class woman. Their degradation was transferred in the minds of these romantics into innocent delight. From the cult of woman as emotion and sensuality came such ideas as those of 'crude communism'. They were the equivalent to the romantic idea of a lost state of nature personified in the noble savage, the peasant, or later the worker.

In rejecting an idealized Fleur de Marie Marx thus makes a significant break with romantic socialism. He indicates the possibility of an actual Fleur de Marie realizing actual human appetites and propensities in a real communist society. But unfortunately Fleur de Marie never organizes. She knows no solidarity. She is symptomatic of oppression, not the agent of her own liberation. Prostitution is seen as a particular cultural expression of exploitation, a specific form of alienation. It is not simply an affair of individual prostitutes, but a statement about women's condition, and thus about social relations in general. The transformation of the relation of man to woman is thus an essential feature of communist society, but still the action of women themselves does not emerge as an essential part of this process. As to the exact nature of the transformation in the future communist society, both Marx and Engels were too great respecters of history to delineate. Communist human relationships and culture are open only to conjecture before the material conditions for their creation exist. There can be no answer, Engels wrote many years later in 1884 in *The Origin of the Family*, until there is 'a generation of men who never in their lives have known what it is to buy a woman's surrender with money or power; a generation of women who have never known what it is to give themselves to a man from any other consideration than real love, or to refuse to give themselves to their lover from fear of the economic consequences'.[6]

These earlier statements in the 1840s were undoubtedly over-optimistic in seeing prostitution and the degradation of women in a direct relation to strictly economic factors. Our subsequent experience has shown that the phenomenon of prostitution continues to survive long after there have been changes in the structure of institutions and the removal of immediate economic necessity in the nineteenth-century sense. However, Engels's later comment shows that he saw economic transformation only as an essential precondition, and the cultural and psychological aspects of prostitution as needing to be worked out subsequently. What we are bound to ask now is whether the connection between change in the institutional structure *can* lead to the cultural changes envisaged, without the mobilization of Fleur de Marie at the point of her own prostitution, before the revolutionary transformation of society. This becomes rapidly an argument about the cart before the horse, in which it is not clear whether Fleur de Marie is pulling or being pulled into history.

In *The German Ideology* (1845–6) Marx and Engels created a basis for a more concrete study of women's condition as an historically changing aspect of the material situation. The assumption is again that the particular relation of human beings to nature affects not only their own nature, but the way in which they relate to one another. The extent to which man can modify nature historically will be reflected in his consciousness of other human beings. '... Man's consciousness of the necessity of associating with the individuals around him is the beginning of the consciousness that he is living in society.'[7] With this association arises division of labour, 'originally nothing but the division of labour in the sexual act'.[8] The distinction is made here between division based on sex, natural pre-disposition, physical strength, accidents, and a formal institutional division, based first on mental and material activity, then on the ownership of property. The determining factors in historical change are seen as the production of material things to enable human beings to live; the creation of new human needs in the process of satisfying old ones; and in the process of reproduction. 'The production of life, both of one's own in labour and of fresh life in procreation, now appears as a double relationship; on the one hand as a natural, on the other as a social relationship.'[9] It would follow then that a study of the social relations of reproduction is as essential for historical understanding of the human condition as the study of the social relations of production. Instead Marx went on to examine the latter and subsequent Marxists have followed him. However, Engels in *The Origin of the Family* took up this idea again.

'According to the materialistic conception, the determining factor in history is, in the final instance, the production and reproduction of the immediate essentials.'[10] He went on to say this had two sides, the production of the 'means of existence' and 'the production of human beings themselves, the propagation of the species'.[11]

From this Engels attempted to work out social stages relating to various modes of production and reproduction. He connected changes in the family to changes in the ownership of the means of production. He argued, for example, connections between ownership of the means of production, such as cattle, and the position of woman in relation to man in society. He believed that human society had passed through an era of matriarchy and that women had never regained the ascendancy they enjoyed then.

The study of geology, archaeology, prehistory and anthropology was still relatively new and had only developed really from the 1860s as anything more than a rather dilettante pursuit. It had faced similar opposition to Darwinian concepts of biological evolution because it provided an alternative to Genesis, and a chronology which made nonsense of the theological calculations of biblical scholars. At the time Engels was writing there was considerable argument about how to classify the new discoveries made through excavation. There was also controversy about whether anthropological evolution could be observed as corresponding to biological evolution. Arguments about alternative utopian futures had even earlier produced an alternative account of the past. Utopian socialists in the 1830s and 1840s quite often produced their own versions of human evolution. They frequently argued an anthropological golden age and provided their own ideas of Eve's part in the Fall. Because of this feminism and socialism were often connected in popular imagination with the horrors of evolution.

Coming out of the utopian socialist tradition but utilizing the new methods of study, Lewis H. Morgan published his *Ancient Society* in 1877. It was subtitled 'Researches in the Lines of Human Progress

*But feminism does here to do with the evolution of the species.*

68

from Savagery through Barbarism to Civilization'. Morgan drew on studies of American Indians and worked out a progressive sequence of man's anthropological evolution. This was particularly interesting to Engels because he and Marx had been exhaustively studying anthropological data in an effort to document the interaction between human beings with nature in the period before recorded history. Subsequently anthropologists have found that Morgan's sequence is over-simplified and that Engels was arguing a case from insufficient data. The fact that Engels thought it possible to reach conclusions about early societies from evidence about contemporary primitive societies also affects his conclusions. Unfortunately, an academic controversy, opposition to the evolutionary school, and political issues, the general dismissal of any attempt to find historical connections between man in relation to nature and in relation to society, have confused the issue. Engels provided a valuable synthesis of existing anthropological material at the time, which gave Marxists at the end of the century a much more sophisticated understanding of mankind's early history than that available in the utopian socialist movement. However, to try to defend his classification, regardless of new evidence, would be to miss the point. Many of Engels's conclusions can be endlessly discussed in the air because so much is ultimately unverifiable. The fact that his anthropological data is inadequate does not mean that the ideas he expresses and the attempt to integrate his Marxism with an anthropological study of the family should be ignored. To dismiss his anthropology as simply outdated is comparable to the complacency which says of Marx's *Capital* that the economics are old-fashioned. Having understood the limits of *The Origin of the Family*, the most important question, that of method, remains. The arguments against Engels very quickly become arguments against any attempt to discover historical pattern and any factors for change. This is the equivalent of the approach to history which argues about the length of a king's nose and ignores the economic circumstances which could allow his nose to be important. Not only have liberal anthropologists failed to consider the problem of the interaction of modes of reproduction and production, and the relation of this to the position of women and change in the organization of society; but Marxists themselves have ignored the important point about reproduction, as part of the material world, being a determining factor in history. Only comparatively recently has the social situation of the child in the family become a part of an effort to develop a Marxist psychology which can communicate the process of the individual's early consciousness of society, the family. As the separation of production-work and reproduction-childbearing and the family have become physically separated in space, and the period of reproduction reduced by contraception, there has been a tendency in sociology to study these areas in isolation. Similarly Marxist sociology has tended to concentrate on work relations rather than family relations. The worker's consciousness is seen as developing only at the point of production. It is forgotten that the worker came from a particular family, and that we conceive the world through the relationships in the family, describe it in language first learned in the family, and through eyes which grew accustomed to other human beings first in the family. The implications of study of the social relationship of reproduction are of immense importance for a theory of consciousness. Many of the questions raised in *The German Ideology* as well as *The Origin of the Family* need to be re-examined, not as dogma, but in relation to the new knowledge and experience gained since they have been written. The Women's Liberation Movement directs attention to precisely these areas which have remained in theoretical obscurity within Marxist theory.

It is not surprising that the attention of Marx and Engels was directed towards historical change in the nature of the family. In the mid-Victorian era dramatic changes were evident in relations between the sexes, and between parents and children; just as now it is apparent that social changes in production have immediate effects on the family. At one side there was the idealization of the bourgeois family. The formidable family groups which confront us in the mid-century portraits and late-century photographs are immediate symbols of Victorianism. Increasingly, from the mid-nineteenth century the family becomes the last refuge of all those human qualities unable to survive in the outside world of capitalism. Home Sweet Home and the roses round the door are the abode of true feeling. The Angel in the House guards the sanctity like one of the old household gods. Froude in *The Nemesis of Faith* in 1849 described how, when men return home, they lay aside 'our mask and drop our tools'. They are no longer forced to act out the characters forced on them by their work. 'We fall again into our most human relations.' Home shields the man from the destructive effects of struggle and

Write about
companionship.
How erotic feeling is involved
in companionship + vice
versa.

## Dialectical Disturbances

competition. It is the only place left in which he can simply be 'himself'. This concept of the bourgeois family did not just confine the woman physically to the home. It created a role for her in which she existed only to bolster up the man. Ruskin described this in *Sesame and the Lilies*: 'Her great function is Praise.' She does nothing on her own initiative. But because the man must inevitably be wounded, subdued, harshened 'in his rough work in the open world', he protects woman from contact with his harsh world. In exchange she creates home as a haven of peace for him. Such an ideal of the family of course never questioned the continuance of the competitive society outside. On the contrary, it made man's inhumanity to man more bearable by allowing him to be human at home, though at the expense of the humanity of the woman. The womblike crinoline cushions his aching spirit. Fleur de Marie was the lie to all this, and it is this conception of the 'family' that Marx and Engels ridiculed in the *Communist Manifesto*.

*[margin note: How can he be human if she isn't? But it is good for a person to be supported like that. Perhaps not as good as having a companion – but easier.]*

At the opposite extreme there was the effect of the break-up of traditional agricultural communities and the move to the industrial town on the working-class family. Amidst all the horrors of over-crowding, appalling sanitation, low pay, exhaustion, little food, and the escape of drink, violence, and brutalized sex, most working men enjoyed no haven and most working women enjoyed little protection and had little time for praise. As for parental affection, workers were bound to see their children as 'hands'. Children went out to work early. They often left their parents to fare as well as they could as soon as they could earn enough to live independently. They could be the main breadwinners because their parents would be refused employment. There are frequent references to couples setting up at fourteen and to young teenagers living and stealing in gangs. It was often these aspects of urbanization which shocked middle-class observers more than the conditions at work. Complaints about the break-up of the family combine with strictures on the insolence, immorality, and love of tawdry finery and independence of factory girls. Their ignorance of domestic wifely matters is contrasted with an ideal of agricultural housekeeping. But also within the emerging labour movement, men who protested against the evils of the factory system believed these evils to be magnified in relation to women. This was partly based on a knowledgeable sympathy for women's physical weakness and the fact of reproduction, partly on a conception of womanliness which saw her place as in the home, and also on the strong feeling that women should not take away work from the men. When they worked, it only intensified competition for jobs. These attitudes appear in the comments of a local chartist, P. J. Richardson, when he found women carrying heavy wet calicoes. He tells them:

> This is the work of men . . . and you ought not to perform it; your places are in your homes; your labours are your domestic duties; your interests are in the welfare of your families and not in slaving for the accumulation of wealth of others, whose slaves you seem willing to be; for shame on you! Go seek husbands, those of you who have them not, and make them toil for you; and those of you who have husbands and families, go home and minister to their domestic comforts.[12]

Richardson is far from supporting the subordination of women. But he appeals to a traditional conception of a proper sphere for women. He believed factory work and heavy work subordinated them and that the vote and equal rights were essential if women were to end this degradation. There was quite a strong vein of retrospection in popular radicalism and chartism. Marx and Engels created a very different way of seeing woman's role in the family and at work. In *The Condition of the Working Class* in 1844 Engels writes about the pregnancies of factory women, the return to work after a few days, leaving the baby and rushing home in the dinner hour. Nursing mothers themselves speak of their difficulties and describe the pain in their breasts. The effects of the factory system on such apparently intimate matters as menstruation and sexual intercourse are patiently documented. Certainly in Engels's description of the effect of nineteenth-century capitalism on the working-class family, an idealization of home still combines with a popular memory of the pre-factory situation. This is not surprising because the sources he used, middle-class commentators and working-class witnesses, contained both attitudes. He echoes middle-class observers in his criticism of the moral consequences of large numbers of men and women working together in close proximity: a view he was to reverse later. But in his own observations he makes it clear that he does not think some return to a lost state is the answer. Nor does he believe that change in the family can somehow be abstracted from general changes in society. The neglect of children when the woman works, the upside-downness of poor Jack who can't get work, unsexed and degraded, mending his wife's stockings while she is the wage-earner, indicate that 'both sexes have been placed in a false position from the beginning.'[13] The binding tie of the family before its physical break-up through factory work was still based on property, on who contributed most. The change the factories have produced is to turn the economic control of the family topsy-turvy. Personal relations are reversed while the other social conditions remain unchanged. There is no basis for an alternative idea of dignity. Jack is simply deprived of his manhood. Engels concluded that this partial change only degraded both sexes. In this sense he saw capitalism destroying the working-class family. Admittedly the witness was obviously one of Jack's mates and we don't know what his wife thought about it.

*Blacks, too.*

In *Capital*, along with many specific observations on the working conditions of sewing girls, silk workers, bleachers, straw-plaiters, and other women, and on the effects of machinery on the various trades, Marx takes up this theme of the dissolution of the family again. He connects this to the factory system and the physical separation of home and work. The family ceases to be a unit of production and becomes only a unit of consumption. 'Modern industry, in overturning the economical foundation on which was based the traditional family and the family labour corresponding to it, had also loosened all traditional family ties.'[14]

With this separation of function and loosening of ties gradually came the replacement of the individual family by the state in several spheres of authority. This served further to break down the individual inviolability of the family. The legislative acceptance of government responsibility for the hours women and children worked, and the 1870 act for education, implied that the father's authority could be superseded. They also implied that women and children had rights which could not be included in the rights of the father. In the case of working-class women this recognition was only possible after the full horrors of factory work and life in the new towns had been exposed. Indeed, one of the arguments used by people who wanted to oppose the movement to ban women working in the mines was that they had always worked there, long before the factories. There were too some women who feared that protective legislation would mean they couldn't get any employment. It was a painful contradiction that Marx grasped very well. Marx supported protective legislation as a limitation on the capitalist's right to exploit the worker. But he never accepted the view of many English radicals, and the followers of the French socialist Proudhon, that it was unnatural for women to work. Quite the opposite, he saw the process he identified as the dissolution of the family under capitalism as being a necessary precondition for new forms of relationship between men and women, parents and children. In 1866 he brought a resolution in favour of child labour, as well as women working, before the International, with the proviso of protective legislation, because he believed work should not be separate from education and was beneficial to the human personality. In *Capital* he wrote that 'however terrible and disgusting' this was in its immediate effect, ultimately, 'by assigning as it does an important part in the process of production outside the domestic sphere to women, young persons, and to children of both sexes, it creates a new economical foundation for a higher form of family and of relations between the sexes.'[15]

It was all very well to argue in this way if you believed capitalism's knell had already sounded. But subsequently Marxists have found this statement somewhat problematical. From the later Engels onwards it has been argued that women must be involved in production as a precondition for emancipation. But this has been seen rather as the only way in which they could exercise control as workers, rather than a basis for a new family and changed relations between the sexes. There has been an understandable nervousness about child labour as a precondition for emancipation.

The comment which comes later in the passage makes it clear that Marx has already jumped mentally into the communist future. 'Moreover it is obvious that the fact of the collective working group being composed of individuals of both sexes and all ages, must necessarily under suitable conditions become a source of human development.'[16] A hundred years later this is less obvious. First of all it means sharing a philosophic commitment to activity, association and work as a means of developing human consciousness. Second, whether this is anyway synonymous with the inclusion of individuals of both sexes and all ages in production is open to speculation. Third, the only sense in which we can interpret the phrase 'suitable conditions' is to imagine work in which there is no element of compulsion. Production would have to be inseparable from play. It is almost impossible for us to visualize such a condition.

Generally both Marx and Engels were very guarded about making pronouncements about the future, because they were all too aware of the dangers of rigid utopian schemata. However, there are scattered about their works various observations about the nature of communist sexual relations. They both wrote romantic love poetry as young men. Engels translated Shelley whom he greatly admired and Marx sent Jenny three volumes of love lyrics. They lived very differently from each other in later life, Marx respectably settled with Jenny, but having an illegitimate son Frederick; Engels in free union with Mary Burns and then with her sister after she died, both women Irish proletarians and fiercely republican. But philosophically their attitude to love was consistent with their central commitment to human growth and development. They believed that individual sex love would reach a much fuller expression in communist society because the old pressures of economic necessity present in capitalism and the alienation of all social relations would disappear. They were opposed equally to the idealization and the cult of women, as natural emotional feeling, and the vulgar mechanical materialism which reduced all human sexual relations to a simply physical response. Marx in *The Holy Family* saw love as essential to the fulfilment of all human beings. He says it was the experience which 'first really teaches man to believe in the objective world outside himself'.[17] He equated the intellectual tendency to dismiss love as suspicion of 'everything living, everything which is immediate, every sensuous experience, any and every real experience the "whence" and "whither" of which are not known beforehand'.

Capitalism was held guilty not only of the exploitation of labour power. It had appropriated sense-experience. This was all too evident in the ideology of the bourgeoisie as much as in how they lived. In *The Origin of the Family* Engels pointed out much later that it was most ironical that the right to marry whom you pleased was enjoyed by the oppressed class, the proletariat, rather than the oppressors. The latter were encumbered by the responsibility of their property. Believing like Shelley and the early radicals that love between the sexes was a social affair, and did not escape the influence of social institutions, Engels argued that monogamy created the preconditions for women's liberation historically. The love marriage was as much a right of woman as a right of man in bourgeois theory. But in practice the rights of lovers were subordinated to the rights of property. Similarly the young Marx in the 1840s also believed that possessive love indicated the desire for a slave as partner rather than another human being. 'The jealous person is above all a private property owner.'[18]

But they did not argue from this that sex relations would become a more public affair. Communism was the means of enabling every individual to enjoy a far richer personal life than was possible under capitalism because the old economic subordination will no longer exist. 'It will transform the relations between the sexes into a purely private matter which concerns only the persons involved and into which society has no occasion to intervene.'[19]

As to the forms of such relations, in *The Origin of the Family* he felt it was only possible to see what they would not be. All that was certain was that the generations who had never known alienation or domination 'will care precious little what anybody today thinks they ought to do; they will make their own practice and their corresponding public opinion about the practice of each individual and that will be the end of it'.[20] Such a generation is still unborn.

Marx and Engels left an important theoretical commitment to the liberation of woman's potential as a human being and the connection of this to communism. Between them they added greatly to an understanding of the nature of women's oppression in the nineteenth century, both in the anthropological and in the economic sense. However, as Juliet Mitchell points out in *Woman's Estate*, the liberation of women has remained marginal in Marxist theory – dependent on the emancipation of the working class. There were many questions they left open and they took some ideas for granted which appear incredible now. They were of their own time. They could not envisage the extraordinary transformation of social revolution, the startling conclusions of bourgeois psychology, the new technology of contraception or a movement like women's liberation. Many really crucial questions are unanswered. If these are to be resolved it is not by annotating their writings specifically on women but by extending Marxist theory in general as part of revolutionary feminist praxis.[21] Does it follow that changes in the ownership and organization of production in fact change the social relations of production, and consequently effect a revolutionary change in women's position? Given that women's oppression pre-dates capitalist society, can it be assumed that a revolution which changes the economic basis of society in a socialist direction would affect her sexual role? Is it not rather necessary for women to organize round their specific experiences as women actually in the course of revolutionary struggle against capitalism? The question remains what form should such organization take to be most effective. How far can the revolutionary argue for women's involvement in productive work when for working-class women this is invariably the most boring and lowest paid? While Engels recognized the separate and specific oppression of women and compared women to the proletariat and man to the bourgeois, he does not work out any sense in which the description of women as a class can be related to the concept of class in Marx's writing. Nor does he have any idea about the kind of action women can take. Similarly they both presumed women would take their part in the general struggle to change society as equivalent to the men, although their general position in society was in no sense equal. Personally they were ready to accept the activity of women in revolutionary work on a completely equal basis. Marx supported the women's section in the International for example. He specially singled out the women in the Commune, praising their heroism. He always encouraged the intellectual development and activism of his own daughters. Engels also obviously respected and learned from the republicanism and class consciousness of Mary and Lizzie. But the more general problem remained. The subordination of women in society as a whole could be reflected in revolutionary organizations. Many revolutionary men were not able to cast off a deep contempt for women, when they became socialists. They didn't apply their other ideas to women.

This was one of the great unresolved dilemmas and it was to be debated fiercely throughout the revolutionary movements as part of the continuing question of women's emancipation.

## CHAPTER 4

# Dreams and Dilemmas

---

The wife who married for money compared with the prostitute is the true scab. She is paid less, gives much more in return in labour and care, and is absolutely bound to her master.

Havelock Ellis

Why can't we men and women come near each other, and help each other and not kill each other's souls and blight each other's lives.
. . . When passion enters a relationship it does spoil the holy sweetness. But perhaps those people are right who say no such thing as friendship is possible between a man and a woman, only I can't bear to think it so.

Olive Schreiner, Letters to Havelock Ellis

History tells us that every oppressed class gained true liberation from its masters through its own efforts. It is necessary that woman learn that lesson, that she realize that her freedom will reach as far as her power to achieve her freedom reaches.

Emma Goldman, 'Women's Suffrage',
in *Anarchism and Other Essays*

---

Women's liberation was a live and explosive issue in the emerging socialist movements at the end of the century. However, this was not so much because people dutifully sat down and read Marx and Engels. Most of their writing which dealt with women's oppression was not widely available until a relatively late date. In various ways women themselves put considerable pressure on the new movements and were able to put their case within the general arguments for socialism. Also there were other writers and thinkers who popularized the connection between women's liberation and revolution, both in the Marxist and anarchist tradition. Undoubtedly too the organization and activity of bourgeois feminism, especially in England and America, forced socialists to consider the issues and clarify their own approach to the question.

From the start there was little uniformity. In Russia for example, where the revolutionary movement was deeply committed both to women's emancipation and personal cultural transformation, apart from the earlier influence of George Sand on Herzen, Chernychevsky's novel *What is to be Done?*, published in the 1860s, was the central text for a generation. It was a story of an emancipated heroine, a lofty 'free union' and a cooperative sewing workshop. Women like Vera Figner played an important and frequently heroic part in the general movement and a separate bourgeois feminist movement only developed long afterwards.

In America on the other hand the feminist movement came out of the anti-slavery campaign and two tendencies emerged. One group restricted its demand to the vote and were willing to settle for a compromise on total suffrage. But another group based in New York, with Susan B. Anthony and Elizabeth Cady Stanton, not only refused to compromise over the franchise but connected emancipation with change in marriage, clothing, morals and the organization of labour. They produced a short-lived journal called *The Revolution* in 1868. In the same year Victoria Woodhull arrived in New York. She swiftly became a notorious figure, propagating free love, feminist Marxism (her own variety), spiritualism, and universology – the key to all knowledge. The main wing of American feminism was far more cautious and far more conservative. Its advocates were at once ignorant and contemptuous of organized labour, though later, in the 1890s, a social feminism, connected with the settlements, developed. This was concerned rather to improve the working conditions of girls and women in factories and sweat shops rather than the problem of connecting the liberation of women with the idea of revolution.

The 'woman question' caused some argument in the European socialist movement. In the First International the French anarchist-socialist Proudhon and his followers in the sixties were quite opposed to Marx's ideas. Proudhon also came into conflict with socialist feminist women in France. In Germany the followers of Lassalle argued against the semi-Marxist groups led by Bebel at a congress in Gotha in 1875. Bebel had proposed equal rights for women as part of the official party programme. But the congress rejected this on the grounds that women were not yet ready for equal rights – a familiar argument.

Bebel's book *Woman and Socialism*, published in 1879 in Germany, although received with the utmost horror by the German bourgeoisie had an important effect. Both he and Engels also personally encouraged the growth of a separate socialist women's movement in Germany, which published its own papers and had its own organization. However, only in 1891 did the German party officially accept women's equal rights, and then only in a very limited legal sense. It would seem too that at a grass roots level they did not emphasize these questions very much in their propaganda. Adelheid Popp, a trade union militant in the Social Democratic Party, describes this in her autobiography:

I had no notion yet of the 'Woman Question'. There was nothing about it in my newspaper, and I only read Social Democratic publications. I was held to be an exception, and I looked upon myself as such. I considered the Social Question, as far as I then understood it, as a man's question, just like politics. Only I would have liked to be a man, to have a right to busy myself with politics.[1]

She discovered that Social Democrats supported equal rights for women but still didn't realize that women themselves could share in the work of the party. When she read a reference to the exploitation of women workers in her party paper, she was so excited and overjoyed she couldn't sleep. It wasn't until she went to a branch meeting where there were three hundred men and nine women from the party that she managed to speak out herself and take an active part in revolutionary politics. She was much encouraged by Bebel's book *Woman and Socialism*.

Bebel argued like the utopian socialists that the liberation of women was inseparable from the release of all human beings from 'oppression, exploitation, want and misery in a hundred shapes. . . . The so-called women's question is therefore only one side of the whole social question . . . only in connection with each other can the two questions reach their final solution.'[2]

Neither could be separated, and neither could be resolved except through the creation of a socialist society. This was partly because he believed the practical conditions for women's liberation, communalization of housework, facilities for looking after children, were dependent on socialism; but also because the relationships of exploitation and domination connected with capitalism, and within which women were subordinated, could only be dissolved by a fundamental change in the social structure. Bebel was aware that woman's oppression pre-dated capitalism, and that her consciousness of subordination went very deep and was expressed in areas where habit and nature were so ingrown they were almost indistinguishable. She was 'a slave before the slave existed'. Thus like Engels he did not believe that women's liberation could be created in a utopian way in the moment of revolution. Revolution was only the beginning. There was a long process afterwards. This did not mean, however, that he put off any movement for short-term changes, or dismissed the immediate real conflicts actually between men and women within capitalism. Beginnings don't come from nowhere. You have to do a lot of work before you can even begin. Arguing that women were doubly exploited, he saw them fighting against capitalism and against their own oppression. Bebel follows the radical tradition which puts the oppressed firmly in charge of their own liberation. Women's interests could no more be included with the interests of men than the workers could be included in the interests of the employers. From Mary Wollstonecraft to Flora Tristan, revolutionary women had finally looked to men to free women. But Bebel believed there was little likelihood of men as a group taking up the cause of women's emancipation. Why should they try to end women's dependence in the family and society, when this dependence directly benefited them?

It gratifies their vanity, feeds their pride, and suits their interests to play the part of master and lord, and in this role, they are like all rulers well nigh inaccessible to reason. This makes it all the more imperative on women to exert themselves in bringing about new conditions, which will enable them to free themselves from this degrading position. Women have as little to hope from men as the workmen from the middle classes.[3]

This passage indicates the transformation Marxism made of

utopian socialist assumptions, while at the same time leaving un-solved many of the essential dilemmas of the earlier movement. There was no question of convincing oppressors as a group suddenly to become reasonable, or kind. Revolution was not a matter just of reason or human sympathy; it involved also the power to effect change. True, some radicals understood this before Marx. Much of the suspicion towards Owen from root and branch reformers was his early flirtation with the rich and powerful, ostensibly in the cause of the poor. But Marx's ideas provided a clear theoretical and historical basis for this understanding. Thus Bebel argues that women must make their own struggle. However, the crucial difference which Marx made in his writing between previous exhortations to the workers to make revolution was to show how acting from their immediate situation the working class could not help but carry a potential alternative to capitalism at the very points at which they opposed the existing system. Bebel's conception of women's need to struggle is still a *moral* imperative. The imperative remains volun-tary, an exertion of will. Here the break with utopianism is not made distinctly. There is no apparent way in which women could not help but act in some manner towards a socialist society. Like earlier revolutionary feminists Bebel could only appeal to women to see the light of reason. This is consistent with the more general theoretical and practical deadlock within German social democracy at this time and the lack of any strategy for the revolutionary seizure of power.

The immediate importance of his book was the application to the predicament of women of an historical approach combined with a very clear refusal to gloss over the awkward areas. He brought the argument right home into the socialist movement:

There are socialists who are not less opposed to the emancipation of women than the capitalist to socialism. Every socialist recognizes the dependence of the workman on the capitalist, and cannot understand that others and especially the capitalists themselves should fail to recognize it also; but the same socialist often does not recognize the dependence of women on men because the question touches his own dear self more or less nearly. The effort to defend real or imaginary interests, which of course are always indubitable, and unassailable, makes people so blind.[4]

It was to Bebel's credit that he could searchlight the murky areas of his own movement. Blindspots were not peculiar to revolutionaries when he was writing; they had appeared long before, and are with us long afterwards. But it has usually taken a separate movement to force socialists to look at them long and clear, without flinching. There is nothing more incongruous than the innocent surprise of a Marxist when he finds his own theoretical conclusions confirmed within his own movement. Comradeship can become a kind of camouflage, obscuring rather than resolving the particular consciousness of sex, race and class. It can often mean that people just pretend to cast off the selves produced by the outside world. Bebel would not accept the disguise of comradeship. He believed that real contradictions within the movement had to be confronted openly.

He is much less aware of contradictory and opposing interests among women themselves. He neglects the problem of class conflict, which cuts right through any sense of women as a group. In the 1880s and 90s the class interests of upper- and middle-class feminists which emerged so clearly in the war were less evidently opposed to working-class women and to socialism. Bourgeois feminism could still appear as part of a vague human movement towards a better society. Its later manifestations evoked an understandable hostility among socialists, though in its crudest form this was to be expressed as a straightforward contempt for middle-class women, in which sex prejudice became confused with revolutionary zeal.

But Bebel can be much more open. There is real sympathy in his description of the way these women were 'trained as dolls; fools of fashion', and the insight with which he traced their frequent illnesses to the meaningless course of the lives they could lead. Internationally the prominence and activity of women from middle-class backgrounds is very marked in the socialist movement of this period. Undoubtedly the consideration of their particular experience of oppression was a product of their revolutionary activity and at the same time contributed to their participation in it.

The implications of his view that the women's question was inseparable from the whole social question have still to be worked out:

> The question as to what position in our social organization will ~~Bebel~~
> enable woman to become a useful member of the community, will put
> her in possession of the same rights as its other members enjoy, and
> ensure the full development of her powers and faculties in every

direction, coincides with the question as to the form and organization which the entire community must receive, if oppression, exploitation, want and misery in a hundred shapes are to be replaced by a free humanity.[5]

The liberation of women thus demands its own specific forms of socialism, which come out of the experience of women in oppression. Subordination has a hundred shapes; it needs innumerable combined transformations. Socialism is not only the ending of class oppression or exploitation at the work place, but in every area of human experience. The regions of consciousness are not capable of tidy delineation, and the spheres of subordination interact.

Bebel follows Marx and Engels in his commitment to human development and his faith in human potential. Right at the end of his book sits a surprising passage. It has been dismissed as quite unconnected to his general argument for women's emancipation, and impossibly utopian. He suddenly branches out into a discussion of the authoritarian education which serves to compartmentalize and limit human beings' capacity to become conscious of the world around them. He sees this as part of the division of labour and sees socialism as involving the disappearance of both. 'There will be no musicians, actors, artists and scholars by profession, but by spontaneous choice, by right of talent and genius.'[6]

In fact this was quite closely connected to his conception of the break up in the distinction between men's and women's roles. He thought socialism would mean that the individual cellular existence of the household would be reduced. Human beings would lead an extremely sociable existence. There would be innumerable halls for eating, for games, reading rooms and libraries, concert halls, theatres, museums, playgrounds, green parks. Behind these proposals was a conviction common in the socialist movement that not only would the internal world of the family merge with the outside world of society, but that the division between work and play, play and education, education and work, work and love-making, love-making and work, would completely disappear. Of course the revolutionary re-creation of boundaries between public and private could not be solved by these passages in Bebel or in Marx's and Engels's approach to love. It had to be worked out in practice. The extent to which the personal life of human beings could or should be socialized was to cause much controversy in the Soviet Union after the revolution. It related to the more general argument about what should be preserved from the pre-revolutionary culture, and what had to be created anew.

The socialist movement which developed in England from the 1880s onwards was one in which women's emancipation was extremely important. The reasons for this are various. The agitation of middle-class women for higher education, legal changes, the participation of radicals in the movement against the Contagious Diseases Act, and for birth control, inevitably raised women's right as a living issue which socialists could not ignore. Though the liberal feminist movement for equal rights culminating in the struggle for the vote has often been chronicled, it has suffered from adulation or outrage. The feminists appear either as great and noble heroines, or frustrated and ridiculous battle-axes. Many of the crucial questions about liberal feminism as a political and social movement are only just being asked. One of these must undoubtedly be the nature and extent of the interaction between liberal feminism and the various socialist groupings, both in terms of individuals and in terms of the influence of ideas. One obvious change was the emergence of the Pankhursts, minus Sylvia, as quite explicitly on the side of the ruling class, conservatism and the Empire in the period just before the war. The split was apparent when Sylvia's attempt to link the women's cause to that of the working class met with her mother's and her sister's determined opposition.

In the eighties and nineties the situation was much more fluid. Division was less clear and the points of agreement blurred. There were also aspects of the English radical and socialist traditions which aided an understanding of the women's struggle, and immediate factors in the history of the reawakened interest in socialism which account for the prominence of the 'woman question'. It was not so much the economic arguments of *Capital* (which were little known until the early 1900s), but the moral condemnation of the alienation of human relations in capitalist society (which came from the poets, from the romantic movement, from millenarian religion, from the writings of Carlyle and Ruskin) which provided texts for socialists. While Marx expressed the same horror of the inhuman effect of capitalism on human beings, in his later writing he quite explicitly subordinated moral concern to the attempt to work out a means of changing society by understanding its actual historical and economic basis. But within the socialism of the 1880s it was the immorality,

85

the ugliness, the narrowness, the absurdity of capitalism which pre-occupies socialist discussion. There was also less interest in theories of organization and little grasp of strategy, which was to emerge after Lenin's influence had been felt. As women's emancipation was still a moral issue, and one which related to ideas about consciousness and cultural change, this emphasis meant it was considered a great deal in the wide range of subjects which were felt to be important. More immediately, the fact that secularism was closely linked to the growth of socialism, and that religious doubt led many middle-class intellectuals towards socialist ideas, questions about spiritual or material changes, figured prominently.

For example, the grouping which included many of the original members of the Fabians, the Fellowship of the New Life, split on this issue. The controversy about internal spiritual change and external political transformation was often fought out in terms of 'either-or' just as it is today. But there was quite a strong tendency among the early socialists to attempt to argue for both. To some extent this involved an immediate reaction against the emphases of Marx's and Engels's later life and produced a strong current of romantic socialism. Again this helped the question of women's oppression to emerge clearly, because of all subordination this was precisely one in which the personal merged with the political. Though a cheap translation of *The Origin of the Family* was not available until the young rebels against Hyndman in the Social Democratic Federation started to import it from America in the 1900s, Bebel's book was quite widely read in socialist circles, and had considerable effect.

In 1885, when it was published in England, Marx's daughter Eleanor reviewed it with Aveling, the man she lived with, under the title 'The Woman Question, A Socialist Point of View' in the *Westminster Review*. They criticized the various feminist campaigns because they did not touch the economic basis of women's oppression or have any real idea of a fundamental change in sex relations and in society as a whole. They followed Engels and Bebel in making a parallel between the worker and woman:

> The truth, not fully recognized even by those anxious to do good to woman, is that she, like the labour classes, is in an oppressed condition, that her position like theirs is one of unjust and merciless degradation. Women are the creatures of an organized tyranny of men, as the workers are the creatures of an organized tyranny of idlers.[7]

They acknowledged that women experienced a specific oppression from men. They argue again like Bebel that women must organize themselves:

Both the oppressed classes, women and the immediate producers, must understand that their emancipation will come from themselves. Women will find allies in the better sort of men, as the labourers are finding allies among the philosophers, artists, poets. But the one has nothing to hope from man as a whole, and the other has nothing to hope from the middle class as a whole.

They use 'class' in connection with women in the same rather ambiguous sense as Engels and Bebel. Their debt is apparent. The most interesting aspect of their article is as a response within the English socialist movement. The other sources they draw upon to support their case – Shakespeare, the *Vindication*, Shelley's 'Notes on *Queen Mab*', Mill, Olive Schreiner's novel *Story of an African Farm*, and Ibsen's *The Doll's House* – were characteristic texts for socialists who argued for the emancipation of women. They emphasize very much the connection between socialism and the creation of a new morality and new ways of living together. In the 1880s commitment to sexual frankness and opposition to the secrecy, silence and hypocrisy of bourgeois personal relationships still required a great deal of courage. They believed that under socialism marriage would be a purely personal affair; there would be no need for divorce. They thought like Engels that monogamy would be the form of relationship in the future, but a monogamy based on free choice. Women would be independent in every sphere, prostitution would no longer exist in any form. 'There will no longer be one law for the woman and one for the man.'[8] Whatever sexual standards apply for him will apply for her. 'Nor will there be the hideous disguise, the constant lying that makes the domestic life of almost all our English homes an organized hypocrisy.'

Eleanor's tragic free union with Edward Aveling and her eventual suicide are well known. If she glimpsed the possibility of a more honest way of living and a greater love, she faced the dilemma of 'free' women before and since, the impossibility of living and loving honestly in the existing world. Less is known of the work she did as a trade union organizer, both among East End dock workers and in forming women's branches of the Gas Workers and General

87

Labourers Union. She was also active in the international socialist women's organization which was becoming increasingly important, and in which revolutionary women from Germany, Russia and Italy, like Clara Zetkin, Alexandra Kollontai, Angelica Balabanov, were to play a prominent role. Eleanor Marx's own interest in Shelley and in Ibsen, whom she translated, related closely to her commitment to a rejection of dishonesty, and the smothering destructive features of women's situation in the 'Doll's House' of the bourgeoisie.

In the eighties and nineties there was considerable overlapping and interaction between socialists and people in a progressive cultural circle, who were concerned in a purely personal way with what they sometimes described as 'the new life'. This meant a vague aesthetic rejection of the ugliness and commercialism of nineteenth-century capitalism. It could mean sandals, Buddhism, cottages, market gardening, communal living, cooperative villages, acute bouts of self-consciousness, and the occasional free union. It could also mean the 'New Woman' and 'Ibsenism'. Though socialists often reacted impatiently against the refusal of the new lifers to go further, admit class exploitation and accept the necessity for revolution, this cultural milieu had much more influence on the socialist movement in this period than is generally recognized. The main conflict between them was how far it was possible to effect a personal spiritual transformation of the self within capitalism, or whether such transformations had to wait until long after the revolution. There was a strong tendency for socialists in the 1880s to argue that cultural changes could only arise after the revolution, but then in practice to behave as if such changes were at once imperative and imminent. Indeed, they regarded their own organizations often as the new society of brotherhood in microcosm. This meant a favourable climate for understanding the interpenetration of private and public, psychological and material, characteristic of the 'woman question'.

William Morris followed Shelley in his ideas about free unions, in his belief that people should not pretend to love, and in his hope that friendship would persist after sexual love had gone. He wanted to reduce romantic love to its proper proportions; it had become puffed out as other feelings of affection had been made impossible. He laid down no rules at all for human relationships in the future society, but saw infinite variations and great flexibility. Yet he is very firm in his commitment to women's absolute equality and independence, and abhorrent of jealousy and possession. Perhaps more than any other socialist of the period he had an ideal of the natural healthiness of human sexual relations. In 'The Society of the Future' he wrote, 'I demand a free and unfettered animal life for man first of all. I demand the utter extinction of all asceticism. If we feel the least degradation in being amorous, or merry or hungry, or sleepy, we are so far bad animals and therefore miserable men.'[9] His ideal of the socialist society was one in which people would be able to encounter one another in what he felt would be a more natural manner.

The publication of Edward Carpenter's *Love's Coming of Age* in 1896 did much to popularize the connection between the liberation of women and the socialist movement. It was based on the theories of Morgan, Engels and Bebel, and on pamphlets and lectures Carpenter had been working on for some time. Carpenter's life and ideas expressed forcibly many of the prevailing tendencies current amongst a section of the progressive intelligentsia. He had moved from Broad Church Anglicanism to radical agnosticism in the seventies and made some study of the history of religion. He was attracted by eastern religion, especially Buddhism, and by primitive religion and an early interest in anthropology grew from these. In the early 1880s he became a socialist. A great admirer of Walt Whitman, Morris and Tolstoy, he was part of a diffuse group of intellectual socialists interested in a wide range of artistic, literary, psychological and anthropological questions. Carpenter for a few years became a link between the explicit revolutionaries, and workers in the labour movement, and men and women who were more concerned about internal spiritual enlightenment.

Carpenter believed in natural, uncluttered living. He called this simplification of life. He was opposed not just to the economic exploitation of capitalism but to the degradation and ugliness of cultural and spiritual life. He met some working men who were connected to a communal farm Ruskin had established near Sheffield. They were utopian socialists and influenced his already awakened radical class guilt. He determined not to be a parasite and live on anyone else's labour. He took some land and grew his own produce which he sold in the market in town. Slowly he made contact with the tiny group of Sheffield socialists who met in the Commonwealth café, and his cottage outside Sheffield became a point of convergence for an extraordinary variety of people. Carpenter's own personal life

89

was complicated by his homosexuality, but this forced him to confront problems which many upper-middle-class men of the period ignored. He was among the earliest socialist writers to identify with a sympathetic attempt to understand the sexual needs of homosexuals, whom he called the 'intermediate sex'. Through his friendship with Havelock Ellis he was in touch with developments in the early study of sex psychology, and in his lecture notes he refers to Krafft-Ebing and Albert Moll.

In *Love's Coming of Age* his concern with internal spiritual processes, his socialism, and his anthropological and psychological interests combine. He was enthusiastic about the women's movement, which he saw as much as the growth of a new consciousness as specific campaign. He connected this to the workers' movement, though he recognized that most working-class women were unaffected by the ideas of the new womanhood. He believed that ultimately only in a communist society could women have real independence because this must imply security in motherhood and no necessary dependence on a man. He shared similar ideas to Bebel about the communalization of housework under socialism. He thought this an essential part of the liberation of working women. It was of course very much an aspect of the crop of cooperative cottages in 1880s. He followed the utopian socialist and Marxist tradition too in imagining a more fulfilling and complete love in the society of the future.

But the real impact of *Love's Coming of Age* was not so much in its predictions for the future but in the way it attempted to consider the psychological aspects of female sexuality at the time. Carpenter dwells on the effect of pregnancy, on the need for information about sex for the young. There is a vague cerebral commitment to female sexual enjoyment, though this is expressed in very high-flown language about primal nature. He felt existing forms of contraception to be unsatisfactory and unnatural, apart from the rhythm method, and advocated instead emotional sublimation. He favoured what he called 'soul unions' – protracted sexual intercourse without the male orgasm.

Both Carpenter and *Love's Coming of Age* are forgotten now. His language, style and psychological theorizing have dated. The fashionable watery mysticism which appealed to many of his contemporaries now appears only mawkish. What has lasted, however, is the 'entire and unswerving refusal to "cage" another person', the insistence on 'free' and 'spontaneous' relationship between human beings – despite the knowledge that this 'must inevitably bring its own price of mortal suffering with it'.[10] This freedom in love was impossible between people who were socially, economically and psychologically unfree. Thus he urged women to take the name 'free woman' proudly.

> Let her accept the term with all the odium that belongs to it; let her insist on her right to speak, dress, think, act and above all use her sex as she deems best; let her face the scorn, the ridicule; let her 'lose her own life' if she likes; assured that only so can come deliverance; and that only when the free woman is honoured will the prostitute cease to exist.[11]

Thus he saw the liberation of women as being as much a conscious act of cultural commitment as an end product of social revolution. It was undoubtedly this emphasis which appealed to women at the time. It may be comforting in a distant sort of way to be told that far, far in the future, long, long after everyone else is free, a new world for women will be created. But it is unlikely to move anyone to action. Carpenter's stress on the act of voluntary commitment and individual choice had a powerful emotional effect. 'Too long have women acted the part of mere appendages to the male; suppressing their own individuality and fostering his self-conceit. In order to have souls of their own they must free themselves, and greatly by their own efforts.'[12]

We know very little about the impact of these ideas amongst women in the socialist movement at a grass roots level. A copy of *Love's Coming of Age* travels around now with the T.U.C. history exhibition of 'Things'. It belonged originally to a young woman who was a clerk and a member of the Hackney Social Democratic Federation in the early 1900s. But we have little information about the kind of people who bought the many editions of Carpenter's book between 1896 and 1918; nor do we know whether these ideas within the socialist movement and the impact of the suffragettes meant that women in any numbers began to see themselves and each other in a different way. There is an interesting hint to be found in Carpenter's correspondence that women who rejected some aspects of feminism and the new womanhood nevertheless were questioning the basis of marriage and the family, and the hypocrisy of conventional morality.

A woman called Edith A. Macduff wrote to Carpenter in 1894 having read some of his pamphlets. She was more interested in the personal and social aspects of women's emancipation than the strictly political question of the vote. She makes an interesting comment on the need for female solidarity, discouraged by 'the disloyalty of the average woman to her sex and to its cause. I suppose it is a survival from her days of slavery – an indirect flattery to her tyrant. Oh, if women would only be true to themselves and to one another I believe they could move mountains.'[13]

Carpenter's book upset many socialists at the time. There was considerable nervousness about connecting the idea of socialism with 'free love'. Many, like Robert Blatchford, felt that they should make the social and economic changes first and let free love and women's liberation creep in quietly when no one was looking later.

Not surprisingly revolutionary women were not willing to take this advice. Angelica Balabanov, the Italian socialist and feminist, once told Louise Bryant, an American journalist, 'Women have to go through such a tremendous struggle before they are free in their own minds that freedom is more precious to them than men.'[14] This is a dangerous generalization to try to stretch but it fitted the kind of women coming to a consciousness at once of the need for socialist revolution and of a transformation of women's situation in this period. It was very difficult to procrastinate with such women. They were too determined and too impatient to be fobbed off with vague promises. They retained too the close connection with tragedy which existed in the earlier period. If it was true of sections of the male socialist movement that personal life-style was as much a political statement as their theory, and indeed the two were quite inseparable, this was often even more true of women. Here the connections were painfully inescapable. Marx's daughter was by no means alone in this discovery.

One of Eleanor Marx's closest friends, Olive Schreiner, was part of the Carpenter circle. Brought up in South Africa, her novel *Story of an African Farm* is about adolescence and the passionate rejection by a young girl of the traditional role for women. The strong autobiographical element is apparent throughout the novel. She came to England in her early twenties, and through Havelock Ellis, with whom she had a brief unsuccessful love affair which was to develop into a life-long friendship, came into contact with Carpenter and the vague intellectual grouping which combined political concern with intense involvement in experimenting with new ways of living.

It is difficult to categorize Olive Schreiner's ideas. So much of what she started remained unfinished and unresolved. Carpenter in his autobiography, *My Days and Dreams*, describes a duality in her nature, a 'mobile and almost merry-seeming exterior' but underneath a 'vein of intense determination' and 'ineradicable pessimism'.[15] Her commitment to the liberation of women was not so much a political decision as part of her whole being and life. Because·she could not restrict her conception of liberation to political reform, she was forced to live out the tragic contradiction of emancipation. Because she felt 'the evil lay deeper than any accusation against men could explain, or any mere reform of the suffrage could mend',[16] she remained somewhat apart from the feminist movement. Similarly, though she was involved in the 1880s with the socialist groups, and subsequently active in the campaign against the Boer War, she remained both in her life and her ideas distant from the organized left. Her ideas about the relations of women and men are expressed in the form of mystical stories in *Three Dreams in a Desert*. In one of these she describes a vision in which the man and woman are bound together in pain.

In her own life she experienced intense and acute emotional suffering which often paralysed her completely. She wrote to Havelock Ellis in 1885, 'Life is a battle to be fought quietly, persistently at every moment.'[17] She shared the intellectual loneliness, the emotional despair and the nervous diseases and tension common to women of the period, who broke away from convention not only politically but socially and sexually. Unable to identify with the women's movement in the eighties and nineties, she disliked the timidity, respectability and attachment to Mrs Grundy which she found in 'women's rights'. The range of her interests was much wider and more explosive. She wanted to find out exactly why she felt tense before menstruating and noticed she couldn't work. Eleanor Marx was the only woman she could discuss this with. Then there was the dilemma of her own sexual nature. She had discovered in one relationship with a man that she had a strong streak of masochism. Under Havelock Ellis's tutelage she explored the existing works on sex psychology. Olive Schreiner insisted too on finding out the actual conditions and feelings of women with vastly different experiences from her own.

*I am uncomfortable with and distrustful of happiness — it still is a foreign thing, not a comfortable familiar easy thing.*

Women, Resistance and Revolution

She observed and recorded black South African women, London prostitutes and Lancashire mill girls because she wanted to learn from them about their situation.

But amidst her search to discover 'Woman' she displayed distaste for her own womanliness. She resented the constraint of her own femininity. She felt herself at war with many of the characteristics of women of her own time. When she was young she longed to be a boy, and the heroine of her novel *From Man to Man* dreams ' "How nice it would be to be man". She fancied she was one, until she felt her body grow strong and hard and shaped like a man's. She felt the great freedom opened to her; no place shut off from her, the long chain broken, all work possible for her, no law to say this and this is for woman.'[18]

There was still too great a divide between the assertion of the dignity of women and the hope of human possibility for women and the realization of that dignity in the life women had to lead. 'Oh, it is awful to be a woman,' she wrote to Havelock Ellis in 1885, and added, 'I've not been a woman really though I've become like one.'[19] A denial of some aspect of her femininity was almost inevitably the lot of the 'free woman'. As she struggled against political, economic and social subordinations she found that her traditional sexual role was irreconcilable with the liberation she demanded at other levels. But sexual unorthodoxy could mean that all other forms of activity were barred to her, and she was still very isolated among women. One response was to curb and control her own sexuality, and to live without having a family. Olive Schreiner's way was rather a mystical connection to other women with whom she could communicate only through the common experience of pain. There seems no way to transcend, no way beyond masochism as the consciousness of women.

In 1908 she wrote to Frances Smith about her sympathy for the English suffragettes who were being forcibly fed in jail:

My heart feels so tender over a baby girl because of all the anguish which may be before it. I have done all I can to help to free women, but Oh, it is so little. Long ages must pass before we really stand free and look out at a world that is ours as well as man's. . . . You know when I was a young girl and a child I felt this awful bitterness in my soul because I was a woman, because there were other women in the world. I felt [like] the wonderful kaffir woman who once was talking

94

Dreams and Dilemmas

to me and said, 'There may be a God. I do not say there is not; but if there is he is not good – why did he make woman?'[20]

In her book *Woman and Labour*, published in 1911, she is hopeful that a life of wider activity will end woman's role as a 'parasite'. She still emphasizes the difficulty of woman's liberation, and the very deep nature of her oppression. But she attempts to trace this historically rather than describing it in a timeless mystical way. She connected the historical process of the exclusion of privileged women from labour and their consequent sexual parasitism to class parasitism – the dependence of one class on the labour of another. Her account resembles those of Bebel and Engels. The difference in her approach is not so much in what she said but the way she said it. She illustrates her points with very vivid personal descriptions. For instance, when she is exposing the hypocrisy of upper-class men who oppose their own women entering professions,[21] she describes 'the lofty theorist' standing 'before the drawing-room fire in spotless shirt-front and perfectly fitting clothes', holding forth about women as child-bearers. Immediately a very real 'lofty theorist' appears before your eyes. Undoubtedly Olive Schreiner had encountered many like him. Rather mischievously she sends him to bed. There is nothing like bed for reducing a theoretician to human proportions. She observes that when he wakes in the morning he will not say to the 'elderly house drudge, who rises at dawn while he sleeps to make his tea and clean his boots, "Divine childbearer! Potential mother of the race! Why should you clean my boots or bring up my tea?" '[22] He doesn't object to an arrangement of society which means that working women labour for him. He is as incapable of seeing a connection between the woman who ages prematurely, 'the haggard, work-crushed woman and mother who irons his shirts or the potential mother who destroys health and youth in the sweater's den', and his own pampered object, as the bourgeois man in the 1840s was of connecting the fate of Fleur de Marie to a situation of women. The whole concept of femininity is so manifestly a projection of man's distorted fantasies. There is nothing unfeminine about women on all fours scrubbing for him. But there is something unfeminine in his eyes about the woman doctor, or even the woman in an office. It is the independence of his own woman working he doesn't like. It is not women working he objects to, but women working for a decent wage with some leisure.

95

Though she can point out the contradiction in the way bourgeois man sees the two worlds of women, Olive Schreiner is incapable of indicating the common interest of the two kinds of women, worker and parasite. Nor is it clear how labour is going to be transformed for all women. She drifts off at this point towards the end of the book into a visionary flight of the imagination of the garden of Eden. It was the real weakness in her approach that her capacity for insight can be used to cover up the weaknesses in her ability to analyse and work out alternatives.

In 1889 Emma Goldman with a small bag and a sewing machine landed in New York City from Russia. A few years later 'Red Emma' had been transformed by the press until she became in popular imagination the anarchist bogy. Occasionally the image of another Emma came through. A writer in the *St Louis Mirror* in 1908 wrote about her revolution: 'The dream is the reality to which we move . . . universal peace and beauty, Emma Goldman, the daughter of the dream.'[23]

Her *Anarchism and Other Essays* was published in New York in 1910. In several of the essays she discusses questions relating to the liberation of women. Her criticisms of the feminist movement were similar to those of Olive Schreiner. She disliked not only the narrowness of their ideas of change, but she also disapproved of their lack of understanding of labour movement struggles. She rejected too their dismissal of sexuality, the tendency to connect emancipation with celibacy. She did not have much sympathy with a concept of liberation with meant the emancipated woman had to be a 'compulsory vestal'.[24] Instead she wanted an emancipation which 'should make it possible for women to be human in the truest sense. Everything within her that craves for assertion and activity should reach its fullest expression, all artificial barriers should be broken, and the road towards greater freedom cleared of every trace of centuries of submission and slavery.'[25]

Such a commitment to women's liberation was obviously closely bound up with her anarchism. She draws on many influences, including Carpenter, Havelock Ellis, Ibsen, but the emphases in her thinking on the question of women are integrated within her general political ideas. In the anarchist movement at the time, even more than among the socialists, there was a very strong tendency to try to live out the ideals of the future society within the existing world. For a woman this was doubly difficult. Emma Goldman mentions the problems the free woman faced in relation to men. 'The average man with his self-sufficiency, his ridiculously superior airs of patronage towards the female sex is an impossibility. . . . Equally impossible for her is the man who can see in her nothing more than her mentality and her genius, and who fails to awaken her woman nature.'[26] She faced both these herself. Part of this attempt to live now as you imagined everyone would live in the future was a process of cultural creation. In criticizing the 'women's rights' movement she wrote, 'They thought that all that was needed was independence from external tyrannies. The internal tyrants, far more harmful to life and growth – ethical and social conventions – were left to take care of themselves; and they have taken care of themselves.'[27]

While this was a valuable insight and a useful corrective to a simply institutional idea of change, there are moments when she is so concerned to assert the personal subjective features of liberation that she loses all contact with the interaction between partial reforms, like the vote, the actual and immediate circumstances and the developing consciousness of women. Liberation becomes simply a personal act of will. She pursues a similar theme to Carpenter's. The free woman has to assert and declare herself. But she puts it more extremely. She demanded that the emancipated woman should assert herself as 'a personality, and not as a sex commodity'.[28] She must refuse to bear children unless she wants them. She must also refuse to be a servant to God, the state, society, the husband, the family, etc. She must disregard 'public opinion and public condemnation'. This was a lot to ask in 1910. A few turbulent, courageous spirits like herself might achieve it, but most women had too great a stake in some form of social acceptability to follow. Emma Goldman expected all women to share her ability to throw herself totally into exposed situations, and was too zealous a puritan to understand that some people can hold ideas and still not be willing to live their lives through them as she did. The daughters of the dream were biding their time. They talked about the vote, not about Emma Goldman's liberation – or Olive Schreiner's or Karl Marx's.

None the less Marxism and the revolutionary movement which developed towards the end of the nineteenth century had a fundamental effect on the terms of the debate about the connection between women's liberation and the socialist revolution. From this framework directly arose the discussions in the Soviet Union in the twenties.[29] And in subsequent revolutionary movements, in places and contexts remote from the circumstances and experiences of nineteenth-century revolutionary thought, women have been and still are returning to that past. It is necessary to keep a balance between connecting with a tradition and seeing the inadequacies of that tradition. An apparant certainty is imposed as dogma which makes us feel secure. We ignore the chinks and crevices which don't fit, but through which light comes. We must always examine the chinks and crevices and look into the light.

We are left with questions. From what basis and in what manner can women act together as a group which can be the agency of revolutionary change? Where is there a necessity to act from the logic of women's own socio-historical situation? In what sense can women be regarded as a group with interests in common? What are the particular experiences of oppression peculiar to women? Are there such experiences? If so how can these be expressed in terms of revolutionary struggle? In what way does the conception of a communist society imply the liberation of women? How far do existing socialist societies approximate to this? What is the manner in which women can participate fully in a revolutionary movement? And ultimately can the essentially personal and emotional understanding of pain be translated into political action, or is the tragic vision the only consolation for the daughters of the dream?

Emma Goldman thought equal rights were 'just and fair' but that the most 'vital right is the right to love and be loved'.[30] But the revolutionary woman knows the world she seeks to overthrow is precisely one in which love between equal human beings is well nigh impossible. We are still part of the ironical working-out of this, our own cruel contradiction. One of the most compelling facts which can unite women and make us act is the overwhelming indignity or bitter hurt of being regarded as simply 'the other', 'an object', 'commodity', 'thing'. We act directly from a consciousness of the impossibility of loving or being loved without distortion. But we must still demand now the preconditions of what is impossible at the moment.

It is a most disturbing dialectic, our praxis of pain.

## CHAPTER 5

# Bread and Roses

Come all you false young men
That leave me here to complain
For the grass that is now trodden underfoot
In time it will rise again.

'The Seeds of Love', early English ballad;
first recorded version, seventeenth century

How hard is the fortune of all womankind;
They're always in fetters, they're always confined;
Bound down by their parents until they're made wives,
Then slaves to their husbands the rest of their lives.

Popular song; first recorded version, eighteenth century

The woman who comes forward now in the streets is strong, loyal,
tragic; she knows how to die as she loves, because of that pure and
generous vein which, since 1789, has run richly through the heart of
the French people. She who was before a partner in life and work now
wants to share her man's association with death. . . . She does not hold
her man back; on the contrary, she thrusts him into battle, bringing
soup and linen to him in the trenches as she did when he was out at
work. Many women do not want to go back home, but take up a rifle. . . .

Lissagaray

The hands of Jeanne-Marie are strong
Dark hands tanned by summer's heat,
    They have gone pale
Under the sun of burdened love . . .

Rimbaud

No matter what your fight
Don't be ladylike.
American trade union organizer, 'Mother' Jones

99

That man over there says that a woman needs to be helped into carriages, and lifted over ditches, and to have the best place everywhere. Nobody ever helped me into carriages, or over mud puddles, or gives me a best place. . . . And ain't I a woman? Look at me. Look at my arm! I have plowed and planted and gathered into barns and no man could head me. . . . And ain't I a woman?

> Sojourner Truth: Speech before Women's Rights
> Convention, Ohio, U.S.A., 1851

As we come marching, marching in the beauty of the day
A million darkened kitchens, a thousand mill lofts gray,
Are touched with all the radiance that a sudden sun discloses,
For the people hear us singing: 'Bread and roses! Bread and roses!'

As we come marching, marching we battle too for men,
For they are women's children, and we mother them again.
Our lives shall not be sweetened from birth until life closes;
Hearts starve as well as bodies; give us bread, but give us roses!

As we come marching, marching, unnumbered women dead
Go crying through our singing their ancient cry for bread.
Small art and love and beauty their drudging spirits knew
Yes it is bread we fight for . . . but we fight for roses too.

As we come marching, marching we bring the greater days
The rising of the women means the rising of the race.
No more the drudge and idler – ten that toil where one reposes,
But a sharing of life's glories: Bread and roses! Bread and roses!

> James Oppenheimer, inspired by banners carried by young
> mill girls in the 1912 Lawrence Massachusetts textile strike

---

Not everyone learns from books. Not everybody's story is written down. There is a world of experience that belongs to the women who were not given to prophecy, who knew nothing of the privileges of education, who read no novels, who never heard of the innumerable utopias which promised them freedom, and were innocent of Marxist or anarchist theory. It is this world which is the most difficult to recapture and recreate. Yet it was through the interaction of this experience with the ideas of revolutionary feminism that the beginnings of answers were made. The silent people of no name, the ignorant and ignored, move reluctantly into 'official' history which reflects those who have power in the world as it is. An essential task of a revolutionary feminist movement is the investigation of the past of the women of the people who have been neglected because of their class and because of their sex. As yet we are only able to touch the outermost limits. We only know what was happening to these women in a superficial way. But we can watch something of the growth of a radical and ultimately revolutionary consciousness, we can see what actions and demands and forms of organization came from their specific situation as women. We can also note the particular problems and dilemmas which women encountered as a result of this activity; note too the resilient face women put against change, the persistent traditional fatalism carried through in folk song into the dramatic economic and political changes of nineteenth-century capitalism – and beyond. The timeless tragedy of the continuing cycle of love, loss, encounter, parting, birth, joy, sorrow, pain, life and death. Repeatedly revolutionary political movements proved incapable of relating to this.

The woman confronts the man personally. The essential difference between them is his freedom and her bondage. Here it is the fact of reproduction that holds the woman and governs her consciousness:

> They'll kiss you and they'll court you
> And tell to you more lies
> As the hairs upon your head, love,
> Or the stars in the skies.[1]

Pretty girls are warned not to place all their affection on a green willow tree. All sweetness carries its own bitterness:

> He gave me honey all mixed with gall
> He gave me words and vows withal.
> He gave me a delicate gown to wear,
> All stitched with sorrow and hemmed with fear.

Childbirth traps the woman in her pleasure:

> When my apron strings hung low
> He'd follow me through frost and snow,

> Now my apron strings won't pin,
> He'll pass my door and not come in.

Hopeless love entangles her. She wonders:

> Must I go bound and he go free.

Songs of girls who were easily led, who yielded gently to delight, forgetful in the dark night of love; girls easily persuaded, who believed handsome wanderers with false promises, who waited for soldier boys who never returned, whose lovers picked up their clothes and left them to face pregnancy alone. Some of them bargain like the lass of Islington, 'her hand on the Cellar Door'.[2] Occasionally they combine. The miller's wife and the servant girl he is pursuing change beds and he enjoys his own wife. In Jamaica the same joke was played on the white slave-owner. More often they try for a brief escape from womanhood; like sweet Polly Oliver, dressed as a boy they join the army to find their man or lie disguised beside their pressganged sailor lover:

> In pulling off my britches, to myself I often smiled
> To think I lay with a hundred men and a maiden all the while.[3]

But for every Polly (or in real life Hannah Snell, a marine in the East Indies) or Mary Reed, a female pirate, there were thousands who didn't escape and didn't want to, thousands who had no idea of making their own lives, of controlling events, of getting out of the rut of what had always been. The essentially distinct experience of women was encountered by its nature alone, and this traditional consciousness was a lonely consciousness which did not think in terms of future and had no idea of how to act upon the world. It knew only a protective, defensive women's lore. Before any form of reliable or widespread contraceptive methods it was impossible for women to take the control of their sexuality into their own hands.

It is really from women's relationship to consumption that the experience of collective action emerges. Most important was the price of bread, the basic item in the diet of the poor. With a primitive communications system local supply was all important. A bad harvest meant scarcity and hoarding on the market to raise prices. The food riot and price fixing which often went with it was a popular means of controlling distribution. Thus in Nottingham in 1812 it was reported that:

several women in Turncalf Alley sticking a half penny loaf on the top of a fishing rod after having streaked it with red ochre and tied around it a shred of black cloth, emblematic, it was said, of 'bleeding famine decked in sack cloth'; by the elevation of this and the aid of three hand bells, two carried by woman and one by a boy, a considerable crowd of people, chiefly women, soon congregated together.[4]

They demanded that flour should be reduced to 6d per stone. Their example was contagious. Mobs set to work in every part of the town. One group carried a woman in a chair who gave the word of command and was given the name of 'Lady Ludd'. Such actions were half ritual, half political. They came naturally from the role of women in the family. Their organization was based on the immediate community. They did not require a conscious long-term commitment like that of joining a union or a party, nor were they feminist in any explicit sense. However, during the nineteenth century the context of the food riot changed because of the development of other forms of political action. In the case of women too, certainly in France, the traditional action of women in relation to consumption became intertwined not only with revolutionary events and ideas but also with the emerging popular feminism of the streets and clubs.

In the months immediately before the march to Versailles the women were growing impatient with what they felt to be the men's ineffectiveness. The bread crisis was peculiarly their own. In September they stopped carts and besieged the town hall. On 5 October the revolt started from several central markets. In the Faubourg Saint-Antoine women were in the lead – fishwives, stallholders, working women along with smartly dressed bourgeoisies. Again in 1792 and 1793 laundresses from the Faubourg Saint-Antoine invaded grocers' shops. Though women were present they were less active in military operations like the taking of the Bastille, or the political demonstrations. Individual women like Constance Evrard, a cook arrested on the Champ de Mars demonstration, were conscious of the political significance of demonstration and petition. Predominantly though the women were moved by economic concerns which affected them in their position as housewives. This continued to be the pattern during subsequent periods of revolutionary agitation. The history of popular action in 1848 has still to be written. But in the Commune of 1871 women again were involved in price fixing and in attacks on the food shops. This is hardly surprising for they had to face the endless queueing. A popular song described this hopeless quest for food and provisions:

> Not a single shop or store
> Has got anything on show,
> And whatever way you go,
> Knock at each and every door,
> It won't do you any good.
> There's not even any wood.[5]

In 1871 too they possessed an added element, a revolutionary memory of women's earlier collective action. The idea of a march of women to Versailles to stop the bloodshed spread in April 1871. Beatrice Excoffon, the daughter of a watchmaker who lived with a compositor, told her mother she was leaving, kissed her children, and joined the procession at the Place de la Concorde. There were about 700 to 800 women. Nobody was clear about the aims of the march or knew definitely what they should do, but there were political rather than strictly economic motives:

Some talked about explaining to Versailles what Paris wanted. Others talked about how things were a hundred years ago when the women of Paris had gone to Versailles to carry off the baker and the baker's little boy, as they said then.[6]

Also the role of women had been raised. There was a dispute about whether women could only ask for peace or whether they should defend their country as much as the men. For although the women had been taking action they had been taking action from their traditional position as women. Rather similar was the way in which they walked ahead of their men in the Commune to meet the soldiers, saying 'Will you fire on us? On your brothers, our husbands? Our children?'[7]

These actions were still from a quite customary definition of womanliness. Although revolutionary political ideas were impinging on these women and although they acted with conscious historical memory, they were not challenging in any way their role as women. However, very easily in such moments the new conception of commitment could upset what had been regarded as the woman's sphere. A head-on clash could ensure between what the women felt to be their duty and what the men felt it to be, as wives, daughters, mothers. Thus in 1792 when the women's battalions were formed in the

French Revolution there was opposition from the men. In challenging the men's sole right to patriotism and glory the revolutionary women moved into a form of feminism. There was a similar development in 1871. One source of feminist consciousness here came from the attempt to equalize revolutionary struggle. A women's battalion was not allowed but the women of the Commune accompanied their husbands or lovers and often fought with them. *La Sociale* reported on 5 April: 'A band of women armed with chassepots today passed by the Place de la Concorde. They were going to join the Commune fighters.'[8]

Often the dividing lines between nursing at one of the first aid posts, serving as a 'cantinière' or being a soldier were not clear. On the battlefield Louise Michel, a schoolteacher prominent in the Commune, looked after the wounded and took part in the fighting. The accounts these women leave describe their complete commitment to the Commune. They lived only for the revolution in a way which is only possible in times of extreme crisis. But they were not always well regarded by the officers. André Leo, a revolutionary feminist who was a journalist, described how obstacles were put in their way by the officers and surgeons who were hostile even though the troops were in favour of them. She believed that this division was because the officers still retained the narrow consciousness of military men while the soldiers were equally revolutionary citizens. She felt this prejudice had had serious political consequences. In the first revolution women had been excluded from freedom and equality; they had returned to Catholicism and reaction. André Leo maintained that the republicans were inconsistent. They did not want women to be under the sway of the priests, but they were upset when women were free-thinkers and wanted to act like free human beings. Republican men were just replacing the authority of Emperor and God with their own. They still needed subjects, or at least subjected women. They did not want to admit any more than the revolutionaries of the 1790s that woman was responsible to herself. 'She should remain neutral and passive, under the guidance of man. She will have done nothing to change her confessor.'[9]

Yet this was the very antithesis of all the claims of revolutionary ideas. It was evident that 'The Revolution is the liberty and responsibility of every human being, limited only by the rights of all, without privilege of race or sex.' Thus by taking the revolution seriously the women of the Commune also found themselves forced to take up feminist positions in that they had to struggle not only against the enemy at Versailles but to confront the prejudice and suspicion of some of the men on their own side. The experience was one which was subsequently to be repeated in other revolutionary movements. It is at the point when the revolution starts to move women out of their passivity into the conscious and active role of militants that the mockery, the caricatures, the laughter with strong sexual undertones begin. It is one of the most effective weapons against women's emergence. It is one thing to be the object of hatred and insults, and another to be the object of scorn and hilarity as well. It produces its own self-mocking defences and its own peculiar paralysis.

If there was some ambiguity in the attitude of the men of the left there was none in that of the men of the right. Here class hatred, political elitism and sexual authoritarianism united in hysterical denunciation and acts of atrocity. Listen to Maxime du Camp on the women:

> Those who gave themselves to the Commune – and there were many – had but a single ambition: to raise themselves above the level of man by exaggerating his vices. There they found an ideal they could achieve. They were venomous and cowardly. They were all there agitating and squawking: inmates from Saint-Lazare out on the spree; . . . the vendors of modes à la tripe de Caen; the gentlemen's seam-stresses; the gentlemen's shirtmakers; the teachers of grown-up school-boys. . . . What was profoundly comic was that these absconders from the workhouse unfailingly invoked Joan of Arc, and were not above comparing themselves to her. . . . During the final days, all of these bellicose viragos held out longer than the men did behind the barri-cades. Many of them were arrested, with powder-blackened hands and shoulders bruised by the recoil of their rifles; they were still palpitating from the over-stimulation of battle.[10]

The penalties were severe. Beside the names which are well known, like Louise Michel, sentenced to transportation to a penal settlement, there were innumerable others. A concierge, Louise Noel; a parasol-maker, Jeanne Laymet; a cook, Eugenie Lhilly; the seamstress, Eulalie Papavoine; Elizabeth Retiffe, a cardboard maker; the rag-picker Marie Wolff – they were transported, given hard labour and executed. They had gone to join their lovers on the barri-cades or they had been moved by the sight of the wounded. They loved the Republic, hated the rich, and rose against the years of humiliation they had experienced as workers and as women. Captain Jouenne began the indictment at their trial by calling them:

unworthy creatures who seem to have taken it on themselves to become an opprobrium to their sex, and to repudiate the great and magnificent role of woman in society . . . a legitimate wife, the object of our affection and respect, entirely devoted to her family. . . . But if, deserting this sacred mission, the nature of her influence changes, and serves none but the spirit of evil, she becomes a moral monstrosity; then woman is more dangerous than the most dangerous man.[11]

There was a change too in the way she was treated by the gentlemen of the ruling class. Elisée Reclus, the geographer taken prisoner, described one of the women canteen workers:

The poor woman was in the row in front of mine, at the side of her husband. She was not at all pretty, nor was she young: rather a poor, middle-aged proletarian, small, marching with difficulty. Insults rained down on her, all from officers prancing on horseback along the road. A very young hussar officer said, 'You know what we're going to do with her? We're going to screw her with a red hot iron.' A vast horrified silence fell among the soldiers.[12]

Here expressed in a particularly intense and repulsive form was the hypocrisy which the young Marx had exposed so vehemently. Here is the real nature of the sensibility and gallantry of the men of the upper classes towards femininity. The same issues appeared in other movements which were not specifically revolutionary. For example, in the anti-slavery agitation in the United States Sarah and Angelina Grimke – along with many other women – became convinced of the moral righteousness of the anti-slavery cause and started to write and speak for the movement. They were denounced in 1837 in a pastoral letter which was read from the pulpit and distributed by the General Association of the Congregational Clergy. This letter stated that the 'appropriate duties and influences of women' were clearly put in the New Testament:

The power of woman is in her dependence, flowing from the consciousness of that weakness which God has given her for her protection, and which keeps her in those departments of life that form the character of individuals and of the nation . . .

But when she assumes the place and tone of man as a public performer, our care and our protection of her seem unnecessary; we put
ourselves in self-defense against her; she yields the power which God
has given her for protection, and her character becomes unnatural.[13]

When the Grimke sisters decided to respond by defending the
rights of women they met also with hostility from men in their own
movement. The argument was that it would damage the anti-
slavery cause to be connected with feminism. This argument appeared again and again in various contexts in radical labour and
revolutionary struggles. Ultimately the result of this was women
breaking from those movements not simply organizationally but
politically. In 1881, after months of campaigning for women's suffrage and losing partly because male abolitionists wouldn't support
them, the feminists Elizabeth Cady Stanton and Susan B. Anthony
wrote their 'Message to Future Generations':

Our liberal men counselled us to silence during the war, and we were
silent in our own wrongs; they counselled us again to silence in Kansas
and New York, lest we should defeat 'Negroe Suffrage', and threatened
if we were not, we might fight the battle alone. We chose the latter,
and were defeated. But standing alone we learned our power; we
repudiated man's counsels forevermore; and solemnly vowed that
there should never be another season of silence until woman had the
same rights everywhere on this green earth as man.[14]

They warned young women that they could not rely on men's
advice. They had to depend only on themselves for the transitional
period before they were equal. 'While regarded as his subject, his
inferior, his slave, their interests must be antagonistic.'[15]

There is a difference between having your own movement and
cutting yourself off politically from all other movements. This last
form of feminist isolationism is attractive in its simplicity. It appears
to offer an option which implies that you concentrate on your own
struggle and wait for some absolute future when men and women
have progressed towards equality. It is of course a profoundly liberal
utopian notion. 'Progress' is seen as some kind of single linear
advance towards a goal. There is no sense of a movement living and
working in history, learning through a dialectical interaction of its
own efforts in objective circumstances. It forgets that the consciousness of particular groups amongst the oppressed is only partial.

While this consciousness must be realized and expressed in their own movement, if the attempt is not made continually to extend and connect this partial consciousness to the experience of other oppressed groups, it cannot politicize itself in a revolutionary sense. It becomes locked within its own particularism. This is as true of women as of blacks or workers. The attempt to extend and connect is not one which can be made in some utopian static future, but is part of a continuous dialectical historical process in which all participate consciously. It is only when the feminist (or the black or the working-class militant) understands, perceives, feels themself as pitted against a total oppressive system rather than simply against the indignity which is done to them through the subordination of their own kind, that a revolutionary political consciousness can start to grow.

In practice these connections were grasped by women who by social and political circumstance were involved not simply as women. For a black woman in the Civil War in America, for a Frenchwoman in one of the revolutionary moments, for an English chartist or for an early woman trade unionist to confine their conception of the oppression they resisted simply to their gender was absurd. The isolationism of Stanton and Anthony appeared immediately as a false option because it did not relate to their everyday life or their immediate political practice. In fact it could lead to actions which were explicitly contradicting their experience. Emma Goldman showed how the Stanton–Anthony tendency within feminism remained deliberately blinkered about labour movement struggles even to the point of supporting strike-breaking by women. This earned them the antagonism not only of male but female workers.

The absence of any practical theory of revolutionary feminist action and organization which made explicit the necessity to fight on several fronts rather than isolating one aspect of oppression had serious consequences. The corollary of feminist isolationism was a tendency amongst some women revolutionaries and industrial militants to smooth over and camouflage the specific oppression experienced by women, either because it was felt to endanger movements and causes or because it was felt to be unresolvable in the immediate future. The tension which resulted from this voluntary containment of energy was corrosive and destructive. There was continual pressure on women to compromise in this way. They found themselves having to make choices with nothing but their own feelings to guide them. Each choice appeared as an individual matter because there was no theory to which it could be more broadly referred.

In the 1840s, for example, Jeanne Deroin faced this dilemma in jail. She had worked out with a group of male trade unionists the idea of a federation of all existing workers' associations, a more modest version of Flora Tristan's proposals. She had argued fervently for this idea in her feminist socialist paper *L'Opinion des Femmes*. But the union meetings were stopped by the police and she was arrested on a conspiracy charge. While she was in prison and before she came up for trial the lawyer for her male colleagues came to visit her. He brought a request from them. They asked her not to disclose her part in the idea of a federation because knowledge that a woman who was an ardent feminist had been the initiator of the scheme would damage its chances of success. Jeanne Deroin was caught in a strange irony. She was being asked to step back, to confirm the passivity of women's role, her inability to initiate and participate in a movement designed to benefit women as well as men workers. She spent a troubled night but finally decided to pretend ignorance of the plan for federation. Though she compromised on this occasion she continued to argue socialist feminist ideas.

Other women have found the attempt to struggle on several fronts too exhausting. Rather than face the often crippling and painful agonies of fighting not only the enemy without but the enemy within, they have chosen to deny their own oppression as women. As individuals their talents have earned them men's respect for their service to revolutionary movements. But they have contributed nothing to the theory or practice of revolutionary feminism, and they have not been able to move women in large numbers to take up the revolutionary struggle, because they were distrustful of those women favoured and praised by revolutionary men who still despised women as a group.

If the contradiction is painful it is an essential one to maintain both within the labour movement and in the revolutionary movement, for the exclusion of the broad mass of women means inevitable failure. Elizabeth Gurley Flynn, known as the 'Rebel Girl', who organized with the Wobblies, Industrial Workers of the World, describes this very well in the context of a textile strike in Lawrence, Massachusetts, in 1912. Italian, Polish, Russian and Lithuanian women played an active part. They picketed in freezing weather, pregnant women and others with babies in their arms marching with their placards for 'Bread and Roses'. But despite their enthusiasm they came up against the feeling of the men that their place was at home:

> We had special meetings for the women. . . . The women worked in the mills for lower pay and in addition had all the housework and care of the children. The old world attitude of men as 'the lord and master' was strong at the end of the day's work . . . or now of strike duty . . . the man went home and sat at ease while his wife did all the work, preparing the meal, cleaning the house, etc. There was considerable male opposition to women going to meetings and marching on the picket line. We resolutely set out to combat these notions. The women wanted to picket. We knew that to leave them at home alone, isolated from the strike activity, a prey to worry, affected by the complaints of trades people, landlords, priests and ministers was dangerous to the strike.

If women's involvement is to become real rather than pious exhortation, the specific problems and experiences of working-class as well as middle-class women and of women engaged in revolutionary struggle have to be studied and understood. If this is to be done with honesty it means learning from the women themselves. All too often the words 'worker' or 'revolutionary' are used in the sense of *male* worker or *male* revolutionary. Now while women shared some of the experiences of their men, they also found themselves in new situations which were peculiar to women. The sameness and the separateness are so integrally bound together that sometimes they were scarcely aware of the conflict which was going on. Women found themselves, like men, in Europe and in America, confronting the new forms of alienation and exploitation produced by the factory and large-scale machinery. They reacted like men with a hatred of the factories, 'Bastilles', and with a persistent hankering after the old days of domestic work and peasant economy, which seemed in retrospect golden. In the 1830s girls in Lowell, Massachusetts, fresh from the countryside, paraded boldly through the streets singing:

> Oh isn't it a pity that such a pretty girl as I
> Should be sent to the factory to pine away and die.
> Oh I cannot be a slave
> For I'm so fond of liberty
> That I cannot be a slave.[16]

The early nineteenth-century English folk song nostalgically takes up the same theme:

> Where are the girls? I'll tell you plain,
> The girls have gone to weave by steam,
> And if you'd find 'em you must rise at dawn
> And trudge to the factory in the early morn.

The women responded like the men not only with moral protest but with strikes and the organization of unions. In the early nineteenth century these sprang up and collapsed only to start again a few years later. The economic organization of the family was based on the woman's labour as much as the man's; sometimes, with unemployment, it was the women's and children's earnings alone which saw a family through. At the same time as the French women were involved in associations and schemes for federation, Englishwomen were forming their own friendly societies and associations, like the Female Gardeners and Ancient Virgins, or the Female Political Union, or taking part in the attempt at a union of the whole working class in the short-lived and ill-fated Grand National Consolidated Union. Nor did they play a passive part. The paper *The Union* (1842–3) gives an account of the women's part in the strikes of that year in Lancashire, Staffordshire and Yorkshire:

> It is a singular fact that women were in many instances the directors of the strike – women held their meetings, sent their delegates and drew up their terms – and women accompanied the turnouts in immense numbers, in all their marchings and counter-marchings throughout the manufacturing districts. . . . At Halifax these women headed the mob, on some occasions seizing the soldiers' bayonets and turning them aside with the words 'We want not bayonets but bread.'[17]

Women were beginning to be involved in activity which demanded a sustained organizing effort and in which they discovered their own powers, an essential political experience for the oppressed. They started now to keep collective accounts. They were no longer organizing only the household. This large-scale organization at the place of work, at the point of production, was a new way of fighting. It had implications far beyond the bread riot. Women learned to put their own case. In America in 1841 the Lowell factory girls started to produce a paper called the *Factory Girls' Album* in which they complained of long hours, low pay, speed up and store order wage payments (truck). From this the Female Labour Reform Association was formed. While the effort to keep these early trade unions together was often beyond both male and female workers, they formed an essential stage towards the much more solid defensive structures which workers created at the end of the century.

Though sharing the class exploitation of men and, like them, concentrated together in the new factories, there were nonetheless elements in the women's position which made them less able to organize. Reproduction, the long periods spent in child-bearing which interrupted the work routine, and female orientation within the family combined with middle-class propaganda about thrift, patience and individual self-help, to deflect the proletarianization of the working-class woman. The particular relationship of the woman to reproduction and consumption within the family mediated her relationship to commodity production. Women continued to work in the home, maintaining the needs of the family, but work for wages became predominantly an activity which was external to family production. The wife's work outside the home was thus an economic supplement to the family income. Women retained certain features of a pre-capitalist labour force. They never learned fully the rules of the new economic game. The corollary of this was a readiness to accept low pay. Indeed they were often employed when it was convenient to use cheap unskilled labour rather than machines, when employers wanted to dilute the labour force, or when new machines meant a process had been simplified and devalued. The general inferiority of women was thus inseparable from their weak bargaining position at work, and from the social definition of 'women's work' as work which was badly paid and unskilled.

Male trade unionists had two choices. They could either try to integrate women into their unions or they could try to keep them out of skilled work. Throughout the nineteenth century male workers resisted the idea of women working, on the grounds that their place was at home and that they had no business to be taking jobs from men. But ironically capitalism was structured on the fact of women and children working. The conflict appeared in several forms. For instance, men in the traditional craft of book-binding in a dispute in 1845 in which women were being employed at a low rate, complained: 'Females often have not the power to plead their own cause in such matters, and being helpless in many respects whenever their wages are concerned are trodden down.'[18]

It was in the older crafts, which were being mechanized in the nineteenth century, that most hostility broke out. In the printing trade in the second half of the century there was trouble in America, France and England, as men tried to secure the privileged sections of the trade for themselves – for example typesetting, although some American male trade unionists by the 1860s had seen that the exacerbation of this conflict between men and women workers ultimately benefited only the employers, and started to argue equal pay on these grounds. A similar lesson was learned by Russian metal-workers in the early 1900s. They had banned women from the union so that when there was a crisis the men were turned off and the women taken on at half pay. As a result of this experience the women were admitted with a council of their own.

The real difficulty then, as now, in convincing male trade unionists that they have a common struggle with women workers, is that as long as you look at effects rather than causes it makes sense for the men to suspect women. The general subordination of women and the role of women in the family, along with their sexual situation, meant, and means, that they are liable to play a passive reactionary role at work. However, male suspicion and hostility will serve only to reinforce the likelihood of this. It's no good maintaining this by continuing to prevent them from participating in union activity or by maintaining discrimination in pay and other matters. The only way to get a solution is by challenging the total subordination of woman in capitalism. Her consciousness at work cannot be isolated. If attention is confined only to one area the case collapses. In this sense the woman must of necessity fight for bread ·and roses, because the material aspect of her exploitation is integrally related to her own consciousness of what she is. As long as this consciousness is formed in a situation where she continually drops back and lets the man lead, she will continue to do this at work and be less likely to resist her employer. As long as her position in the family does not change, her job as wife will get priority.

The thorny question of protective legislation has always highlighted the dilemma. Bourgeois feminists at the end of the century were opposed to special protections for women workers on the grounds that these were always used to restrict women's chance to work. Indeed, they had a good case. Earlier the Female Operatives of Todmorden had put it well when in 1833 they wrote to the *Examiner* in concern about proposals to legislate against women's work. They pointed out that while their conditions of work were far from ideal, they were better off than domestic servants, and if they were prevented from working they had no one to support them if they weren't married. All they could do would be to set off husband-hunting in 'Van Dieman's Land' and to 'jump ashore' with a 'who wants me'.[19]

It is true the various legislative attempts to cut down the hours and restrict the nature of women's work had a two-edged aspect. They were often used as justification of 'women's work', and welcomed by men not simply as lessening the exploitation of women's labour but reducing competition between men and women workers. This is clearly brought out in the statement of American cigar makers in 1879:

> We cannot drive the females out of the trade but we can restrict their daily quota of labor through factory laws. No girl under eighteen should be employed more than eight hours per day, all overtime work should be prohibited, while married women should be kept out of factories at least six weeks after confinement.[20]

Despite this interested motivation the measures recognized the actual situation of women workers. The feminists forgot that if the women faced the danger of industrial segregation, they also carried the double role of wife and mother as well as worker. If you argued for an abstract equality, the abstract right for workers of both sexes to be equally exploited at work, without remembering that the woman worked at home as well, you in fact subjected working women to an intolerable oppression. The only way out was to connect feminist criticism of the sectional privileges of male workers with an attempt to change conditions for all workers. Thus protections won for women could be extended to include all workers and minimize the possibility of conflict between workers of different sexes.

There was need for an analysis which showed that the work situation of women could not be arbitrarily divided into work for pay outside and work for no pay inside the home. The particular areas of women's oppression and exploitation were completely inter-connected. The woman worker was in a position inferior to that of the man at work, although they were of the same class. Her situation in the family served to maintain this subordination. The general cultural oppression of women conditioned them to accept their economic and social position. It was a vicious circle which could only be broken by an alternative theory which took into account all aspects of women's oppression. Such a theory could not come either from a specifically feminist consciousness, or from trade unionism; it required a way of thinking that could extend beyond the particular to a general analysis of society. From working women, in their insistence on bread and roses, in the possibility of changing society so that people not only had more to eat but encountered one another in completely new ways and developed a radically different consciousness of each other, came a glimpse of such a total alternative. It was only a glimpse. They never developed in theory the particular nature of their own situation which made such connections both necessary and apparent to them. Nor were they strong enough to create continuing forms of organization which could give this expression.

It is evident that these problems were by no means peculiar to the nineteenth and early twentieth centuries. They remain living issues today and there seems little prospect of solving them from within a capitalist society.

Just as women revolutionaries encountered suspicion from their men when they seemed to be impinging on male prerogatives, women workers encountered an even more bitter resistance from their men, which was founded not only on the men's jealousy for traditional masculine superiority, but on the economic fact of privilege within the working class. Thus just as the women's revolt in political terms spoke for those who were silent within the revolutionary movement, the economic organization of women (and here the Bryant and May match girls' strike is the obvious example) encouraged the organization of all workers who were low down even within the working class. Both carry the revolutionary possibility of breaking through established caste hierarchies which continually develop actually within those movements which attempt to resist and overthrow the capitalist class hierarchy.

The way in which things can be different emerges very slowly. Revolutionary feminism has been weaker both in theory and practice than the mainstream of the left. Leaders of revolutionary movements have tended to be predominantly men and have seen the world from their point of view. But if the basis of a theory was laid in the nineteenth century, the first tentative steps were also made by women themselves towards an alternative in practice. This has been continued in the various revolutionary movements of the twentieth century. Thus an attempt to find what women asked for and what forms of organization they found most useful helps us to understand the particular oppression experienced by women.

Working women in the national workshops in the 1848 Revolution in France were moving towards the ideas of workers' control. They complained about the differential in the supervisors' pay and emphasized the inefficiency of these women. They also showed a lively class hostility to the role of middle-class women who came to 'improve' them on a philanthropic basis. Conditions were hard in these workshops set up by the government. The women worked twelve hours a day for very low wages in terrible conditions. They were also forced to compete with the women in prisons and religious communities who worked for even lower rates. The women were grouped in divisions of one hundred with delegates to the Provisional Government. Desirée Gay, a shirtmaker, was the delegate for the second arrondissement and used her position to try to change the way work was organized. She also wrote in the socialist feminist paper *La Voix des Femmes* criticizing conditions in the workshops.

Through the associations they were just forming, groups of women – glove-makers, washerwomen – pressed for more pay. But they also went beyond straightforward economic demands about pay at work. The midwives, for example, argued that socialized medicine was the answer to their bad conditions and low pay. Although some of the middle-class feminists tended to feel that improved education alone was the answer to all women's economic problems, working women in the feminist movement were more inclined to seek collective social solutions when they became conscious of the need for change.

Nor did women confine themselves to the work situation. Again this indicated the interlocking nature of women's oppression. *La Voix des Femmes* is full of all kinds of schemes for every aspect of life which affected women. In March 1848 women workers petitioned the Provisional Government for crèches.[21] A plan for the organization of crèches appeared in the paper on 3 April 1848.[22] The women suggested large houses, built in large gardens, for the working population in the area. These would contain a reading-room, bathroom, communal dining-room as well as a crèche where the children would have 'enlightened care'. There would also be a school. The training of young girls and a medical unit are emphasized as well. Evidently the women in Lyons were also discussing how to set up crèches. They wrote to the Paris women asking for news about the organization of work projects and offering information about their organization of crèches.

The ideas about crèches, which were very new in the 1840s, came directly from the needs of women who were working. But they also arose from the intense faith in the educability of human beings, common both in the socialist and feminist movements at the time. The interaction between the practical needs of working women and theories about children's education produced schemes which were very important indications of alternative forms of social living. This concern for education reappears in the Commune. In 1871 delegates from the Society for New Education brought a plan forward which resembled an earlier scheme worked out by the feminist socialist Pauline Roland in 1869. The idea was to make 'young people ready for self-government through a republican education'. This implied not merely a secular education without the old patriotic indoctrination; it also implied experimenting with completely new methods of teaching. There was particular interest in women's technical education and various workshop schools were organized. In some cases these provided homes as well as schools for girls with no families. Maria Verdure and Félix and Elie Ducoudray, representing the Société des Amis de l'Enseignement, had a plan too for reorganizing day nurseries. They should not just be places to leave the children but educative and entertaining. They should have lots of gardens and painted or carved toys representing animals, trees and flowers. They wanted bright colours everywhere and young women to look after the children, ten to every 100 children. Again medical supervision was to be provided. The prominence of women in these educational projects was very noticeable in 1848 as well as in the Commune. It was to be a feature of subsequent revolutionary movements, and was in fact a kind of public extension of the private role of women in the family. It does not seem to have aroused the antagonism provoked by ideas which challenged the basis of the family or by the action in which women broke out of the traditional confines which determined the scope of femininity.

Sexuality was probably the most explosive of issues. The derision which Francis Wright and the Saint-Simonians encountered in the 1820s and 1830s tended to make the women of the 1840s very defensive about the connection between socialism, feminism and free love. There is little about free unions in *La Voix des Femmes*. Divorce was supported but in the interests of public morality. However, there was general criticism about the superiority of the man in marriage. A letter to all women from Henriette D., a working woman, appeared. She demanded that the woman 'should not stay any longer under the power of her husband, [she should] be able to act, sell, buy, contract like him'. She wanted the revision of the Civil Code which stated women must submit to their husbands. She felt this was the most tyrannical of abuses. 'No more slavery, no more masters, equality between married couples, let's destroy abuses, it's time we defended our rights.'[23]

In the Commune various measures were passed which benefited women in the family situation. For example, wives, legal or not, received the pensions of National Guardsmen who had been killed. This was an implicit recognition of the structure of the working-class family and a blow against the authority of the Civil Code. This accorded with the kinds of demands women brought forward in the popular clubs and was justified by communards both on the grounds of justice to the women and on its effect of weakening the religious-monarchical institution of marriage and making a legal fact of the real living morality of workers.

This very important concept of the revolutionary group possessing a superior and more honest moral code which does not need the authority of the upper classes and the state, has always appeared amongst the oppressed in moments of revolutionary confidence. The sans-culottes in the 1789 Revolution were proud of their purity. In the case of the women the ideas of 'free unions', coming from the socialist feminist movement, encountered the rather different very practical facts of the working-class common marriages. From the outside, to the hostile bourgeois, they both appeared equally sinful and immoral. But the idea of a '*union libre*' with its connotations of the rehabilitation of the flesh was very far from the working-class 'their morals and ours' position, which was concerned with security and protection rather than sexual liberation. This contradiction has still not been successfully worked out.

1848 nevertheless was crucial as a time when the theories of socialist feminism interacted with the merging culture and institutions of the French working class. Journals like *La Voix des Femmes* provided a vehicle for women to express a wide range of ideas. The first issue announced proudly that it was a socialist paper. 'We are not only publishing a paper, but we are creating for women a library of practical information.' It was started by Eugénie Niboyet, who soon gathered a group of women around her. The socialists were from the start the liveliest and most decisive influence on the policy of the paper. There was Desirée Veret, a dressmaker and Owenite; Marie-Reine Guindorff, a Saint-Simonian; Desirée Gay, delegate for the women in National Workshops; Suzanne Voilquin, Fourierist, dressmaker turned midwife; Jeanne Marie, Saint-Simonian; Elisa Gremaille, Saint-Simonian, passionately involved in the cause of women's education; and Jeanne Deroin. These women provided not only socialist ideas but considerable practical knowledge about industrial conditions. There was also a group of middle-class republican women who were more interested in literature and artistic questions. The paper came out daily, though sometimes rather irregularly, between 20 March and 10 June. It was circulated in the large provincial towns as well as Paris. The paper was committed to certain general ideas: the belief that work would emancipate women, as long as it was organized in a collective manner, internationalism, anti-racialism, and opposition to all forms of slavery; but there were various other tendencies among the women centrally involved. When Jeanne Deroin and Hortense Wild started *L'Opinion des Femmes* in 1849 Eugénie Niboyet was no longer involved and she started to move towards the right. After 1848 there is a clear division between the socialist and liberal feminist position. This shows in the subsequent feminist papers, some of which were very right-wing.

*La Voix des Femmes* was most successful not only in bringing a diverse group of women together and enabling them to express themselves, but also in serving as a focus for organization, rather in the way Sylvia Pankhurst connected the Women's (later Workers') Dreadnought to the East London Federation of the suffragettes. The clubs also achieved the same result. Women's clubs had arisen in the first French Revolution because women were not allowed to enter some of the other revolutionary clubs. It was still considered rather shocking to have men and women together in the atmosphere of a political club. This situation continued in 1848. *La Voix des Femmes* mentions Cabet's club as one of the few which admitted women. The women's clubs were a means not only of political pressure but of popular education. They sprang up again in the Commune. The discussions were repeated in the revolutionary press and thus reached a wider audience. At a meeting of the Société de la Voix des Femmes in April 1848 questions about the organization of work were discussed. Wages, the role of middle-class women in the associations, the demand of a group of working women that the national workshops should be organized without supervisors, and information from Desirée Gay about the organization of cooperative workshops in the interests of working women in England, were discussed.

The clubs evoked the most extreme reactions. The men of the right could not decide which was the more monstrous, mixed clubs where there was infinite possibility of all kinds of horrors, from women smoking to women talking about their liberation with men, or a club full of women which was undoubtedly hatching a plot not only against property but against male superiority.

During the Commune a correspondent of *The Times* crept into a women's club. The room was filled with women and children of 'the lowest order of society'. The women were wearing 'loose untidy jackets' and 'white frilled caps upon their heads'. At the end of the room there was a table covered with papers and books, with young citoyennes wearing red sashes behind it. A young woman spoke about the need to defend the Revolution. He was not concerned about what she said but notes she was 'young and pretty' – the inevitable sexual note. But he detected a look in her eye which made him feel he would 'not like to have been her husband'. The following speaker was tolerably respectable, but 'rambling and inconsistent'. She spoke of the role of women in the Commune and the Revolution of 1789. She was critical too of the clergy. Another woman attacked society's exploitation of the poor. *The Times* reporter found her speech 'vague and unnecessarily repetitious'.[24]

Innumerable cartoons appeared ridiculing the women in the clubs. Rather as the suggestion that women should fight for the revolution produced an outraged reaction, because it went so much against the traditional passive role of women, the fact that they should actively discuss ideas proved repugnant to conservatives. Not all men shared this antagonism of course. An unsigned letter in *La Voix des Femmes* urged the women not to form a separate club and completely exclude men, especially those who had complete sympathy with the ideas of emancipation. The writer felt that the exchange of ideas between the two sexes seemed absolutely necessary if they wished to arrive at one truth. A compromise measure secured the education period, of women by women, which was felt to be very important, first, and then admitted men by invitation tickets. The women argued that they needed to develop their ideas together to give them confidence, and that fathers and husbands might be uneasy about their wives attending a mixed club. There was also an added problem of male hostility preventing the women from expressing themselves. La Société de la Voix des Femmes was literally brought to a close and the police came in because the men who were admitted caused such a rumpus that the women's voices were completely drowned. Eugénie Niboyet's quiet voice finally penetrated when there was order again. She said it was impossible for self-respecting women to accept the insults hurled at them. 'We don't want to act as playthings, or entertainment for anybody. . . . Behind your catcalls despotism is strengthened. You know very well that we don't want to lower you in any way but you're afraid to see us rise.'[25]

The question of women's clubs arose in quite different contexts. The Russian revolutionary movement at the end of the nineteenth century was passionately committed to women's emancipation. The strong emphasis on personal emancipation along with the movements for economic and political change, and the remarkable participation of women in the revolutionary groups, encouraged a theoretical climate in which women's emancipation was stressed as a crucial aspect of the revolutionary movement. Women from rich families sought higher education so they could go out into the villages as teachers, doctors and nurses. They wanted to live fuller and more useful lives. Many of them flocked to the university at Zurich in the early 1870s. Stepniak in *Underground Russia* describes their politicization: 'But on arriving in the country of their dreams, they found not only schools of medicine there, but also a great social movement of which many had no conception.'[26]

From among the groupings at Zurich came an important basis both in terms of theory and of personal contact for much subsequent revolutionary activity. But even in this situation, which was explicitly sympathetic to the ideas of women's emancipation, and in which every woman had made an exceptional step in actually seeking higher education, women experienced particular problems within the revolutionary movement as a whole. A group of women therefore decided to start their own club from which men were excluded. The reasons given were that in meetings where men and women were present, women mostly remained silent, not so much because they knew less, but because they did not know how to speak and articulate their knowledge. They wanted to develop their confidence and ability to express themselves together without men. The older women opposed this. They thought the exclusion of men would mean that the discussion became one-sided and declined in interest. After six weeks the club split on this issue. Another group was formed of women who lived in the same hostel. They had a self-education and discussion circle in which they discussed social ideas, philosophy, the events of the Commune. Vera Figner, later to become prominent in the Narodnaya Volya group, was a member of the circle, although they had not asked her to join at first because her husband was known to be contemptuous and they mistakenly assumed she shared his attitude. About the same time another women's club or circle was formed in St Petersburg, to which Sofia Perovskaya and the Kornilova sisters belonged. They discussed both the social and personal aspects of women's liberation. When Perovskaya and the Kornilova sisters joined another circle which included men the other women were extremely indignant. However, they all finally merged with the men's circle and became one of the pioneer groups in the popular movement of going to the people.

The functions of the women's clubs extended beyond discussion and organization. They were sometimes also a means of organizing home life in a cooperative manner. In March 1848 *La Voix des Femmes* reported a demonstration of young working women aged between fifteen and thirty, neatly dressed and of respectable appearance, with a banner inscribed 'Vesuviennes'. The Vesuviennes not only formed a club, but having no men to support them, and no families, had organized themselves communally. They had strict rules: wealth was divided, food and lodging were guaranteed, each woman received ten francs a month. Their first commune was in Belleville. They marched in a disciplined manner to the Town Hall where they asked for assistance from the government. The Vesuviennes maintained that women should bear arms in the Garde Civique and form a reserve force for the military forces.

In the Russian revolutionary movement communes also appeared. Chernychevsky's novel *What is to be Done?* had a great influence from the 1860s onwards. In the book the heroine organizes a cooperative workshop and forms resolutely platonic free unions. In St Petersburg workshops and communes appeared modelled on this idea. They were particularly important in providing homes and shelter for women workers and students who had left parents and husbands. It was believed too that it was necessary to create alternative cultural forms of association before the revolution. One of the Kornilova sisters describes these: 'The material conditions of the inmates varied, but resources were regarded as common property. Mutual help was acknowledged as the supreme rule of the common life.'

Not only did the commune make living cheaper and provide companionship and security, it also acted as a kind of educational force; those who were better educated influenced the others. It was seen too as a way of realizing:

. . . our socialist ideas in practice in our private lives, and whilst we were no better housed, but rather worse than the factory workers, we were not obliged to distinguish between mine and thine among comrades. The commune meant much in particular to women from the provinces. Not infrequently there were some among them who had broken completely with their rich and influential families and arrived penniless with the object of studying. Of course they all hoped to find work of some kind. But without acquaintances or connections they very seldom succeeded. Many women would have been utterly lost but for the mutual help within the commune, without in fact the youthful support of youthful comrades. Everything conventional and insincere in our mutual relations was absolutely ruled out, not the smallest regard was paid to outward appearances, and we lived among friends as if in the innermost family circle.[27]

Thus the communes arose partly from the practical needs of women, but they also served to create new forms of the family within the revolutionary movement. They at once served to bind the revolutionaries together by personal as well as political ties and to create in microcosm the beginnings of a new culture. A characteristic of the Russian movement in the 1870s as well as in France in the 1840s was a strong emphasis on personal emancipation. The dangers of this emphasis are apparent. There is a tendency to try to create the new world by a personal act of will and the way in which cultural change grows out of material circumstance is neglected. Very often the energy and heroism which comes from such an emphasis are dissipated in disillusion and defeat. On the other hand, some kind of understanding that revolutionary political consciousness and activity must affect individuals as personal and private beings as much as in their external and public work is necessary if movements are to survive attack and persecution without breaking and dividing into warring factions under the strain. Because of the particular problems women face they have always seen this very clearly as soon as they become involved in any numbers in revolutionary work. The emphasis on the importance of the personal questions of liberation has not only recurred again and again whenever there is a high degree of participation of women, it has almost been a precondition for the mobilization of women in any significant numbers.

An account of a women's prison in the biography of Marie Spiridonova, the social revolutionary, illustrates this well. It was necessary to create their own community if they were to emerge from prison able to play any useful part in revolutionary work. They studied intensively anatomy, biblical texts, Darwin, medicine, mathematics, Nietzsche, Dostoyevsky, Indian philosophy, Pascal, Tolstoy, Marx, Herzen. There were strict regulations about not talking in study times as privacy was impossible. They read anti-revolutionary thinkers with special care. Kakhovskaya, one of the youngest among them, said:

We found ourselves forced to review our whole intellectual armoury, to rethink all our principles, to establish carefully the fundamentals of our philosophy of life. For we had all come into the Revolution very young, taken by the emotional waves of the movement. . . . In our search for spiritual and moral enlightenment we therefore made ourselves thoroughly familiar with the entire artillery of our ideological opponents.[28]

They believed that you only had the right to call yourself a convinced socialist and atheist when there was no system of metaphysics which could confute you and when you carried your principles over into personal life with all their implications.

They tried to overcome the conditions of the prison by imposing not only an external discipline but by internal discipline as well. Every action however small was examined with relentless self-analysis. Every law was not simply to be observed but to be observed without hypocrisy. The enclosed world of the Katorga bred its own introspection. This was encouraged by the predominance of social revolutionaries and anarchists among the prisoners, who tended to think in moral and ideal terms rather than in real and strategic ones.

Spiritually it gave them great strength but politically it carried its own weaknesses. One inmate, Bitzenko, who was later to become a Bolshevik, pointed this out:

> The destruction of all values continued until it threatened complete annihilation of everything. . . . They questioned even the fundamental aims for which they fought and so arrived by degrees at the threshold of all life's mysteries. In the end they found themselves confronted by sheer nothingness and the abyss. What was the meaning and justification of life? Where was truth and what was it? Where and what was the real criterion of good and evil, justice and morality? What was the real meaning of progress? Was socialism really necessary? Where was the true path to the salvation of the world? Could our struggle involving the use of the force of arms be justified? Was it not possible that far more could be attained by another method – the influence of an honourable personal life? Consideration of all those questions from the point of view of the class whose interest they had undertaken to defend did not satisfy them. They would not be satisfied with anything less than the absolute

The conflict between these two approaches to the revolutionary life was to appear in various disguises and under different names in many kinds of revolutionary circumstances. Bitzenko proved for the short term to be correct. But the question of the manner in which the external world of revolutionary practice penetrates the inner world of consciousness, and how this affects the revolutionaries' action, has not been answered satisfactorily. Nor have the consequences of this interaction been seriously discussed in terms of their effect upon organization. Yet the course of revolutionary movements indicates that this is a vital question. Because the oppression of women operated as much on a personal as a public level, of necessity women inclined towards demands and modes of organizing in which these combined. But because there was no theory to connect, explain and extend the practical discoveries of revolutionary feminism, the significance of the women's activity was obscured and forgotten. The women's movements themselves faced not only the difficulties common to all revolutionaries, but a particularly fierce opposition from the right which was sexual as well as political, and an ambiguity among revolutionary men, some of whom agreed with Proudhon that women's role was not in 'la vie exterieure' but belonged to 'la vie interieure'. The implications of sexual repression and authoritarianism could not be worked out convincingly in the nineteenth-century context.

Probably the most difficult problem revolutionary women had to contend with lay not in the attitudes of men right or left, but in their own terrible timidity, the result of centuries of oppression. They dropped back easily into the fatalism which sprang from the impossibility of control over their pregnancies, their inexperience in control, organization or initiative, which meant it was always a desperate struggle not to pass responsibility onto someone else, and in the practical difficulties which continually stifled their aspirations to 'la vie exterieure'.

The German social democrat Adelheid Popp describes how at her first meeting she took every reference to the apathy of working women personally. She felt she had to speak in defence of her sex. She lifted her hand. 'They cried "Bravo" before I opened my mouth; merely from the fact that a working woman wanted to speak. As I mounted the steps to the platform my eyes swam and my throat was parched. I felt as though I was choking.' She dwelt on the mental poverty of working women. 'I demanded enlightenment, culture and knowledge for my sex, and I begged the men to help us to them.'[30]

She reeled under the applause and began the painful task of writing her first article, with only three years of schooling, no notion of spelling, and her letters like those of a child. At home she met bewilderment and opposition. Her mother wanted her to marry normally and be a wife. But she still felt the overwhelming necessity of continuing in her way of trade union and revolutionary militancy, and in the long struggle towards self-education:

When I felt the necessity of writing how I became a socialist it was solely with the wish of encouraging those numerous working women who possess hearts full of a longing to do something, but who always draw back again, because they do not trust their own capabilities.[31]

If women experienced the lack of 'trust' of 'their own capabilities', common to people who have always been despised, this combined with their role in the family and at home to make an active political life incredibly difficult if not impossible. So many of the women who were politically involved had to renounce the normal life of women. This element of renunciation and self-denial bred a kind of stiffness, a lack of humour, which appeared to people on the outside as an unnatural fanaticism. Though sometimes revolutionary women quite consciously chose to combine the internal and external worlds, it was extremely difficult. A Russian comrade wrote to the Marxist and feminist Dora Montefiore just before the Russian Revolution:

> I am a mother. I shall not be spared in this life anything that concerns a woman's lot. In my time of life – I am thirty-two – a woman feels very strongly – though often unconsciously – the want of motherhood, and I am no exception to the rule.[32]

She intended to combine the duties of a mother with those of a revolutionary. All winter she had been giving lessons supporting her mother and as many workless people as she could, until two months before her confinement.

The great emphasis on education which was such a feature of the nineteenth-century movements continues. Just before the Russian Revolution, Alexandra Kollontai, who was to conflict with the Bolshevik leadership after the revolution for her insistence on the need to combine feminism with Marxism, as well as her support for the Workers' Opposition movement which stressed change coming from below, organized a club of about two hundred women in St Petersburg. An interview with her appeared in *The Woman Worker* in 1909:

> Two years ago we made the first effort to interest groups of women in questions specially affecting them and in means to raise their condition. Such for instance as protection from hard work, before and after the birth of children. So step by step we hoped to lead them to socialism. . . . Men visitors are admitted but it is managed by the women themselves.[33]

There was a congress in December 1908 which the authorities expected to be a tame gathering of moderate middle-class women. In fact, out of 700 women forty-five were socialists and thirty of these were factory workers. They had also prepared carefully enough to have an important impact. The working women with Kollontai's help had decided what to say in support of various reforms they urgently needed. Sometimes two or three had studied the same question so that the one who emerged able to speak best for it could get up at the Congress. They were all very frightened, but startled the Congress by holding forth for at least fifteen to twenty minutes and getting their points across. All this was even more remarkable because they were meeting underground, in great secrecy, smuggling speakers out of the back door with handkerchiefs over their faces if the police raided.

Really, because these women had so little experience and confidence, they could only start to achieve anything by producing an atmosphere in which everybody felt it to be absolutely necessary to contribute everything that they had. Women's movements have often been characterized by a stress on self-activity, equal participation and a suspicion of leaders. In the New York shirtwaist strike in 1909, girls of seventeen and eighteen were standing up and addressing meetings; some of the immigrant girls didn't even know how to telephone, they had no idea about the laws relating to pickets, or how to defend themselves in court. A reporter in *The Call* commented:

The most remarkable feature of the strike is the absence of leaders. All the girls seem to be imbued with a spirit of activity that by far surpasses all former industrial uprisings. One like all are ready to take the chairmanship, secretaryship, do picket duty, be arrested and go to prison.[34]

The same has frequently been true of the way women participated in revolutions. Men have sometimes felt that there was some inbuilt anarchic tendency in women. However, the absolute necessity of complete participation is generally characteristic of all people who have long been oppressed and have little experience in continuing organization. Their problem is in sustaining this, but the presence of tried leaders means that they simply drop into their old roles of dependence and any popular movement disintegrates. The contradiction appears not so much in leadership in particular situations based on specific concrete knowledge, but in the leader as figure with all the trappings of authority. Women who have had such an intense personal struggle to escape from male authority have shown a complex attitude to leaders within a women's movement. There is an intense suspicion but also a kind of passive dependence once any authority is asserted. Conversely, women who have fought alone and reached any measure of independence are often passionately jealous about it and unwilling to work with other women. When the women round *La Voix des Femmes* suggested George Sand as a candidate for women, because she had the respect of men, Sand turned on them with contempt and was careful to dissociate herself from any socialist feminist movement.

But a problem could arise when individually prominent women were completely committed to a movement. The existence of the East London Federation of the Suffragettes along with the network of welfare services, the crèche in Bow, the cooperative toy factory, the continued agitation for working women's conditions in the Dreadnought, were all a product of Sylvia Pankhurst's energy and determination. But her presence inevitably eclipsed the other women and meant they played a secondary role within the federation. She was in the ridiculous position of instructing them not to depend on her. When they were going on a demonstration to Trafalgar Square she said, 'I am going with you. I want you not to cling round me, but to do your own business. You must all go around. I am certain that the more there are of us, the more difficult it will be for our opponents.'[35]

The federation showed great ingenuity in organizing. They thought of everything, from women in a boat on Victoria Park to advertise the Dreadnought with the letters written on the top of coloured umbrellas, to the occupation of empty houses by people in workhouses. The minutes are full of the micro world of all groups. An organizer was inefficient, funds were stolen. They negotiated complicated agreements with the Socialist Sunday School Union; they patiently drafted letters to the papers. They led innumerable militant deputations to ministers, organized an exhibition of women's sweated trades, sent resolutions in support of the Russian Revolution, campaigned for equal pay, and for non-interference in the allowances for soldiers' and sailors' wives. But despite all this they did not as a group work out together any theory of the way in which their feminism related to their socialism.

One point became perfectly clear however, and that was their fundamental difference from the Women's Social and Political Union. They were very much frozen out:

Their [the W.S.P.U.] view of the difference between the E.L.F. and headquarters was that we had more faith in what could be done by stirring up working women than was felt at headquarters, where they had most faith in what could be done for the vote by people of means and influence. In other words they said that they were working from the top downwards and we from the bottom up, that is with regard to wealth and influence.[36]

Mrs Parsons struck a more personal note; she 'thought it a good thing to have a separate party in the East End from the West End, as they did not say anything about our work in the East End at the meeting at the Empress Theatre and that Sylvia Pankhurst was the leader down here; they had their two leaders'.[35] Sylvia Pankhurst, who was clearly embarrassed, 'said we would not talk about that as we did not bother about those things'. Mrs Parsons apparently took the hint and subsided.

Historically though the split was of tremendous significance. The First World War and the Bolshevik Revolution forced feminists to define clearly which side they were on, while the extension of the franchise removed the single unifying issue which had bound them together. After 1917 no political movement could be quite the same. This was as true for the woman as for anyone else. Ironically it was the action of women which was crucial. On 23 February there was a peaceful women's demonstration on International Women's Day. The women decided, against the advice of all organized political groups including the Bolsheviks, who expected the police and troops to be called out and futile bloodshed, to go on strike. But when the women sent delegations to the factories thousands came out and were joined by working-class and middle-class housewives who were affected by the shortage of food and high prices. The army was called out but did not fire on the women. Encouraged by their success workers came out on to the streets in great numbers the following day.

There are obvious similarities in the action and organization of women. At one side there is action which comes from a particular need in a specific situation; at the other there are new needs which the extraordinary events of revolution make possible to conceive but not to realize. While these are common to movements which are not specifically revolutionary, the ideas of democracy, equality, liberty and comradeship provide a theoretical justification for the women's claims. The weakness of revolutionary feminism was a failure of coherence, both in practice and theory. True, they organized internationally in the early twentieth century on a scale far beyond that of any equivalent groups now in terms of formal organization and congresses. But they did not find a means of overcoming the traditional fatalism, the passivity, the timidity and lack of confidence which were characteristic of women in normal times. The spasmodic heroism of exceptional moments of revolutionary and industrial militancy could sweep this aside momentarily but as a long-term problem it was not solved.

Similarly they did not achieve a form of organization and a theory which could relate and clarify the specific aspects of women's oppression, and the more general oppression which they shared with men, which could serve as a basis for action. They did create in innumerable different ways though an historical memory of the collective action of women, organizing from the point of their femaleness, their class, and their commitment to the idea of a society in which there would be no indignity, and in which no one would be despised or ignored. Subsequently this tradition of revolutionary feminism has been obscured. All that remains is the memory of the other feminism that came from the top down, and which was concerned to accommodate privileged women within capitalism. But persistently, against incredible odds and often with opposition from men, the same kind of demands, which immediately raised many questions often ignored by male revolutionaries about ways of living together, about authority in the family, about the toys children first learn about the world from, recur.

At the same time all the women involved, whatever their class, found themselves fighting the enemy within as well as the enemy without. They had to overcome their own silence, their own paralysis, their way of shrugging off the responsibility for the world to the men. There was no denying this for them. They couldn't fight just for bread, because their own hearts had been starved for so long they hardly knew how to begin:

> Sisters, don't say you can't do anything . . .
> No more lack of confidence
> No more hesitation.
> Let us ask ourselves clearly this question,
> What do we want?
> We want total and complete liberation.

Let them mock us, a day will come when they will no longer laugh.
Is this day far away?
What does it matter.
We will have difficulty, suffering, struggles.
Happiness will be for our sisters, for the women born after us.

Women reply to men who ask 'What do you want? What are you trying to do?

'We want to reconstruct a new world with you, where peace and truth will reign, we want justice in every spirit, and love in every heart.'[37]

CHAPTER 6

# If You Like
# Tobogganing

23 February 1917:
In spite of all directives the women textile workers in several factories
went on strike, and sent delegates to the metal workers with an appeal
for support . . .

It had not occurred to anyone that it might become the first day of
the revolution . . .

The February revolution was begun from below, overcoming the
resistance of its own revolutionary organizations, the initiative being
taken of their own accord by the women textile workers, among them
no doubt many soldiers' wives. The overgrown bread-lines had provided the last stimulus. About 90,000 workers, men and women, were
on strike that day. The fighting mood expressed itself in demonstrations, meetings, and encounters with the police. A mass of women,
not all of them workers, flocked to the municipal Duma demanding
bread. It was like demanding milk from a he-goat. Red banners
appeared in different parts of the city, and inscriptions on them
showed that the workers wanted bread, but neither autocracy or war.
Women's Day passed successfully with enthusiasm and without
victims. But what it concealed in itself, no one had even guessed by
nightfall.

L. Trotsky, *History of the Russian Revolution*

The woman's road – threshold to stove.

I thought I saw two people, but it was only a man and his wife.

Russian proverbs

To all citizens of the village of Verteyevka of the male sex who are
married, from all citizens of the village of Verteyevka of the female sex
who are married. Ultimatum.

# If You Like Tobogganing

Whereas all we married women, citizens of the village of Verteyevka, live under difficult conditions, our husbands beat us, we hear no decent words from them, they treat us like cattle, we therefore have no more patience to endure such insults, and we hereby write the present ultimatum. We agree to work at home and be our husbands' helpers, but demand in return that we shall not be given over completely to our husbands' wills, that they shall not be so free with their hands, and call us such names as 'old hag', 'bitch', 'slut', and other unmentionable ones. And this too we add – we shall not disperse, and not return to our husbands until they have all signed their names to this paper.

> Reported by Aksinya Karaseva in the village of
> Verteyevka, Briansk Gubernia, mid 1920s

On all sides the men are being blamed. But it is often the women's fault when the family breaks up. . . . Some young fellow comes along with his songs and his accordion. . . . They are always running to the Genotdel, and slandering their husbands. There a whole women's commission gets together, the husband knows nothing of it – and he is disgraced.

> Tovarish Motish, from Siberia. Congress, 1925

You are surprised that I live with men, not wanting to fall in love with them? . . . I have read many novels, and know how much time and strength it takes to be in love. . . . But when, these past years, has there been leisure for us? . . . If you are attracted to someone he is called to the front, or to another city, or you are so busy yourself that you forget – what harm to cherish the few minutes that may mean a little happiness to you both?

> Genia, in *Love of Three Generations*, by
> Alexandra Kollontai

Love should make you build bridges and bear children. . . . Only text-books on horticulture have anything about roses, and daydreams are dealt with only in medical works.

> Vladimir Mayakovsky, *The Bedbug*

> We do not like romance
> In our present time – to us
> It reeks of flowered screens
> Over garbage cans, of pretty words
> Bringing hollowness, not flesh,
> To every skeleton . . .

But you are a girl
Your problem cannot be denied.

In the Russia of the past
Women once pinned flowers
To their shoulders, chained to lovers,
Flogged by snarling guards
In the exile of Siberia.

And in the Russia of today
Men and women, proud of working-hours,
Sturdy, far from blood-steeped tinsel,
Take their summer vacations
On the steppes, in cleaner games,
In flowers, pledges, loyalties,
Clear-growing, inevitable,
Deepening in their youth.

Steal, for an hour now and then,
To your time of violets, the hope
Of less impeded tenderness
In a freedom yet to come,
Then fold it in your heart for unapparent,
Secretly unyielding strength
On every picket-line throughout the world,
Revolutionary girl.

'To a Revolutionary Girl', Maxwell Bodenheim, in
*New Masses*, U.S.A., 1934

Ukraine girls really knock me out
They leave the west behind
Moscow girls make me sing and shout
And Georgia's always on my mind.

Beatles, 'Back in the U.S.S.R.'

---

The images of women which have come through to us from the Russian Revolution are arbitrary and distorted. Quite often they are descriptions of the women's role which are completely constructed in manipulative terms. Men have given us their version of what women should be. There are pictures of those round, rosy Soviet Stalinist heroines of motherhood, all sunset and tractors and socialist realism. There are memories of an old Trotskyist lecturing on the 'women's role', and telling how the women fraternized with the troops. There are the women the right has created in the west, like the sinister butch Cheka women who inhabit spy novels – gnarled, stiff and unhandled in the night, sitting behind desks in uniforms and judging men mercilessly, their breasts hollowed with hatred. There are the beautiful women rescued from the grim stern discipline of the party or the horrors of revolution – Garbo in *Ninotchka* is delicately seduced and falls gracefully in elegant inelegance, or you see Julie Christie and the daffodils of *Dr Zhivago*.

Love and daffodils are always on the other side. The things a woman 'really' wants come from the 'free' west. Women are completely external to the revolution. Here the images of left and right merge. Women are regarded as too fragile or too backward, they lack the discipline necessary for serious politics. The revolution happened despite them.

It is true that the telephone girls John Reed describes in *Ten Days That Shook the World* recoiled from the workers; true too that Louise Bryant met girls who fought for the whites. But other women came out in the spring of 1917, pushed not only by working conditions but by high prices. They wanted bread and peace, demands for the here and now. We know that much, but where they came from and who they were and how they felt and what became of them has vanished now. We inherit a kind of silence. All the stills have been faded out, some are substitutes. It's hard to piece our own picture together because we have to see through layers of subsequent political interpretation, and because the story of what women did has been shuffled into the background. Many other questions have appeared to interpreters of the Russian Revolution as more important. Yet the effect of the revolution on women has implications wider than those of specific interest to women's liberation. The world the revolution opened for women is inseparable from that which it opened for men. Because the Russian Revolution is described through the men's eyes this has been forgotten:

> It is quite true that there are no limits to masculine egotism in ordinary life. In order to change the conditions of life we must learn to see them through the eyes of women.[1]

Those women who came out on Women's Day were not just crucial in terms of the political events which followed; their action has tremendous significance as a symbolic break from their own oppression. If we knew more about the history of the women workers' movement we would be able to piece together the slow growth in consciousness and organization which enabled them to send for delegates and initiate the strike themselves. But it *is* possible now to understand the kind of stake poor women had in 1917, to grasp the odds against them and realize that we take for granted so much of what they were fighting for that we've forgotten the enormity of what they almost won.

Passivity and fatalism were particularly close to Russian women; their subordination was so absolute and bound up with the backwardness of the country, and their poverty was so extreme. They rose from such a long and deep sense of being nothing, of knowing no hope in change. It is not really surprising that in a society where serfdom had only ended comparatively recently, women should be regarded still, quite openly, as property. Nor that the physical contempt for all human life general in that society should be acted out almost ceremoniously on the bodies of the women. Russian proverbs read like hymns of social and sexual flagellation. Public oppression and indignity reproduced itself in the private part of living. The family was a little sanctuary of authoritarianism and suffering:

A chicken is not a bird – and a baba [peasant woman] is not
a human being.
Beat your wife for breakfast and for dinner too.
I will love you like my safe and beat you like my fur coat.
A wife isn't a jug – she won't crack if you hit her a few times.

She had her own kind of vengeance:

It is easier to manage a sackful of fleas than one woman.

The realities behind such ironies were grim. In peasant families it was customary for the bride's father to give the groom a new whip so he could exercise his authority if he wished. It hung over the marriage bed and was eloquent of the way in which the young girl passed from the control of her father to the control of her husband. Tsarist family law declared the wife's duty was 'to obey her husband as the head of the family, to be loving and respectful, to be submissive in every respect and show him every compliance and affection'. In practice this meant the wife had to follow her husband wherever he went. She could not get a passport or take a job without his permission. Resistance was almost impossible. The husband took over any property which she inherited. Divorce was very difficult because it was decided by the church and only on very limited grounds. It was moreover extremely expensive and quite beyond the means of the poor. In the eastern provinces women were still veiled and polygamy continued. But even in the rest of Russia peasant women were often sold to the highest bidder. They had little choice as to whom they married. To their husbands they were working hands, part of the livestock, as much as sexual partners. The young girls were soon worn down with work and childbearing. They cooked, carried water, washed clothes in the river, made fires, milked the cows, toiled in the fields, and did the spinning and weaving. In the winter the *moujiks* were often at home with nothing to do but drink vodka and have sex with their wives. There were no contraceptives. Secretly the women went to the local wise woman who operated with nails or buttonhooks or carrots. Childbirth was a kind of nightmare. Infant mortality was high, there were only a few midwives. 'The mother lay among the cockroaches and pumpkins on the stove, and gnarled and dirty hands delivered her baby.'[2]

In the city women worked long hours for less pay than their men, concealing their pregnancies until the last moment. Years later an old worker remembering these conditions told how as soon as anyone was pregnant they were sacked on the spot:

The women workers used to hide it until their mouths foamed and the child was born at the bench. And after the confinement – back to the bench. What could be more terrible than for a mother not to be glad to have her child? And there used to be many women workers who cursed their children.[3]

There was no legislation to protect women in industry, until a very limited social insurance scheme was introduced in 1912. Casual prostitution was part of the life of working women; the brothels were blessed by the priests – to protect the rest. Infanticide was common. On the other hand the world of middle- and upper-class women was very protected. But although they lived in comfort they were just as powerless as the others. Young women were meant to be accomplished, not educated. Higher education was regarded as almost synonymous with indecency. Secretly they pursued their affairs – discovery meant disgrace. When they were married any property they owned was managed by their husbands. Although a few women in the intelligentsia had broken away and joined the revolutionary movement, to the rest they were outcasts.

First the war and then the revolution shattered all this. Families were broken up. The women took over men's work, they learned new skills. Some women from rich homes became nurses. But instead of this being simply reversed when the men came home, the revolution carried it farther. In April 1918 the Petrograd Council of Trade Unions issued an extremely significant declaration:

> The question of how to combat unemployment has come sharply before the unions. In many factories and shops the question is being solved very simply . . . fire the women and put men in their place.[4]

The Petrograd Council maintained that such a solution was incompatible with the new manner in which the working class was going to organize the economy. They held that the only way to end unemployment ultimately was by increasing productivity on a socialist basis. In the meantime dismissals which were necessary because of the economic crisis should be related to each individual's degree of need – regardless of sex. 'Only such an attitude will make it possible for us to retain women in our organizations and prevent a split in the army of workers.'[5]

Women were admitted with full rights into the working class. Thus an essential principle of women's equality at work was established and a completely different criterion introduced for redundancy. Women benefited particularly from this assertion of the value of workers as persons rather than things, because single women with young children were regarded as among the most needy.

It was obviously necessary too to provide protection for pregnant women. Alexandra Kollontai had spent a considerable time before the revolution studying maternity provision. Partly as a result of her pressure the first working women's conference was held in Petrograd within a week of the formation of the Soviet government and more than fifty thousand women were represented. Although her proposals for the new maternity laws were the basis of discussion, the working women formulated its actual outlines on the basis of what they themselves had experienced. The Decree on Insurance in Case of Sickness, 22 December 1917, was the first of a series of protective measures. An insurance fund was set up without deductions from wages and workers' wives were covered as well as women actually in industry. In January 1918 the Department for the Protection of Motherhood and Infancy was officially organized and functioned in close connection with the department of social welfare. It secured sixteen weeks' free care for women before and after pregnancy. Expectant mothers did light work and could not be transferred or dismissed without the consent of a factory inspector. Night work was prohibited for both pregnant and nursing women. Maternity homes, clinics and advisory centres were set up. These seem like unspectacular and extremely fundamental reforms now, but in the Russian context they were an extraordinary achievement. Although women benefited from the general legislation for all workers, Jessica Smith says it was the maternity insurance law which they always mentioned as the most important change in conditions.

Most extraordinary was the legislative transformation of the family. Six weeks after the revolution the former ecclesiastical control of marriage was replaced by civil registration; within a year the new Matrimonial Code established before the law complete equality of rights between husband and wife, as well as dissolving the distinction between legitimate and illegitimate children. The husband's legal domination in the family was ended and women could decide on their own names and citizenship. They were no longer obliged to go wherever their husbands went if they didn't want to. Divorce was made easy and a relationship could become a marriage simply by mutual agreement between the two partners; equally, mutual agreement could end it. If both partners did not want the relationship to end it was left to the decision of the courts, until 1926, when both partners were able to get a divorce by applying to the Registrars' Office instead. At first both partners were obliged to pay alimony for six months after they separated if one of them was unemployed or not able to earn a living. Property was at first divided equally. The 1926 Family Code changed this. It attempted to secure the rights of peasant women and housewives by regarding all property as jointly held. Women were thus entitled to remuneration for work during marriage. This code also made explicit provisions for women living in unregistered marriages. Although the marriage laws were not uniformly applied – the recognition of *de facto* marriages for instance never penetrated the eastern areas – combined with the industrial legislation they brought an extraordinary transformation in the lives of Russian women.

Nor were the women merely passive spectators to all this. The organizational results of the Petrograd conference was the setting up of special committees to instruct women in the use of their rights. These were found to be inadequate and in 1919 the Working and Peasant Women's Department of the Communist Party was formed. It was known as the 'Genotdel'. There was opposition to this at first: some Bolsheviks were against it because they thought it was too feministic.

The Genotdel did not simply act as a means of educating women; it actually brought them into political activity. At first it mobilized women for the civil war and the famine. Thousands of emergency 'red nurses' went to the front, did military service, dug trenches, put up barbed wire or carried on political and educational work along the firing line. There were women in the Red Army who fought as guerrillas; in some cases they were in charge of men. Vera Alexeyeva, a social revolutionary cigarette worker turned Bolshevik, was made captain of a guerrilla group and spent weeks in the saddle, day and night, hunting whites in the Ukraine. Later she became leader of a local Genotdel, and found herself organizing peasant women who had just started work in a textile factory. She told Jessica Smith how difficult she had found it to adjust at first:

When peace came they requisitioned me to work among women. Everyone laughed. They didn't think of me as a 'baba' at all. I didn't think much of the idea much myself at first – I was so used to chasing around like a man and wearing men's clothes. . . . I remember the first women's meeting I called, how I tried to draw the women out to discuss the problems before us. One after another got up and talked of her own troubles. Each one had to tell how she had suffered during the revolution and the famine. How could she get bread and clothing, how could she get work, why should so much misfortune have been visited on *her*? Now they are talking about *our* problems – how we can organize day nurseries to take care of *our* children and how we can improve *our* condition. That is a great advance, to have got the women to think and act collectively.[6]

The Genotdel drew women in often on a practical basis at first. 'When we can't get 'em one way, we try another!' said Vera Alexeyeva.

'There are plenty of women we couldn't get to come near a meeting – but when we give them something practical – look how they come.'[7] Sometimes they came to sew and heard lectures on politics or babies or sex. Discussion circles grew from these. Kollontai helped to organize a network of women's clubs which penetrated even into the eastern regions. The women's congresses brought members of the local groups together. The experience women gained from their separate organization helped them to assert themselves in trade unions, public debates and in the party. Kollontai told the American journalist Louise Bryant that the women's congresses were important not simply for the direct political work they did, but also for increasing the confidence of the women themselves and preventing their needs from being ignored by the men.[8] A peasant woman who had been to one of these congresses returned home to her village with pamphlets, posters and a new important understanding of a world beyond the old boundaries. In 1925 Kayer Nissa, a girl of twelve from the Muslim East who had attended one of the women's clubs, been cast out of home and supported by the other women, spoke as a delegate at a conference: 'We have had enough of having our faces covered . . . of being imprisoned, in stuffy ichkaris, sold at the tenderest age to old men, maimed in body and soul, and degraded to slaves.'[9]

Sometimes this new confidence meant that the women criticized the men. They felt insulted by attitudes they had not even noticed before. In the discussions which preceded the 1926 Family Law a peasant woman said:

We are still in the dark, we were enslaved for centuries. All we know is priests' gossip – which we are only now beginning to forget about. 'The wife must fear her husband.' . . . Our men comrades, they know a bit more than we do. You must teach us, you must not just laugh and giggle; that is no use, particularly on the part of the enlightened comrades, the party men. I do not consider this the way of comradeship. . . . To us that is very insulting.[10]

Commitment among party leaders to women's emancipation was real enough. But there was considerable confusion about how it was to be achieved. Theoretically specific reforms at work were fairly straightforward. The relationship between the sexes presented more problems. It was generally accepted that 'The proletariat cannot achieve complete liberty until it has won complete liberty for women.'[11] It was also apparent that liberty for women implied not merely change at work but in the family. The revolution had to reorganize at the point of reproduction as well as production. The need to free women from the drudgery of housework was a common theme. It was hoped that they would be able completely to collectivize these private tasks with public restaurants, communal kitchens, laundries, cloth-mending centres, collective housekeeping arrangements and facilities for children, crèches, nurseries, kindergartens, children's colonies. By releasing women from this private work in the family, they could become involved in production. Lenin emphasized the effects of work on women's consciousness. He believed they could discover a new active and public world in place of the isolation and fatalism of the little world of the family.

The involvement of women in production had another aspect though which tended to predominate after his death. Soviet economists did elaborate calculations to show the amount of labour hours spent in inefficient private housekeeping. It could be argued that the emancipation of women from the family was economically necessary if the material preconditions for socialism were to be created. The slogan 'Abolish the Family' could thus be justified in terms of economic efficiency as much as of women's liberation.

Kollontai tended to see the family more as a cultural institution which maintained the old values of authoritarianism and domination. While the family in its traditional form continued it was impossible for the workers to achieve full social emancipation. 'The capitalists themselves are not unaware of the fact that the family of old, with the wife a slave and the man responsible for the support and well-being of the family . . . is the best weapon to stifle the proletarian effort towards liberty.'[12]

Trotsky takes up the same argument in *Problems of Life*, lectures he gave to workers, and carries it farther with the sensible observation:

Unless there is actual equality of husband and wife in the family, in a normal sense as well as in the conditions of life, we cannot speak seriously of their equality in social work or even in politics. As long as woman is chained to her housework, the care of the family, the cooking and sewing, all her chances of participation in social and political life are cut down to the extreme.[13]

For all these reasons, in the early years of the revolution it was generally assumed that the family would wither along with other institutions which had persisted from capitalist society. The real argument was how long it was going to take, and how much effort you needed to put in to help yourself out of the transitional period. In the early twenties Trotsky was arguing that though new kinds of family could only develop after a more highly developed material base had been created, because economic backwardness continually held back the provision of public facilities, voluntary initiative in making cultural precedents was still important. He recommended that people should 'group themselves even now into collective house-keeping units'. These should be very carefully thought out and coordinated with the local Soviets and trade unions. He envisaged a new architecture – housing built round the needs of these communal associations. 'We can escape the deadlock at present only by the creation of model communities.'[14] He saw these as one means of releasing the 'creative imagination and artistic initiative'[15] of the masses, through changing the 'complicated net of inner relations in personal and family life'.[16]

Very quickly, when people began to emphasize the liberation of women, they became involved in the cart before the horse, chicken before the egg dilemma of new culture versus material base.

Naystat in *Youth Communes* makes it all seem a simple problem, the delineations in theory of the transition to the transition seem clearcut:

The new *byt*, like the new family, will be able to grow up only when all the necessary economic conditions are fulfilled. For that reason it is not yet time to consider a complete reconstruction of life on a socialist basis. . . . We begin by building up the fundamental conditions of a socialized life, the commune is the model of the future socialist *byt*. But even now marriage in a commune is different from marriage else-where. For it anticipates the marriage of a socialist society in that the economic tie has ceased to play a part in the mutual relation of husband and wife. The same applies to the question of the children, although the communes have little experience in this matter at present. During their early years the communes did not desire children for material reasons. But now there are a considerable number of commune children.[17]

He glosses over the actual manner in which a new society is to be communicated through transitional institutions. As Reich points out, it was quite possible for the new families to revert to old values because of material scarcity and lack of any theory about the actual mechanism by which economic and social change connected with sexual liberation. In a youth commune which was formed originally in 1924 to solve the problem of the housing shortage, he describes how overcrowding led to the attempt to enforce sexual asceticism. Couples wanted a room of their own. The other communards resisted marriage which they thought would constitute a faction in the collective. Eventually they gave way but banned offspring because there wasn't enough space for them in the commune. They struggled with practical circumstances but finally gave way on the issue of human, sexual liberation. It was regarded as wrong to want privacy to make love. They did not try to guarantee the prerequisites of sexual happiness; instead they made unhappiness into a virtue. Because it was not made an explicit and integral part of the revolution, sexuality was subordinated to immediate economic necessities. Reich asserts in *The Sexual Revolution* that it was no good saying 'economic base!' *then* 'new way of life!', as the forms of sexual and personal life could not simply be correlated with economic changes. He believed the original attempt of the revolution to create the external means for the liberation of women was on the right lines.[18] But the revolutionaries faltered at the very moment when those external changes started to penetrate the inner consciousness.

Within the Communist Party conflict emerged about the means by which the new culture should be created. Kollontai describes this in her novel, *Free Love*, sometimes better translated as *Red Love*. The heroine Vasilissa, an ex-trade union organizer, tells a rather bureaucratic party member about the house-commune she has lived in.[19] There had been great difficulties because the people living in it retained the old ideas of competition and selfishness. She says house-communes must be transformed from short-term solutions to the housing shortage into 'schools, and foster the Communist spirit'. This was in line with educational ideas at the time which saw education as completely integrated into social life and the specific educational institutions withering away. However, the other party member was completely bewildered; for him education was something that happened at school or in the university and had nothing to do with housing methods. People reverted to the old forms because it was the only thing they knew.

It was the same with the family. Externally everything had changed. Internally people's attitudes remained the same. The women clung on to their individual pots and pans – communal substitutes were viewed dubiously. A communard complained in the day-book, 'I have brought my electric kettle with me to the commune but they use it carelessly. Why did I bring it?'[20] Sexual matters were less discussed but it was apparent that women still fell into the old relationship of submission. Yaroslavsky, a party official, commented, 'It is one thing to write good laws, and another to create the actual conditions to bring the laws into life.'[21]

Lack of any theory which could explain the personal and sexual aspects of life combined with persistent economic difficulties and the heritage of social and cultural backwardness. In the case of women these problems were magnified. For example, women did not become involved in industry in the way it had been imagined that they would. After the period known as War Communism, when ration cards were issued on the basis of employment, the drift of women into social production was slow. During the N.E.P. (New Economic Policy) period there were often simply no jobs. Nor was most women's work much of an alternative to household drudgery. It takes time to train skilled workers, and most of the women were unskilled. New factories were built but the old continued, and with them the same bad old conditions. Although the law said equal pay for equal work, women were doing the same work as men in the 1920s for less pay because it was graded differently. In some cases the men workers ignored the official trade union directives and refused point blank to work with women at the same rates. Although officially again the women were meant to have the same say in trade unions as the men, in practice this was often not the case. Kollontai in *Red Love* describes how the women workers couldn't express themselves, and how their needs were always dismissed by the men as trivial. Vera Alexeyeva told Jessica Smith of the problems of relating the Genotdel to the trade unions:

> Originally all work among women in the factories rested on the shoulders of a woman organizer responsible to the Genotdel. As a result it often happened that the Factory Committee failed to take any initiative in work among women, and refused to put subjects of special interest to women on their programs. When the women did come to meetings they were met with, 'Well, let's hear what the babas have to

say!', and were afraid to express themselves, which made it necessary to organize special women's meetings. While that had some good effects in stimulating women's interest, it also led to a 'we' and 'they' attitude, so we decided to change our method. The last Trade Union Congress voted to place the responsibility for the work among women on the factory committee as a whole and instructed the unions to include questions of special interest to women on their general program. That has had a very healthy effect, and the unions have since been much more active in drawing women into their work. There are still Genotdel organizers in every factory, but they concentrate on the delegates' meetings and party work, while the union takes care of all general and cultural work. It's the Genotdel, however, which prepares the ground for the union work.[22]

But if it was difficult to overcome economic problems, female passivity, and male contempt at work, it was even worse in the home, where traditions had a firmer hold, and public facilities were often quite inadequate. During the early period, War Communism, the communal houses were often grim and depressing, the shared kitchens chaotic, the crèches makeshift. In the N.E.P. years, when the need to produce efficiently was given priority, directors and managers were frequently very unwilling to spend money on crèches and allow the women time off with their children. It was a question of attitudes too. Trotsky describes how house communes collapsed:

Many homes which had been allotted to families living in communes got into filthy conditions and became uninhabitable. People living in them did not consider communistic housing as a beginning of new conditions. They looked upon their dwellings as upon a barracks provided by the state.[23]

In the villages the contrast between the old ways and the new ideas was even more extreme. Jessica Smith explains how peasant women responded to the idea of a day nursery in the late 1920s. Almost all the older women were against it. Children had never been brought up in nurseries before – why start now? They had heard they bathed the children every day and believed this would mean they wouldn't grow up strong. The young women on the other hand, especially one girl whose child had been killed, were in support of the idea. They arranged for a house to be turned into a nursery and painted it white, hanging bright posters round the walls. The other women were shocked. 'Surely they're not going to let children into a clean place like that.'[24] Gradually they changed and accepted a nursery as a matter of course.

It was not only the women who resisted changes in the home. Even men who would accept reforms like equal pay were opposed to the emergence of women from the inner life of the family. In some cases their opposition was outright. Men were known to throw the papers of the Women's Department on to the fire because they resented the time their wives spent on political activity rather than on housework. More serious was the resistance in the eastern parts of Russia.

'In 1928, a twenty-year-old girl, Zarial Haliliva, escaped from her parental home and began to call meetings for the sexual emancipation of women; she went unveiled to the theater and wore a bathing costume on the beach. Her father and brothers sat in judgement over her, condemned her to death and cut her up alive.'[25] Nor was this an isolated case. In Uzbekistan, for instance, in 1928 there were 203 cases of anti-feminist murder. Girls were also beaten and punished severely simply for attending the meetings of the women's clubs.

There were many men in the party who were shocked at this kind of open persecution, but who were responsible in more subtle ways for keeping their wives in their old oppression. Lenin deplored how few men, even among the proletariat, would realize how much effort they could save their wives if they helped in the home. Some years later Lunacharsky wrote that he would shake the hands of a comrade, 'an honest Leninist', who would rock the cradle so that his wife could go out to a meeting or study.[26] More common than these honest Leninist cradle-rockers were the party militants who would make a great show of their revolutionary commitment to the liberation of women but wanted their own wives to stay under their thumbs. One woman described how her husband had put an end to her work and political activity:

And in those very meetings which he forbids me to attend because he is afraid I will become a real person – what he needs is a cook and mistress wife – in those very meetings where I have to slip in secretly, he makes thunderous speeches about the role of women in the revolution, calls women to a more active role.[27]

All these difficulties provoked intense discussion and argument. There has probably never been a time when great masses of people

discussed openly questions which affected women so much. Naturally, in these public debates on alimony, or the divorce laws, women
themselves played an important part. Sometimes they criticized very
freely. 'If Comrade Ryazanov intends to abolish *de facto* marriages,
why has he not in the sixty years of his life arranged matters in such
a fashion that we begat children only after registration.'[28] It was
apparent that certain questions evaded the party's decrees and were
beyond the competence of the most zealous of moral organizers –
Comrade Ryazanov not excepted.

But equally by the mid 1920s it was clear that an approach which
regarded relationships of men and women as a personal affair and
which just secured equal rights by legislation could only provide an
external guarantee for the free development of an internal process of
liberation. The real contradictions existed in the contrast between
the aspirations for the emancipation of women and the real situation
of the women before freedom. The women in the harems of Turkes-
tan who burned their veils and lost their homes and children as a
result, or the peasant women suddenly deserted by their husbands,
were in an impossible situation. It was clear that liberal freedoms
were quite inadequate here. In a debate on the Family Code in 1925
one woman, Comrade Shuropuva, spoke about this:

> What is the position of a peasant woman? She looks after the house,
> she sews, she washes and she helps her husband take in the harvest,
> while he – forgive me, comrades, for saying so – he will not go to bed
> alone and she has to obey his pleasure. And if she does not, he kicks
> her out. [Laughter.] We should think about these problems. The
> comrade just said: 'Who forces him to take two wives?' I can prove it
> to you. He took two wives, each gave him a baby so he must pay for
> them both. It is nobody else's fault. If you like tobogganing you must
> like pulling your sledge uphill. But comrades here are saying that
> some women have three or four [men]. Maybe, but we peasant
> women have no time for that.[29]

Marxist ideas about the family assumed a completely different
historical tradition from the cultural realities of Russia after 1917. In
an under-developed country, traditionalism, superstition and the old
authorities had a real hold. In a situation of economic crisis, post-war
chaos, and revolutionary upheaval it would have been extraordinary
not to find considerable psychological tension and familial insecurity.
Experience kaleidoscoped, people moved away from one another. It

was very difficult to hold fast to the original motive of complete liberation on the woman question while preventing the innumerable distortions which appeared within the existing situation. The struggle was herculean and tragic. Suddenly there were so many orphans. So many children's homes were needed. Dandies were reported to be sponging off the well-paid working girls. The women from the old upper classes reappeared, were mysteriously well dressed, became secretaries to the 'specialists' in industry, and cared nothing for emancipation. It is in this context that the struggle against prostitution, the practical attempt to liberate women in the household, communal kitchens, house communes, cooperative playgroups, the improvements in women's working conditions and the legislation protecting them appeared. The problem was of course to meet the immediate extraordinary situation of scarcity in a way that could ensure the growth and creation of a new liberation in women's position and consciousness in the future. The very new is extremely frightening. People watched with apprehension.

In 1924 Trotsky commented on what seemed to be the move 'from the old family to the new':

Some viewed it with great misgivings, others with reserve, and others still seemed perplexed. It was, anyhow, clear to all, that some big process was going on, very chaotic, assuming alternatively morbid or revolting, ridiculous or tragic forms and which had not yet had time to disclose its hidden possibilities of inaugurating a new and higher order of family life.[30]

It was difficult for people to keep their nerve throughout this process of sexual-cultural revolution. The original guide-lines seemed inadequate. The belief that the creation of new economic forms would allow men and women to make their own communist culture, and that personal relations could not be subjected to the same kind of organization as the external affairs of life, gave way under pressure. Possessiveness, jealousy and domination did not disappear with public ownership of the means of production, or even with communes and crèches. There was no alternative theory. Party officials religiously lectured on Engels as though circumstances had not changed. Or like Yaroslavsky they declared, 'We don't want to be forever looking under the bedsheets.'[31] There was an awkwardness and embarrassment about sexual questions, a feeling that they were somehow irrelevant to the serious work of the revolution. The liberation of female sexuality is such an important part of the politics of women's liberation that this neglect of the mechanisms of sexual and personal transformation had serious consequences in allowing a great narrowing in the definition of what constitutes liberation. But the gap was obvious more generally to practical party workers.

The functionary Koltsov complains, 'These questions are never discussed; it was as if for some reason they were being avoided. I myself have never given them serious thought. They are new to me. They are extremely important and should be discussed.'[32]

Similarly a comrade called Tseitlin said:

In the literature, the problems of marriage and the family, of the relations between man and woman, are not discussed at all. Nevertheless these are exactly the questions which interest workers, male and female alike. When are such questions going to be the topic of our meetings? The masses feel that we hush up these problems, and in fact we do hush them up.[33]

In the first half of the twenties there was an implicit assumption that guilt and repression belonged to the old order, but sexuality was still euphemistically called 'the family'. It was often treated in a 'scientific' no-nonsense manner like a cold bath, rather than in terms of how men and women experienced each other and how this affected their whole consciousness. There was little attempt to understand the conditions necessary for women to make love in active enjoyment. The material circumstances of female orgasm received as little real attention as they did in the west.

Though the revolution rather avoided discussion about making love, there was a great deal of debate about 'love'. Some communists dismissed love as bourgeois mystification. A Komsomol organization circular announced it was a 'physiological phenomenon of nature'.[34] Human experience was thus reduced to physical sensation. There was a spurious radicalism about such an attitude, which went sometimes with opposition to attractive clothing and formal politeness like hand-shaking. It was popular with the younger communists. Their casual attitude to sex – described in one novel as similar to going to the cinema – shocked the older generation, who had come to their ideas of 'free unions' painfully and earnestly in desperate and stark situations while they had been opposing the old regime. They recoiled from what seemed like the brashness of the young, the nonchalant way in which they trod over feeling.

Lenin spoke for the older generation of party members in his conversation with Clara Zetkin. He condemned the hypocrisy of the old bourgeois morality with its double standards, and he recognized the significance of the changes which the revolution had brought in personal relations. He stressed that 'Communism should not bring asceticism.' He told her, 'New boundaries are being drawn.' He did not elaborate on who was to have the power nor on how boundaries were to be drawn. He identified the young communists' rejection of tenderness and feeling as simply a reversal of the old hypocritical romantic attitudes. He understood how they could impose their own kind of tyranny. He attempted to distinguish between what he called the 'glass of water' theory which conceived 'free' love as being simply the satisfaction of desire, and the 'free' communist unions which implied deep feeling and comradeship. Not surprisingly he reacted impatiently to the accusation of young communists that his ideas on the sex question were 'survivals of a Social-Democratic attitude and old fashioned philistinism'. He snorted indignantly against 'yellow-beaked fledgelings newly hatched from their bourgeois tainted eggs'.[35]

His statements, though obviously not carefully thought out, expressed an important contradiction. Theoretically the revolution was committed to release, to the development of free, unrepressed human beings, but practically the immediate task of creating a communist society from the chaos of the Soviet Union in the twenties required a great effort of self-discipline – in fact the good old virtues of the bourgeoisie in early capitalism: hard work, abstinence and repression. To ignore this was to take cover in fantasy. Communism perhaps should not bring asceticism, but communists certainly needed a strong dose themselves if it was ever to be brought into being at all. The chaos of an unruly love life seemed to be completely unproductive for socialist reconstruction, so the shutters started to come down.

Alexandra Kollontai became notorious as one of the defenders of sexual freedom. In fact her ideas were quite different from the 'glass of water' theories described in novels like *Without a Bird-Cherry Tree* by P. Romanov, and *The Dog's Lane* by Lev Gumilevsky. Instead she followed the tradition of the young Marx and Engels in *The Origin of the Family* in imagining that love would develop rather than disappear under communism:

> In the achieved communist society, love, 'the winged Eros', will appear in a different, transformed, and completely unrecognizable form. By that time the 'sympathetic bonds' between all members of the new society will have grown and strengthened, the 'love potential' will have been raised, and solidarity-love will have become the same kind of moving force as competition and self-love are in the bourgeois order.[36]

Rather later she said in a letter to a young comrade that she hoped in the future proletarian morals would be based on:

> 1. Equality; disappearance of the overpowering masculine self-sufficiency and the servile submission of women.
> 2. Mutual and reciprocal recognition of rights, and disappearance of all feelings of property.
> 3. Fraternal sensibility, together with an art that will allow the assimilation and comprehension of the psychic developments taking place in the soul of the beloved. [In bourgeois ideology, the woman alone was expected to possess this sensibility.][37]

What is really important about Kollontai's approach is the attempt to relate changes in sexual relationships to the total social emergence of women. In the preface to *Free Love* she wrote:

> This novel is neither a study in morals nor a picture of the standard of life in Soviet Russia. It is a purely psychological study of sex relations in the post-war period. Many of the problems presented are not however exclusively Soviet Russian; they are world-wide facts which can be noted in all countries. These silent psychological dramas, born of the change in the sexual relations, this evolution, especially, in the feelings of women, are well known to the younger generation.[38]

It is this 'purely psychological study of sex relations', this interest in the 'silent psychological dramas', this connection to an international sexual revolution, and the examination of the 'evolution, especially, in the feelings of women' – young women, too – which made Kollontai unusual and necessarily suspect. Left communists who wrote about the withering away of the family in a far distant society upset no one. Communist feminists who concerned themselves with what particular women were experiencing at that moment upset many.

The plot of *Free Love* is simple. Vasillissa, a knitter, forms a free union with Volodia, an ex-anarchist, who becomes a member of the party and takes on a job as director of a large industrial concern. He has an affair with Nina, a non-political ex-bourgeois woman who is very beautiful. Eventually Vasillissa leaves him. However, the real interest of the book is in the four conflicting themes which run through it, and the tensions behind them. At one level there is a political clash. The first signs of a break betwen the two appear in their very different ideas about politics, not in their original argument about centralism which was only superficial, but a much deeper difference about the extent to which commitment to the revolution penetrates the way you live. Vasillissa was distressed by her husband's liking for a grand style of living, which involved dubious deals during the N.E.P. period with non-party bourgeois. This explodes with particular intensity when some of the workers under her husband complain about working conditions. They come to the great house of the director and start talking to Vassillissa. She forgets her role as his 'wife', becomes her old Bolshevik trade union bargaining self again, and begins excitedly to plan ways for them to fight back. He returns, sees this, and furiously drags her inside. At another level, as they move away from one another the relationship becomes increasingly dishonest. When she finds he has secretly slept with Nina she feels he has done wrong, not in going to another woman but in deceiving her about it. At the same time she is jealous of Nina, who possesses the traditional attributes of women – beauty and elegance. She begins to feel that her union with Volodia is a charade:

> There was no longer comradeship, no longer affection, between them. . . . She was wife in the house merely to serve as hostess, to act as a cover. I live, she said, in wedlock with a Communist, but another woman is the wife for delectation, for love in a secret little house.

At the same time Kollontai explores the way in which it is impossible for Vassillissa to retain her old independence. She has only a borrowed existence as his wife, she no longer has her work, especally her political work in the factory and the party. When she tries to leave him she says, 'I have panted enough in this cage, I have played the Directress enough. . . . Take for a wife one of those who value such a life.'[39] When she finally goes she throws off 'a skin which did not fit me'.[40]

But in fact the skin held her to him for a long time. Kollontai brings out the clash between the struggle for identity and the ties which had developed over the years when they were together, as well as the very real sexual passion. At first her sexuality was in harmony with the other ways she communicated with him. But ultimately there is opposition between the desire he can still arouse in her and their obvious incompatibility. It is as if her sexuality might swamp her separate identity. The political, emotional, intellectual and sexual factors combine. The only solution is to leave him. But Vasillissa's choice simply ignores the basic causes of tension. She goes away, and is able to rid herself of her jealousy of Nina the traditional feminine, in an understanding mixed with compassion. She has a child and plans to rear it 'in the communist way', cooperatively. She finds her identity thus only by denying the existence of the man and her own sexuality. The only solution possible is no real solution.

But this was precisely what Kollontai meant in *Free Love*. She wanted to:

... teach women not to put all their hearts and souls into the love for a man, but into the essential thing, creative work. When I look through my works I can see that it was this aim that inspired most of my writing on the sexual question. Love must not crush the women's individuality, not bind her wings. If love begins to enslave her, she must make herself free, she must step over all love tragedies, and go her own way.[41]

It was a negative freedom: a freedom of non-attachment which tended to appear in feminist thought in the period. There was a sense in which very strong personal emotion almost inevitably appeared in opposition to the liberation of the women because traditionally such emotion bound women. But this tended to force women to accept that emancipation meant denying part of themselves. When Kollontai was writing it seemed as if this was the only way out. Unfortunately the tendency could result in a dismissal of the personal and sexual dimensions in relationships. There is a trace of the stiff upper lip. Just as Kollontai could share the easy optimism characteristic of communists in the period – that 'intelligent educators' would somehow escape the taint of the past and teach the values of solidarity and comradeship in their revolutionary purity – she shows a hint of that self-denying strain which simply cut itself off from awkward emotion very common in the revolutionary movement. The

If You Like Tobogganing

rejection of the cellular individualism and the passionate egotistic possessiveness of the bourgeois family came to imply the necessary superiority of external social activity to the inner personal life. Such a rejection, which arose naturally from the need for intense political commitment in the revolutionary period, was elevated into an impossible and restricting moral principle.[42]

It was not that Vassillissa should have continued a relationship which became only formality, but that the points of tension, the struggle of the woman for independent identity in relation to the man and the apparent contradictions between her intellectuality and her sexuality, are too facilely resolved. Such questions were and are still crucial.

In *Love of Three Generations*, the young communist Zhenia tries to solve the problem by divorcing strong emotion from her sexuality. She slept with two men, and was in love with neither. The situation was complicated by the fact that one of them was her stepfather. She told her mother, 'But I liked them and I felt they liked me. . . . It's all so simple. And then it does not tie you down to anything.' She argued with her mother, who was shocked, that there could be nothing wrong in this as 'I did it voluntarily and willingly. As long as we like each other we remain together; afterwards we part. No one is the loser.' She points out that her mother would not be so critical if Zhenia were a boy.

In fact Zhenia's case is ostensibly eminently reasonable. But on the question of her relationship with her stepfather her justification becomes immediately glib and insensitive. Her mother asks if she has considered *her* feelings. Zhenia claims the sexual act is only an extension of her friendship for her stepfather: it takes nothing away from her mother:

As to our kissing. . . . Well, you have no time for kissing anyway. And then, mother, you can't want to tie Andrey exclusively to yourself and not let him have any pleasure apart. That would be a nasty proprietary attitude. It's this grandmother's bourgeois upbringing coming up.[43]

Zhenia is described honestly. She undoubtedly expressed feelings which were shared by many young communists. She was to be denounced as the symbol of depravity by innumerable party moralists. But it is important to keep her situation in perspective: Zhenia

157

presents the statement of the dilemma and attempts a particular way out.

Kollontai makes her own position clear: 'Many of the opponents of my writings tried to impose on me an absolutely false postulate that I was preaching "free love". I would put it the other way. I was always preaching to the women, Make yourself free from the enslavement of love of a man.' Alexandra Kollontai never solved the dilemma in her own life. She said she 'tried to combine romance and work. But it was and still is difficult for a woman to combine a profession and married life.' After an early unsuccessful first marriage she entered a civil marriage with a man much younger than her, Dubenko, because he put pressure on her by saying she felt too superior to marry him. This also collapsed. A friend, Zoja, who shared her ideas, called her 'la dernière grande amoureuse'. But Alexandra Kollontai said her 'love affairs always ended in the breaking down of romance. The hour of separation was inevitable.' She concluded that friendship was a more sociable emotion than sexual love.[44]

She wrote, in *The New Morality and the Working Class*:

The longer the sexual crisis lasts, the more difficult it becomes. With every attempt at a solution things become more and more difficult. . . . The frightened people fall from one extreme into the other, and the sexual problem remains unsolved. It would be a tremendous error to assume that only members of the economically secure classes are caught in its toils. The sexual crisis creates dramas among the working people which are no less violent or tragic than the psychological conflicts of the refined bourgeoisie.[45]

Instead of presenting people with a new formula, she thought always in terms of growth. She saw the new morality being created, not imposed, in the process of development towards a communist society. Communism was about the releasing of the potential for responsibility; it implied widening the scope for the practical self-activity of masses of people. The new morality could not be mugged up from ethical manuals of do's and don'ts. It had to come from people experiencing each other in totally new surroundings.

By the end of the twenties a strong counter-tendency had emerged which questioned this way of defining the areas which had to be left to individual responsibility. Instead of emphasizing human liberation, social usefulness became the moral criterion. Zalkind produced a way of apparently solving the contradiction which Lenin had hinted at in his conversation with Zetkin. He was concerned to prevent the diversion of energy for social reconstruction into sexuality. He borrowed selectively from Freud to produce a theory which justified the redirection of sexuality into social reconstruction. The embarrassing passages about individual sex love in Engels were hustled out of history. There was no place any more for clouds in trousers – or skirts for that matter. Now 'every joy must have a productive purpose'.[46]

As the practical difficulties multiplied ideas like this became more popular – not because they were profound but because they were made to measure. The opposition was always on the defensive. It became easier to dismiss the demand for individual freedom as petty-bourgeois. There were powerful practical short-term factors which came from the old authoritarian regime which gave their arguments an added force. The understanding of the connection between the authoritarian state and the patriarchal family, strengthened by religious and legislative sanctions, tended to be implicit in revolutionary thinking. But at the point of affirming positively a cultural revolution in sexual relationships the revolutionaries' theory broke down. There was a drawing back, a concern. Significantly, in a discussion of doctors in 1927 about the effects of the law of 1920 which had legalized abortion, the case for legal abortion was nearly always made in terms of social poverty. Only one doctor, Selinsky, accused them of failing to distinguish 'the real socio-economic and mass-psychological conditions under which abortion has become epidemic'. He stated:

No one of us men would accept a decision by some commissioners as to the social interest in his being married or not. Do not prevent women from deciding for themselves a fundamental issue of their lives. Woman has a right to a sexual life as freely realized as is that of a man. We need no mass-produced class of spinsters which would be merely harmful to the community.[47]

In 1929 the Genotdel was abolished. The official explanation was that an independent women's movement was no longer necessary. In reality, quite the reverse was the case. Gradually new moral authorities were imposed. In the 1930s official policy rehabilitated the family. Concern to stabilize Soviet society, the threat of war, operated as further incentives. Nobody talked any more about the family withering. Instead the official attitude was that it should be as secure as possible. Legal abortions were abolished in 1936 rather than merely discouraged. Referring to the new law a *Pravda* article stressed the responsibility of parents for their own children:

> The State in no wise relieves the mother or the father as the social educator . . . parents' responsibility for the education of their child will be increased and a blow will be dealt at the lighthearted negligent attitude towards marriage.[48]

The whole series of legislation which constituted 'the new family policy' was a complete reversal of the laws passed in the 1920s which had concentrated on women's emancipation rather than strengthening the 'socialist family'. The right of an unwed mother to appeal to court for the child's support from the child's father, without being legally married, was stopped. Divorce was made more difficult and more costly. It was not a coincidence that homosexuality was made a criminal offence in 1934. Non-reproductive sexuality came to be seen as a deviation from socialist reconstruction. Individual pleasure had to be subordinated to the needs of the state. Trotsky in *The Revolution Betrayed* noted:

> The triumphal rehabilitation of the family taking place simultaneously – what a providential coincidence! – with the rehabilitation of the rouble, is caused by the material and cultural bankruptcy of the state. Instead of openly saying, 'We have proven still too poor and ignorant for the creation of socialist relations among men, our children and grandchildren will realize this aim', the leaders are forcing people to glue together again the shell of the broken family, and not only that but to consider it, under threat of extreme penalties, the sacred nucleus of triumphant socialism. It is hard to measure with the eye the scope of this retreat.[49]

The new family policy was justified not on the grounds of necessity, but elevated into a communist morality. This was a very serious distortion of the original commitment to try to seek a means of liberating women despite the economic obstacles. Wedding rings and marriage ceremonies reappeared in the mid 1930s, articles appeared in the papers praising marriage, elevating the family and encouraging fertility. Inevitably these affected the position of women.

Under Stalin it was as if a new place was being given to women.

Just as the Victorians combined the spiritual elevation of 'woman-hood' with an institutional framework which made her powerless, in the Soviet Union under Stalin the elevation of Soviet motherhood, the praise of the wives of the engineers in heavy industry, who set about organizing canteens and child care centres in the mid-thirties not for their own efforts but for their possible influence on their husbands' productivity, provided a new form of paternalist contain-ment. As one Moscow woman commented, 'He wanted us to work hard and fulfil the Plans. But he kept us in our places, never appointed women to high political office.' While *Pravda* denounced 'free love' along with all 'disorderly sex life' as 'bourgeois', and claimed that the enemies of the people had introduced 'the foul and poisonous idea' of liquidating the family and disrupting marriage', Stalin visited his old mother in Tiflis, and the Soviet papers carried articles on his children's reaction to the jam their grandmother made.[50]

The result was considerable ambiguity. The mere statement of equality and its legislative existence meant a fundamental trans-formation for millions of women. The unquestioned patriarchal right could exist no more:

Bit by bit Father stopped beating Mother, but sometimes he threatened her that he would be put in prison for it. He would shout: 'If they put me in prison I will not rest there from you.' But even at such shouting she would say 'We are equal.'[51]

Young women were brought up with strange aspirations. 'At meetings, at lectures they constantly told us that women must be fully equal with men, that women can be flyers and naval engineers and anything that men can be.'[52] Many women had been educated, had become skilled workers. Village women had got a nursery – they didn't take the children into the fields. There were improved facilities for pregnant women. Some women too were undoubtedly pleased with their wedding rings – they were glad to have a marriage ritual again. But all this was very far from the hopes of the early years of the revolution when so many women had started suddenly to be able to imagine a completely different way of being women.

The Second World War forced an elite of women out into public life but it completed the reversal of women's position in the family. Large families were encouraged because there was anxiety about the birth rate. A change in the inheritance laws in 1945 gave greater influence to the father as the head of the family. Women lost their rights in the family: no longer could they choose to limit the number of children they could give birth to. Women who were not legally married enjoyed none of the rights which had been won with the revolution. They no longer had their own organizations through which they could put their case and press for change. The new consciousness which had been developing, of real equality between human beings and the possibility for women of not knowing themselves subordinate and dependent in relation to men, was eroded and almost extinguished. The only kind of emancipation was one which served the interests of the state, and those interests were unquestionably defined by the men in power.

In 1932 an incident occurred which symbolized most precisely the nature of female containment. Stalin's wife, Nadia Alliluyeva, the daughter of the workman Alliluyev:

hitherto blindly devoted to her much older husband, began to doubt the wisdom and rightness of his policy. One evening, in November 1932, Stalin and his wife were on a visit at Voroshilov's home. Other members of the Politbureau were there too, discussing matters of policy. Nadia Alliluyeva spoke her mind about the famine and discontent in the country, and about the moral ravages which the Terror had wrought on the party. Stalin's nerves were already strained to the utmost. In the presence of his friends he burst out against his wife in a flood of vulgar abuse. Nadia Alliluyeva left Voroshilov's house. The same evening she committed suicide.[53]

Indeed, the fate of ideas about the liberation of women and the slow retreat is a sensitive barometer of the revolution itself. How could you demand equality when 'equality mongering' had been declared 'leftist' by the party and denounced, and when differences in income and power were approved? How could you demand the right to control the circumstances of your own reproduction when coercion at work was open and accepted? How could you demand the liberation of women when the possibility of human liberation had been indefinitely postponed? Why should the revolution extend to women when it had failed to become international? The space within which people could define themselves slowly decreased. Authority and repression closed in. The public world of the state penetrated the private world of the human spirit with armed force, torture and death. Why should women expect equality or love?

Russia was groaning under epidemics, famine, forced collectivization, political terror, the trials, the loss of twenty million men in the Second World War. The effects of such devastation inevitably possessed the lives of women. Meanwhile people were given new shrines to worship at, baubles, badges, medallions to value themselves by. The mummified body of Lenin became an object of cult veneration, socialist realist workers dwarfed and humbled actual men and women. People wanted a place to hide. The family became somewhere to go to escape from the horror of the world outside. The dummy 'happy Soviet family' rang like a slogan, reconstructed from the shell of frightened childhood. The liberation of women was submerged, the notion of female activity pressed down. 'Woman' was resurrected instead – as the heroine of motherhood, under the benign whiskers of Uncle Joe.

Later, when people were trying to eradicate Stalin and the cult of his personality, they superimposed a new myth – that of suffering Soviet womanhood, the earth-mother rocking the cradle threatened by the man of steel:

> Everybody weakened. Women didn't –
> Through hunger and sickness, war and drought
> Silently they rocked the cradles,
> Saving our sons.[54]

Where had all those honest Leninists gone?

Out of this slowly came modern Russia. Women's conditions are not those envisaged by the revolutionaries in the twenties, nor are they those which developed under Stalin. In 1955 abortion became legal again – a tacit recognition that its legal prohibition did not affect the birth rate and an attempt to prevent back-street abortions. In 1964 divorce was made rather easier and some of the disability of illegitimacy removed. Similarly birth-control advice is freely available now – though not the pill. As it became easier to criticize the ways in which Stalin's laws did not relate to the needs of daily life, some of the submerged issues surfaced. One aspect of family policy which has often been attacked, along with the difficulty of getting a divorce, is the provision in the 1944 law which made unmarried women completely responsible for bringing up children. The right of men not to be accused wrongfully of being fathers had been protected by this law but it meant that the label 'unmarried mother' carried all its old stigma along with some of the old economic and social disability.

Women have clung on to the two aspects of emancipation for which Russian women are noted in the west – the right to work and welfare facilities for the children. Indeed, emancipation has come to be defined as the right to work – a narrow definition but still an important one. The editor of the journal *Soviet Woman*, Olga Ushakova, said in an interview in *The Times* in 1966, 'Work is so important to us, we cannot imagine life without it.' Another member of the editorial staff, Rodkina, said, 'None of us want to stay at home, not even if our husband earns a million.'[55]

Round the fact of a female labour force and the encouragement of large families a whole network of welfare and community services have developed: leave for both mothers and fathers, arrangements for jobs to be held open during pregnancy, part-time work in factories, crèches on the premises and breaks at work for seeing the children, as well as other extensive nursery facilities and shopping hours arranged for working women. With half the working population women the need for these is apparent. Indeed, the demand exceeds the supply. They are still not adequate. Some children can't get into the nurseries and mothers are forced to make private arrangements. Facilities for dry cleaning and laundries too don't exist in some small towns and villages.[56]

Related to the work situation too is the improvement in the education of women. This is partly at the level of literacy, but there has also been an impressive rise in the numbers of women who receive higher education. The proportion of women to men varies by occupation. Women predominate in the health services and in education.[57] They have also invaded the 'masculine' domains of engineering and science. Some have penetrated into the most complex and highly sophisticated forms of scientific work. Alla Masevich, for instance, chairman of the sputnik tracking group of the International Committee for Space Research, received a symbolic passport at a congress of astronomers recently: 'A place has been reserved for you on one of the astro-ships which will be sent to the moon. In view of your services to science you will be allowed to move freely about cosmic space and to visit any planet.'[58]

Although the revolution is able to grant access to the moon to its women it is still not able to eradicate many of the features of the old inferiority. They are prominent in jobs which reflect 'women's role', and a high proportion of women are in the unskilled sector of industry. The importance of piece-work makes equal pay a reality on paper only. In some factories the average rate for female turners and machine-operators works out considerably lower than that for men on the same jobs. In the last few years there has been discussion about this, and the difficulty of women in industry in being promoted. While men argue that the system operates according to merit and regardless of sex differences, women point out that this tends to reinforce itself. A writer in *Komsomolskaya Pravda* in 1967 maintained that women reached managerial and supervisory posts six or seven times less frequently than men: 'This practice means, apart from everything else, that a woman's average earnings are less than a man's, her creative development is arrested, and she acquires a "female inferiority complex", a lack of self-confidence.'[59]

Evelyne Sullerot in *Histoire et Sociologie du Travail Feminin*, describes how this process is reflected too in the relatively small percentage of women in positions of leadership in the party, the unions and in industry, though even these are high compared with the west.

Undoubtedly, despite welfare facilities many women hesitate to try for jobs which demand total commitment and carry important responsibilities, for in the family Soviet women find themselves in an ambiguous situation. Often they are doing two jobs. Four mothers who work in a ballbearing factory in Sarutov wrote to a Russian paper in 1960 complaining about just this: 'In the factory we work like our husbands often in the same shop. But in the house the duties are unequally divided. . . . And when you ask a husband to help the answer is always the same, "Do you want me to do a woman's work? Why, the neighbours would laugh at me." '[60] Although the revolution in Russia has brought women into the external economy as workers it has not been particularly effective in breaking down the division of labour between men and women. This applies to the home as much as work outside. A recent study of 160 Leningrad working-class couples showed that in 69 families the wife did the housework, in 26 the granny, in 17 the wife plus children, and in 48 the husband helped. An analysis of several such studies done before 1961 indicated that a woman with a family who also has a job will be busy for three more hours, have two hours less leisure time, and one and a half hours less sleep. Undoubtedly the effects of this will build up over the years. Though comparisons with workers' families in the twenties show there has been some shift in the division of labour – men are now more likely to do the shopping and look after the children – the revolution has apparently not really entered the household.

In other ways it has. Male dominance still persists in the older peasant families but the patriarchal pattern has been much weakened. Some of this is just the normal impact of industrialization on peasant society. But there is something more, a consciousness that women have some official support on their side. A peasant woman describes this:

I am your wife. You say, 'You will not go there. I don't want you to go there.' But I say, 'You have no right. I'll go where I please. The husband does not have the right to tell his wife what to do.' There is a law . . . they call it equality of rights. The wife may want to go into the Komsomol or do something, and she does what she wants, not what her husband wants.[61]

But the fact that the Soviet Union is not a society based on equality, that it is probably not any longer a society struggling to become more equal, has affected women's inequalities. There is not just inequality between men and women at work, in education, in the home; there is also inequality between women. Because some women have become privileged they think the liberation of all women is completed. They also use other women to maintain their superiority. Trotsky noted this even in the thirties:

The situation of the mother of the family who is an esteemed communist, has a cook, a telephone for giving orders to the stores, an automobile for errands, etc., has little in common with the situation of the working woman who is compelled to run to the shops, prepare dinner herself, and carry her children on foot from the kindergarten – if indeed a kindergarten is available.[62]

This has continued. Not surprisingly in a meritocratic educational system, professional women value themselves higher than the uneducated and the unskilled. A woman who is a teacher remarks, 'I wanted to get away from the hard thankless work at home. With my pay I could have been able to hire a houseworker.'[63] There is no question about the attitude of the women who have to choose between unskilled work in industry or being the houseworker for someone else. She obviously is at a disadvantage all round. In industry she will on average have a worse position than male workers, at home she carries most of the load, or she can do the 'hard thankless work' which a more privileged woman can escape.

For women who can compete successfully though, there is a definite possibility of turning the normal economic dependency of the female upside down: they earn more than their husbands. Some women are rather embarrassed about this. But this individual dependence in a period of prosperity is having cultural effects. 'The concept of man as a breadwinner for the family is falling by the wayside. A tendency is growing for women to have children outside wedlock, so that they can fulfil their maternal instincts without taking on wifely chores.'[64] Husbands have become a bad investment. Developments like this immediately raise very fundamental questions about the nature of the liberation of women within socialism. Because although having a child without a man could be seen as a gesture towards liberation, in practice it could be in fact women simply taking over the responsibility of being both parents. There has been an economic change which has resulted in a shift rather than a transformation of male/female roles, which has probably also been affected by practicalities like the difficulty of getting a divorce. It would seem from the Russian experience that the existence of a large female labour force, improvements in women's education and the welfare facilities for children, have not been able really to overcome other features of Soviet society in which inequality and competition are marked.

However, these also came under attack in the late sixties. In 1967 a series of letters appeared in the *Literary Gazette*, a writers' paper, in which women readers criticized very strongly the nature of the work they could do. They not only objected to women being pushed into the worst jobs, they challenged the idea of women doing heavy industrial work. The sight of women on the roads has always been a horror theme of observers in the west. In the twenties communists tended to argue that it was not so much the kind of work but its physical effect. But in order to make sure that no workers of whatever sex are employed in a way which makes them suffer physically or mentally, it requires a society which is completely geared to the health of its people rather than to efficient production. As yet the Soviet Union would not appear to be such a society. The reaction of these Soviet women is to assert the separation of male/female work. In terms of its implications this is obviously not going to create a new society for women as a whole, though it may mean that a particular group will benefit.

A very similar response is emerging within Soviet sociology in the last decade. There has been much discussion about the effects of institutional care on young children who have tended to become more backward than those in more direct contact with adults. Instead of leading to a questioning of the type of nursery facilities and trying to improve them this has developed into an attempt to convince mothers that they should stay at home – not, note, fathers. Behind this is also concern for the birth rate. Russian women determinedly have small families despite inducements from the state.

It is hard to predict what women in Russia will do: whether they will try to extend the areas of emancipation and structure them according to their needs, or whether they will simply allow everything to be eroded. It could be that because they have been brought up in an economically fundamentally different society from ours, and because they inherit a rhetoric if not a reality of equality and democratic control, they will be able to envisage and force a way through. The questions raised by the efforts of the revolution in Russia to liberate women are of course indistinguishable from the possibility of human liberation. But the vantage point is different. Women as a group remain in a different material situation from men – they have babies. For them therefore the relations of reproduction are as important as those of production. If the revolution has not solved the second problem, it has barely begun to understand the first.

The only people who could create such a possibility are women themselves. Only they know how they feel, how the external shape of society touches them. A journalist, Larisa Kuznetsova, commented recently on the need for women to define themselves what they wanted. 'If we imagine the "female question" in the form of a sphere, then the women would be looking out from within, while the men would see only the external surface.'[65]

The 'correctness' of what women say they want is not the case. Correctness anyway is subject to alteration and cannot be separated from who has power to say what is correct. The right to make your own mistakes and become responsible to history is an essential, if costly, part in the process of the emergence of the oppressed. The demand by women for control over all aspects of their lives in a society which has not yet solved the problem of combining the socialization of all the means of production with effective means of social and political control for all human beings on an equal basis, would have tremendous implications. Such a demand has not appeared from Soviet women. In the meantime the discovery of what they feel they want now is vital for any attempt to understand the nature of Soviet society. This is not because women possess some mysterious power to solve problems better than men, but because they speak for a section of Russian society which was awakened and then silenced by the revolution, and because their subordination in the external and internal structure of that revolution still continues.

CHAPTER 7

# When the
# Sand-Grouse Flies
# to Heaven

For a fortnight Hsi Men remained with Cinnamon Bud in the house of joy. Not once did he show his face at home.

His five wives felt shamefully forsaken and cast aside. All but Gold Lotus could patiently bear this misfortune. Gold Lotus however could not endure the absence of her mate. Each day she carefully curled her hair, and powdered and rouged her face, and polished as a well-cut-gem she stood at the door of the pavilion and longingly watched for his coming.

She sends him a message which Cinnamon Bud snatched, thinking it was from some new love of his.

> Whether in the pale twilight,
> Or in the sunlit day,
> My thoughts are of him.
> I feel such anguish
> As one hardly feels
> At the sight of the beloved lying dead.
> I grieve for him,
> And am like to die of sorrow.
> Lonely is the pillow,
> Dimly flickers the lamp.
> The moon looks in
> Through the half open window.
> Alas! how can I, wretched one,
> Survive the frosty night?

But Hsi Men tore it into shreds and kicked the boy who brought it angrily and sent him home.

Sadly, Gold Lotus went back to her pavilion. The time passed with intolerable slowness. An hour seemed to her a month. At last she made up her mind. Hsi Men would not come home that night, she was certain. As soon as it was dark she sent her two maids to bed. Then Gold Lotus went into the park, as though she were going to take one of her nightly strolls. But this time she had a definite goal: the cottage of the young gardener, Kin Tung. Quietly she invited him to come to her pavilion. She let him in, carefully bolted the door, and set wine before him. She pressed him to drink until he grew tipsy. Then she loosened her girdle, disrobed, and abandoned herself to him.

> Eternal rules she disregards,
> Rules that nature herself proclaims:
> The high must ever shun the low,
> Noble from the base be strictly severed.
> Emboldened by her desires,
> She fears not her master's wrath.
> Hot with unbridled desire
> She obeys only her own voice.
> In the park of the hundred flowers
> She allows her base impulse to rule her,
> Making a brothel of the house
> Where chastity should prevail.

Hsi Men learns of what she has been doing. The boy is beaten until he is covered with blood. The hair is torn from his head and he is cast out of the house. He takes a horse whip to Gold Lotus and brings it down on her. She manages to lie convincingly, and her maid supports her story. He spares her and Gold Lotus goes to an old wise woman herbalist for help, who sends her to an astrologer. She gives his spells to her husband.

Two days later Gold Lotus and Hsi Men were on the best of terms and enjoying themselves like little fishes in the water. But, worthy reader, it is not without reason that a married man is warned against letting his wife have secret dealings with . . . Tao priests and sooth-sayers, with nurses and matchmakers. A good old proverb runs,

> Let not your guests behold your wife,
> And secretly lock the postern gate.
> Restrict her to courtyard and garden;
> So intrigue and misfortune will pass you by.

From Chin P'ing Mei, *The Adventurous History of Hsi Men and his Six Wives*. Written *c.* 1650 and published in seventeenth-century China, it was banned in the eighteenth century as immoral. Though the law was not changed until 1912 Chin P'ing Mei was very popular and circulated illegally.

> How sad it is to be a woman,
> Nothing on earth is held so cheap.
> Boys stand leaning at the door
> Like Gods fallen out of heavens.
> Their hearts brace the Four Oceans,
> The wind and dust of a thousand miles.
> No one is glad when a girl is born,
> By her the family sets no store.
>
> Fu Hsuan

Our husbands regard us as some sort of dogs who keep the house. We even despise ourselves.

Chinese peasant women

> These well-groomed heroines carry five-foot rifles,
> On this parade ground in the first rays of the sun.
> Daughters of China have uncommon aspirations,
> Preferring battle tunics to red dresses.
>
> Mao Tse-tung, inscription on a photograph of a
> women's militia

WOMAN'S ASSESSOR: Was it because you had different opinions that you fought with your wife?

MAN: No. But because in the past before liberation, I often saw my father beat my mother and I was brought up to think that men should be superior.

JUDGE: When did your father beat your mother?

MAN: In the old society.

JUDGE: And what does the present law say?

MAN: That men and women are equal. But I still think the wife should obey the husband.

JUDGE: But don't you know the law?

MAN: I don't think it matters if a man beats his wife – but he mustn't beat others. In the family it's all right.

JUDGE: What law allows the husband to beat the wife?

MAN: No law.

Felix Greene, *A Divorce Trial in China*, 1960

We apprehended long ago that the women of Asia cannot exact sympathy from the imperialists in their fight to liberate themselves. . . . You have but to witness how the imperialists treat women in their own countries.

Mme Sun Yat-sen

On 14 November 1919 Miss Chao Wu-chieh of Nanyung Street, Changsha, took out a dagger, and, as she was being raised in the bridal chair, slit her throat. Such an event might never have been elevated into history. The suicide of a woman in China was far from unusual. But Miss Chao's suicide became the subject of at least nine impassioned articles by Mao Tse-tung. The event symbolized at once the centuries of hopeless female subordination – the extreme act of suicide was the only way Miss Chao could avoid her arranged marriage – and the critical forces which were being brought to bear on traditional Chinese society.

In order to understand the significance of changes brought by the revolution the nature and degree of degradation and domination which previously existed have to be remembered. While a small minority of the upper classes lived as aesthetic ornaments, most of the women worked ceaselessly and could be beaten and even killed with no hope of redress. Bride-price and wife-selling were normal; so too were polygamy and concubinage. Girls were sold or kidnapped into prostitution. Child streetwalkers could frequently be seen in the larger towns. Within the family the older women disciplined the younger, the mother-in-law beating the young wife. The wife had no rights until she had a son. All women were subject to the authority of husbands, brothers, and finally sons. Although this traditional family was related to the agrarian economy, its effects on women were more severe than in western European peasant societies, because in the evolution of Chinese society women could never inherit. There was no possibility of protection coming from her father's family in opposition to the way in which her husband was treating her, through the property which she owned. In the upper classes she had a trousseau and in the lower classes there was marriage purchase. True, the wife's family might apply pressure but if they weren't powerful wives could be sold as they had been bought and even rented out. Helen Foster Snow, in *Women in Modern China*, says:

the Chinese family resembled nothing so much as a primitive matri-archal clan in which the father had taken the place of the matriarch and spent his whole time trying to hold his usurped position supported by force and strict 'rules' of ancestral etiquette. He calls himself the father and mother of the family, a most indicative term.[1]

Thus conflict between husbands and fathers, sons and fathers, children and parents, was severely restricted. Probably the real strength of this family was in the middle strata of Chinese society. Upper-class women developed the arts of diplomacy and romantic intrigue; the lower peasant woman in the south had a certain independence which came from her economic contribution as a farming hand. There were of course some regional differences too.

The impact of imperialism and industrialization weakened the authority of the father and husband but did not provide a solution for the wife and daughter. Opium brought in by British trade could cause the breakdown of the father and force the mother into a more active role, but it also brought a shortage of food and a permanent escape for the man. Economic development undermined the traditional family cell; though the old structure continued, it became increasingly intolerable to the young. Mao told Edgar Snow in *Journey to the Beginning* that when he was thirteen his father arranged a marriage with a bride six years older than he was. The point of marrying young boys in this way was to use the girl's labour in the household before the boy was mature enough for the ceremony actually to occur. Mao had often come into conflict with his father and taken refuge with his mother, who was also persecuted by the authoritarianism of the father. Rather than marry he ran away from home and wouldn't come back until his father gave in.

The right to a love-match became a really important issue for the young of both sexes, not only in the new bourgeoisie but in peasant and proletarian families. Just before the revolution in the 1940s, Marion J. Levy noted various factors which had eroded male authority in the Chinese family.[2] Amongst them were such diverse factors as women's work in the towns, coeducation, the emergence of a youth culture, romantic love and the Communist Party. She observed that beating had become less common and that mothers-in-law were finding it more difficult to control the young wives. There were frequent complaints of bickering in families. These conflicts were not based on significant issues but rather on the desire to test positions. Wives and mothers-in-law were jockeying for support from male members of the family. Because the institutional authority of the mother-in-law over the young women had broken down but not yet gone, it was difficult to settle these power struggles either way.

Before the nineteenth century, apart from suicide, sexual intrigue, fantasy, and religion were the only ways women could escape. Isolated writers protested against the oppression of women from the sixteenth century onwards and in the eighteenth century women poetesses demanded equality for women in love-making. In 1825 Li Ju-chen wrote a utopian feminist novel in which a hundred fairy-folk turned into women, passed the official examination to become mandarins and instituted a kingdom of women who then oppressed the men. The hero has his ears pierced and his feet bound. But this kind of feminism was all imagining. It could only turn the world on its head in fantasy. Religion was the only other means through which female dissatisfaction could be expressed. Taoist sects, for example, attracted women as an alternative to Confucianism. The convent served as a refuge from arranged marriages. Later, Protestantism with its emphasis on the education of women, opposition to foot-binding and support for a general improvement in women's social standing acted as a means of focusing ideas for change and making articulate female discontent. Indeed, the revolt against arranged marriages reached such a pitch that the government was forced to set up houses for girls disowned by their families. By the early twentieth century though, Christianity was too bound up with imperialism and the attempted invasion of China by the western powers to be a radicalizing force. The Christian women's organizations retained a feministic equality, but rather after the manner of upper-middle-class philanthropizing in Europe and America. By belonging to such an organization women from the upper classes gained social standing and tried to salvage outcast girls from concubinage, prostitution, foot-binding and opium. The women's Christian organizations were part of a more general agitation for female education and by 1917 the state schools were admitting girls – though this still affected only a small privileged minority.

Female resistance emerged in a more popular and radical manner in the context of the general movement against imperialism and the response to capitalism. As women became involved in groups and organizations wanting to overthrow the existing system many aspects of their own oppression came to the surface. For the first time feminism was connected to a social alternative. Before the 1911 revolution secret societies in China served a political function. The ramifications of their influence are difficult to disentangle but sometimes they operated like a mafia through fear and violence, or like social bandits establishing relations with the poor. They played some part in the emerging labour movement in the towns. Within the secret societies women achieved a particular kind of honour. They were not admitted to the very high offices and did not take part in decision-making but they were able to fulfil roles of trust and responsibility not possible in the society outside. The secret society gave its members a rough and ready equality; they were bound together by a common identity which distinguished them from the rest of the world. In the south, women were particularly important as spies and lookouts and known as 'female polished sticks'.[3] Wives and mothers who were not in the societies formed an outer screen protecting the members and attached by loyalty to their men. Possibly to avoid political conflict with the men, women often split off and formed their own autonomous all-female associations with names like 'The Green and Blue Lanterns'. In some cases these were female mutual aid societies, providing security for widows, for example. During the 1911 revolution the secret societies came out in open support. Women fought in the military brigades. From the women's point of view the abolition of foot-binding was the only substantial achievement from the revolution. But after 1911 both male and female societies tended to lose their political content and become a mafia, or they merged with left political organizations.

The growth of capitalism made new forms of organizing possible. It is tempting to reflect on militant secret sisterhoods acting as organizers of women textile workers but this is only speculation. From 1910–12 women silk filature workers in Shanghai came out twenty times. The women were extremely low paid, fresh from the country and without union traditions, though some had formerly been handicraft silk reelers with some form of guild organization. Most likely they were strikes of desperation, which threw up their own anonymous leaders in the moment of need, although they were not strong enough to build a continuing labour movement. The conditions of Chinese workers make resistance no surprise, even if survival was. An unlimited supply of labour, no factory legislation, the possibility of running machinery twenty-four hours a day, made it ideal for foreign capital. Foreign capitalists remained persistently bewildered at the 'xenophobia' of the people they kindly 'helped' by a particularly open exploitation.

Twelve of these strikes were over arrears of pay, or attempts to reduce wages and lengthen hours. The others were over bad treatment from foremen, including beating, and docking of wages. Some involved ta ch'ang [smashing up of plant] and almost all are described as riotous or very disturbing. Those over arrears of pay were generally successful, but only when the women had succeeded in causing so much trouble that magistrates or the police intervened for the sake of public peace, and told the factory owners to pay up.[4]

Short rowdy strikes served the women's interests; because the employers operated in a world of petty cheating and brutality, even if they tried to negotiate they were beaten. In 1911 three years of this kind of action culminated in a strike in which they held out for ten days and apparently were beginning to recognize the advantages of long-term industrial organization. The fact that prices were rising probably strengthened their resolve to stick it out, because they faced the difficulty of making ends meet in the house as well. The weakness of this early labour action in China was really the fact that urban workers were still a small minority. It was very difficult for them to improve their conditions because the peasantry constituted a large reserve army of labour who could serve as strike-breakers. Unless the peasantry were somehow swept into revolution the workers' activity in isolation was relatively ineffective. The anarchists, the only revolutionary group existing before 1911, recognized this but the lesson was forgotten by the Communist Party in the twenties. Probably because of its weakness the Chinese working class was very open to ideas of a complete uprising; they had more hope in revolution than in building up a strong defensive trade union structure and women workers were no exception here.

Amongst the young intelligentsia very different forms of female resistance were appearing. In 1912 a group of young women stormed Parliament, broke its windows and injured its guards in protest against inequality. Ideas about the reform of the marriage laws and changes in the position of women in the family were being discussed a great deal in radical circles during the First World War. Yang Ch'ang-chi, who was later to become Mao's father-in-law, published an article in 1915 called 'Notes on Reforming the Family Institution'. He contrasted the fact that widows couldn't marry and that concubinage still persisted with English marriage customs, which he felt were ideal. More radical was the New People's Study Society founded by Mao and Ts'ai Ho-sheng in autumn 1917. Together with Ts'ai Ho-sheng's sister they swore never to marry because of their hatred of the traditional marriage system. In fact they all did – Mao in 1921. Most of the members were students and teachers from leading schools in Changsa. They were extremely moralistic and intent on reforming the world. The society was concerned to bring to women a consciousness of their revolutionary potential. Ts'ai Ho-sheng's sister, Ts'ai Chang, set up a similar group in Changsha and some girls went to France to study.

The movement against Japanese imperialism (4 May Movement) provided an immediate outlet for the radical energies of these student-teacher groups. In Hunan in 1919 a network of student alliances throughout the province was created with a coordinating body called the United Students' Alliance. Mao participated in this. At first the girls went along with the boys, then they started to take the initiative themselves. Not surprisingly the most liberal schools took the lead. At the end of May in T'ao Yüan Girls' School several hundred students including the principal formed 'Committees of Ten to Save the Nation'. These groups went off to talk in various parts of the city. Sometimes they even involved primary-school children who carried white 'save the nation' flags. They urged their listeners:

Dear compatriots, everyone must awaken to the fact that China is about to be lost and we shall become enslaved just as happened to the Koreans, and our women will suffer extreme humiliation. Taiwan is another example [of Japanese colonization]. Let us all be aware of China's predicament and support native products![5]

Girls from Chou-Nan Middle School also took an important part in this movement against the Japanese along with their headmistress, Chu Chien-fan, who was active in reform circles in Hunan. Early in June the girls formed discussion, investigation and communications groups. Discussion groups of four or five girls went to public places to lecture to women and girls about Japanese imperialism and explain that they should boycott foreign goods. Investigation groups went out into shops and markets to observe what the women were buying and urge them to buy Chinese. The communications group distributed posters and leaflets as propaganda.

The various schools established contact with each other. By mid-June there were eleven schools, mainly girls' middle schools, grouped into an 'alliance'. They extended their demands from the struggle against Japan to the position of poor women in China. They wanted a Half-Day School for Women of the Common People. Politically they were far from revolutionary. They tried to put pressure on businessmen to 'save the nation'. But their activity was very important in contrast to the fatalism of traditional Chinese womanhood, and many women who were later involved in the revolutionary movement took part in politics for the first time as schoolgirls.

In the radical journals which appeared in 1919 Mao wrote frequently on the oppression of women. He opposed fatalism and respect for existing authority, and urged peasants, workers, women teachers and students to join together and oppose aristocrats and capitalists. He said women should have the vote and be allowed to mix with men equally and freely. He was scornful of the double standard of sexual morality. 'What sort of chastity is this, completely confined to women with shrines for female martyrs everywhere? Where are the shrines for chaste boys?'[6]

Many of these journals were explicitly committed to women's liberation. There was the *New Hunan*, committed to undermining the theory of the 'three bonds', to ruler, father and husband, and *Women's Bell*, founded by the student union of Chou-Nan Middle School, and with the aim 'liberty and equality; means: struggle, creativeness, and solution of the woman problem by women'. Articles in this paper covered not only general questions of emancipation but also the conditions of female labour. There were other feminist strains. *New Youth* in June 1918 was completely devoted to translations of Ibsen and studies of his work. The *Journal of Physical Education* argued the importance of physical education for women.

This was extremely radical in the context of traditional Chinese society, when foot-binding had only just been officially ended.

Mao himself wrote about Miss Chao's suicide because it typified not only the hopeless fatalism of women but that of the whole Chinese people. He saw the new culture being created by activity rather than self-abnegation. 'Rather than die by suicide, one should die only after relentless struggle. The goal of struggle does not lie in "wanting someone else to murder me", but rather it lies in "realizing one's own life potential".'[7] He was aware of the implications of the liberation of women:

> If we launch a campaign for the reform of the marriage system, we must first destroy all superstitions regarding marriage, of which the most important is destruction of belief in 'predestined marriage'. Once this belief has been abolished all support for the policy of parental arrangement will be undermined and the notion of the 'incompatibility between husband and wife' will immediately appear in society. Once a man and wife demonstrate incompatibility, the army of the family revolution will arise en masse and a great wave of freedom of marriage and freedom of love will break over China.[8]

A few months after Mao's articles appeared, the case of Miss Li Chi-ts'un received much publicity. Miss Li resisted the marriage her father arranged and ran away from her home in Changsa to Peking where she became involved in the Work-Study Programme. At one side her father maintained traditional notions about women, 'stupidity is the only virtue', and was furious that he had ever allowed her to study; at the other the student press argued that Miss Li was an example of the spirit of struggle which was such an essential element in the new culture the young revolutionaries upheld. The emancipation of women was regarded as inseparable from general social emancipation. Indeed, one writer in 1920, Tai Chi-t'ao, thought a revolution for sexual equality between men and women would precede the workers' revolution for economic equality.

Chinese feminism was thus an integral part of the radical nationalist movement and developed along with it. Politically though the same differences between the communists and the nationalists emerged in the approach to the women problem. A journal called *Women's Voice*, started in 1921 in connection with the newly formed Chinese Communist Party, emphasized the conditions of working women. Organizations like the Hunan Women's Association established some coordination for demands for free marriage, the vote and personal liberation. Nora from *The Doll's House* was the popular symbol of liberal feminism, because she struggled individually and morally against the restrictions of her role as a bourgeois wife. Girls bobbed their hair as a sign of defiance. Enthusiasm for liberation was strongest among the young educated girls in the towns but it spread also to some peasant and working women.

In 1927 the communists and the Nationalist Party broke apart. Communists and their sympathizers were hunted down:

> From the cities came reports that 'the Women's Association was summarily disbanded . . . along with various unions in the city, all of whom were charged with being Red'; and in the countryside, observers claimed that, 'girls and women were killed on the evidence of their bobbed hair alone'.[9]

The nationalists were torn in their approach to women's rights. They needed the support of women, but many of the demands even of the liberal feminists were too radical for their rich male supporters. In the 1930s they tried to reimpose Confucianism through the New Life Movement. In contrast the communists had a clear commitment to the liberation of women and gained the support of non-party feminists in the towns. When they were forced out into the countryside, they passed through places where female emancipation was completely unknown. Here they made contact with peasant women who for the first time were able to express their grievances with the hope of change. When the war against Japan started in 1935 the party continued this work on a greater scale and also made contact with supporters of women's liberation in the towns controlled by the nationalists again. By the time the Second World War ended it was clear that there was widespread sympathy for the communists in very different strata of the population. This was reflected in the women's organization set up in 1949, the All-China Democratic Women's Federation, which included many non-communist women, including the Young Women's Christian Association. It helped to educate and organize women locally and act as a means of articulating the feelings and demands of women to the party organization.

The manner in which feminism interacted with a revolutionary consciousness is well illustrated in the remarkable life of Ting-Ling, whose real name was Chian Ping-tzu. Aged thirteen, after a personal revolt against the family system she led a demonstration of girls from her school – Chou-Nan Girls' Middle School – which surrounded a session of the Hunan Provincial Council and demanded the equality of women and the right to inherit property. Later in the twenties at school in Shanghai she describes how the students helped girl workers on strike in the big weaving mills at Pootaing:

> We collected money on the streets and went out to do propaganda for the strike, to encourage the workers and explain the reasons for their action. We went from one group of girl workers to another, but it was hard to talk with them because of different dialects and some of us had to have an interpreter. The girl workers were surprised to get support from students and much interested in us.[10]

The gulf between the privileged and the disinherited was extreme. Ting Ling says that when she went to factories she was 'a little afraid ... because the workmen in the streets make jokes about us'.[11] For Chinese women revolutionaries there was also the traditional sexual barrier between upper-class women and lower-class men, which made such political work all the more extraordinary. In 1922 she became an anarchist; they were full of dreams of utopias, they wanted to make cooperative villages and do away with government. This was in marked contrast to the Marxists. 'They only said Marx was correct and you must join us because we are the only correct party.'[12]

Apart from her direct political activity, Ting Ling managed to become a failed movie star, a successful novelist and fall in and out of love several times. In the thirties she initiated the New Realist Literary Trend, through a radical literary magazine, *The Great Dipper*, and taught classes for workers who were beginning to write realist stories. When the Sino-Japanese war broke out she returned to political organizing.

Han Suyin, the author of *The Crippled Tree*, *The Mortal Flowers* and *Birdless Summer*, was less explicitly connected with a political movement in pre-liberation China. Child of a marriage between a Belgian middle-class woman and a Chinese railway engineer, she was brought up amidst squalor and conflict – children running after rats to eat them, her mother screaming as a woman thrust a fetid stinking bag of pus under her eyes: it was a child faceless, the nose and eyes gone into one running putrid sore; her mother shouted at her father 'I will go back. I don't want anything to do with this vermin, these yellow vermin of yours.'[13] Han Suyin tried to forget she was half Chinese, until the war against Japan. On board a ship returning to China she met her future husband Paohuang, who was going to serve in Chiang Kai-shek's elite corps. For nine years she submitted to Pao's idea of women in order to be reborn Chinese; he lectured her on virtue, tore up her books and negated her ability to work and create with Confucian morality: 'A woman of talent is not a virtuous woman.' Han Suyin somehow emerged, but not without scars. 'The fundamental ambivalence of our relationship, its extremes of vehemence and hatred, passion and love and cruelty, its obsessional force, hobbled me for a long time.' When he finally allowed her to train as a midwife, Han Suyin saw girl children born and rejected by their mothers. They dared not show the baby to their husbands, it had to be suffocated, strangled, pushed into a water bottle, or just abandoned. It was a girl and hence it was worthless.

She overheard Pao and his fellow officers talking sometimes with a sneaking respect for the strange Red bandits who turned the whole population into combatants, who encouraged slave girls to rebel against their masters, who did not insist on chastity, and who incited peasant women to stand up and denounce their husbands' misdeeds. Han Suyin could see no hope, but slowly came to perceive that China no longer belonged to men of her husband's class, but to the despised and disinherited coolies 'carrying, pulling, tugging, carrying the war and the festering corruption of their masters on their backs'. Imperceptibly such women disengaged themselves from privilege to be born again.

Their experience was just part of a much larger growing consciousness among women, in which personal immediate resentment against particular aspects of their own oppression became connected with the general revolutionary movement. Innumerable new folk tales and dramas now commemorate these 'nameless' women. Millions of women who had lived since the beginning of time only to labour and give birth, carrying Pao and the ancestors of Pao on their backs, serving the imperial invaders, moved for the first time into individuality and history. The Communist Party formed the organizing egency through which very diverse experiences of exploitation and humiliation encountered each other and could be channelled into concerted political action. Ideologically Mao's old indignation about the desperate situation of Miss Chao continued. He had seen her bound by 'three iron cables' (society, her parents and her future in-laws).[14] Writing later on the oppression of women he wrote of 'four thick ropes' binding them down – politics, clan, religion and men – and maintained that these could only be broken by a communist revolution.[15]

However, women were not prominent on the Long March. Some women fought as guerrillas but they were usually kept in the rear in production work. K'uo Ch'un-ch'ing actually went to the lengths of disguising herself as a boy and received the highest award the army had. She was only discovered when she was wounded.

After the communists defeated the nationalists and took power, the beginnings of women's liberation can be seen in three stages – land reform, the revolutionary marriage law, and the experiments in cooperative farming and the commune. At Long Bow, in Luchang County, Shansi Province, in April 1948, women came to report on the progress that had been made in the mobilization of women. There was much disagreement about what was needed but all the women said women should be able to get and keep a share in the land. In *Fanshen* William Hinton describes this: 'In Chao Chen Village, many women said "When I get my share I'll separate from my husband. Then he won't oppress me any more." '

In Chingtsun the work team found a woman whose husband thought her ugly and wanted to divorce her. She was very depressed until she learned that under the Draft Law she could have her own share of land. Then she cheered up immediately. 'If he divorces me, never mind,' she said. 'I'll get my share and the children will get theirs. We can live a good life without him.' Another woman in the same village had already been deserted once. Her second husband was a local cadre, but he oppressed her. When a member of the team visited her, she wept, 'Chairman Mao is all right, but women are still in trouble. We have no equality. We have to obey our husband because our life depends on them.' After the new law was explained to her, she said, 'This is really fine, I can have my own share now.'[16]

The right to a share in the land was only the beginning. Article Six of the Constitution adopted in September 1949 declared: 'The People's Republic of China abolishes the feudal system which holds women in bondage. Women shall enjoy equal rights with men in political, economic, cultural, educational and social life. Freedom of marriage for men and women shall be enforced.'

It is all very well to make constitutions but quite another matter to put them into effect. The Marriage Law was published along with the Land Law on 1 May 1950. The real issue was not sexual relations but the shattering of the traditional family. It ended the superior position of the man over the woman, it ended forced marriage, it secured monogamy and equal legal rights. 'Bigamy, concubinage, child-betrothal, interference with the remarriage of widows and the execution of money or gifts in connection with marriage shall be prohibited.' Husband and wife had the right to free choice of occupation and free participation in work and social activities, and equal rights in the possession and management of property. Divorce was to be granted when 'husband and wife both desire'. Responsibility for formulating and enforcing these new laws which related to women was with the All-China Democratic Women's Federation.

Though women were in complete support of the land laws there was considerable uneasiness among the older women about the changes in the family because they felt these to be a threat to their position of authority and respect. Free choice in marriage, for instance, meant a loss of control over daughters and daughters-in-law. All this was very difficult to change. There was deep hostility between the young wife and the mother-in-law. Propaganda posters showed them going off to night school together. Sometimes intense psychological pressure replaced the old physical restraints; young girls were almost compelled to marry husbands of the family's choosing. When the women and girls came from the Women's Movement and tried to enforce free choice in marriage they met bitter opposition. Some of them were murdered. One father murdered his own daughter. On other occasions in their enthusiasm they forced men to eject their concubines. With nothing to support them these women committed suicide. Because of all these problems the federation was forced to call a halt in some areas and the campaign did not resume momentum until 1953.

However, gradually welfare facilities and improvements in education training and work conditions were giving women an independence which was more than a constitutional affair. In the early 1950s women were prominent in administrative positions. For instance Mme Li Teh-chuan was Minister of Health, Mme Sun Yat-sen,

Chairman of the National Committee in Defence of Children and of the People's Relief Administration and the China Welfare Institute. Miss Shih Liang, a lawyer, was Minister of Justice. This prominence was not without effect. A great deal of work was done. By 1952 744 women and child health centres had been set up and 156 children's hospitals. Besides these the Women's Federation and the cooperatives set up their own health stations. The Labour Insurance Law of 1 May 1951 brought social security in case of accidents, fifty-six days of maternity leave with full pay, made it illegal to dismiss women workers when they were pregnant, and ordered all factories with over 500 workers to set up their own medical service.

Despite all these changes women still found themselves economically dependent on men. Fragmentation of the land only made it economically unviable. Though some women wanted to own their own land, others inclined towards social ownership. Some took the initiative in forming cooperatives. Still the money for work was not paid to the young women but to the father-in-law, because under the cooperative payment for labour was made on the basis of work points, with the whole family as a unit. In the families with the old feudal ideas the women were still controlled by the men. Women too found themselves working in the cooperative all day but still doing all the housework and looking after the children. Here the development of the communes was most important. They provided a real system of social security for women. First there was economic independence. Payment for labour was based on work grades. Each person was paid according to his or her work and the money was paid directly to each individual. With this new-found economic self-determination went a great increase in respect for young women within the family. Also, because the communes provided a truly social environment which through communal restaurants, crèches, houses of respect for the old, gave women the opportunity to play an active role in social and political life, the great problem of abstract 'equal rights' placing women actually at a disadvantage was avoided. Within the social organization of the commune it was possible to recognize the situation of women, as women. For example, the women's committees devised significant health rules. Women were not to work in wet places during menstruation, expectant mothers were to do only light work, and nursing mothers were to work near home.

It would be a great mistake to think of these changes as coming easily. Not only was there great backwardness and poverty but the emergence of women implied a total and permanent cultural re-creation. It demanded a complete reorientation of consciousness, for men as well as women. Such transformations come painfully and with great effort. Hinton describes how in Long Bow a few poor peasant women wives of leading revolutionary cadres organized a Women's Association. They voiced their own bitterness. They dis-covered they could speak and found they had as many grievances as the men – if not more. They began to be conscious of themselves as 'half of China':

> But the women found as they organized among themselves, attended meetings and entered into public life, that they met more and more opposition from the men, particularly from the men of their own households, most of whom regarded any activity by wives and daughters-in-law outside the house as 'steps leading to adultery'. Family heads, having paid sound grain for their women, regarded them as their private property, expected them to work hard, bear children, serve their fathers, husbands and mothers-in-law, and speak only when spoken to. In this atmosphere the activities of the Women's Association created a domestic crisis in many a family. Not only did the husbands object to their wives going out; the mothers-in-law and fathers-in-law objected even more strenuously. Many young wives who nevertheless insisted on going to meetings were badly beaten up when they got home.[17]

Among those who were beaten was the wife of a poor peasant called Man-ts'ang. When she came home from a Women's Association meeting she was beaten as a matter of course. But instead of accept-ing this and staying at home she made a complaint against her husband. A meeting of the women in the village was held and Man-ts'ang was asked to explain himself. Contemptuous and unrepentant he replied that he had beaten his wife because she went to meetings and 'the only reason women go to meetings is to gain a free hand for flirtation and seduction'. The women argued angrily and he answered them. In rage they rushed at him, knocked him down, kicked him, tore his clothes and pulled his hair while he begged for mercy, promising never to beat his wife again. Apparently he kept his promise for his wife was known as Ch'en Ai-lien, her maiden name, from that day.

Having shown their power in this dramatic way, the women were able to persuade husbands not to beat their wives. This kind of conflict developed throughout China. Old ideas went very deep and men in the party were in no sense exempt. In some cases the communist cadres among the men clung to the old ways. Veteran revolutionary fighters thought they deserved young wives. More commonly though they simply did not notice the women's problems until the women pointed them out. In the Rocky Mountain Commune in Greater Peking there was a great public health campaign to clear up the streets and eliminate flies, mosquitoes, rats and the sparrows which eat the grain. Everyone was very busy. Women began to combine in households in order to look after their children. Grandmothers took on these responsibilities. The men remained quite unaware of the facilities needed by the women. The women became exasperated and started producing posters and notices criticizing the men and putting their demands. They stuck these up on the walls. They said to the men: 'You think we aren't needed for socialism? If we are, why don't you help us organize.'[18]

Thus the beginnings of the most fundamental liberation began – women began to think for themselves. All this was a profoundly educative process. The education of women in China since the revolution is not just a matter of going to school or college, or training, though these are of course vital. It is the experience of finding a place and a voice after centuries of belonging to the disinherited and dumb. Li Kuei-ying, a woman in her thirties, a pioneer of peasant origin, describes how when she was made leader of the women's labour group in her cooperative in 1953:

I wanted to get the women as a group moving. I wanted to get them to break away from the past.

That winter I opened a winter school. We helped the women to make shoes and clothes and to improve their agricultural tools. We gave them lessons in feeding poultry and in spinning. We had discussions after the lessons. We tried to get the women to tell us themselves what things had been like before, and how it was now, and how it ought to be in the future. For example, they said: 'My feet were bound so that I could not walk. In the old society, a woman was not supposed to go beyond the threshold of her home for the first three years of her marriage. We weren't allowed to eat on the Kang, but had to sit on a stool when we ate, and if my parents had decided to marry me off with a cur, then I had to be content with a cur. But now you are allowed to see your husband before you marry, and you can refuse to marry him, if you don't like the look of him. The old society was bad and the new is good.' We discussed whether women are men's equals or not, and most said: 'Within the family, man and woman are equal. We help the men when they work in the fields and they should help us in the house.' But many of the older women said: 'Women are born to attend to the household. A woman cannot work in the fields. That can't be helped. It is just that men and women are born different. A person is born either a man or a woman. To work in the fields or in the house.'

Slowly all the women gained confidence. At an open discussion about the future of the cooperatives two of the women spoke. They said, 'The old women still say they don't understand things and are just women, and that it is the man's business to decide and that the women should do as the men decide. But we say that we do understand. We are women and we know what this discussion is about.' They opposed a dividend on land and wanted more investment. An old man tried to silence them. 'We should not listen to women when it is a question of serious business. They understand nothing. After all, they are only women and ought not to disturb our discussions. We don't need to concern ourselves with what they have said.'[19] But Li Kuei-ying's brother disagreed. He pointed out that every other Chinese was a woman. They should be listened to. He felt they spoke sense and agreed with them about investment.

The revolution secured economic independence, equality within the family, social welfare, improved working conditions – but most important, it enabled women to find their own voice. Much more complex is the question of sexual liberation.

For the first time in history the mass of Chinese women are now in a situation where sex can be separated from reproduction. The Chinese attitude to birth control has been much misunderstood in the west. They are steadfastly anti-Malthusian; like the early English working-class radicals they reject the control of population growth as a substitute for social change. However, they discourage large families because they feel the children don't get enough attention and they want the mothers to be able to take part in productive work and political and social life. There has been a shift in tactics however. In the fifties they concentrated on pamphlets, booklets and radio programmes which explained in painstaking detail how to use contraceptives. During the sixties this emphasis was more on public health workers and medical journals and the campaign was more action-oriented: teams of mobile medical workers touring with films, exhibitions, posters, displays in market-places and halls, and meetings of 1,000, or small groups of four or five people. Some meetings took the form of personal testimonies: peasant women who were using I.U.C.D.s or diaphragms would tell other women of their experience with them. They are experimenting with the pill but don't think it safe yet. In the fifties abortions were available in theory though probably not generally in practice for the peasant women. During the sixties, however, as a result of much discussion and experimenting with simple methods, they devised a suction device which can be used in areas where there is no electricity and which results in very little blood loss. Though the peasant women want abortions they are terrified of surgery and Chinese medical journals place a lot of stress on the need to explain the operation and reassure them. Sterilization is just beginning, though lack of medical personnel and the fear of surgery have combined with the men's suspicion not to make it very common. 'It requires the most persuasive thoughts of Mao Tse-tung to convince the average Chinese male that vasectomy is not castration and that he will not experience any loss of sexuality.'[20]

When the birth control propagandists arrive in a town they first try to win the support of the peasant organizations, especially the women's organizations. A member of the women's organization told Jan Myrdal:

In certain families with lots of children, the women would like birth control, but their husbands won't. In these families the husbands say: 'There's not going to be any family planning here.' Then the women go to them and try to talk sense into them. We say: 'Look how many children you have. Your wife looks after the household and sees to all the children and she makes shoes and clothes for both of you and the children, but you don't think of all she has to do or of her health, but just make her with child again and again. Wait now for three or four years. Then you can have more if you want.' Usually, they will eventually say: 'If it isn't going to go on all one's life, then all right. But if she's going to go on with birth control for ever, then I'm not having any.' In these cases, all goes well and usually they decide not to have any more afterwards. But in other cases, the husband just says: 'No'.

Then we women speak to him about it every day, till he agrees to birth control. No husband has yet managed to stand out for any length of time, when we are talking to him. . . . It's only their pride that stands in the way, and we have to tell them that such pride is false and not at all right. But there are, too, families where both husband and wife are agreed that they want children all the time. We can't do anything there. The whole thing's voluntary. The chief thing is to have a healthy family, and that the mother feels all right.[21]

But it is not always just the men who are doubtful. An English surgeon, Joshua Horn, asked many village women about their attitudes after a meeting and question session on family planning:

Their answers revaled two conflicting, but perfectly understandable trends. One was that in the past they had been too poor to raise children, many had died at birth or starved to death and those who survived had gone hungry, naked, unlettered. Now that there was food and schools for all, and life was pleasant and secure, why should they restrict their families? This view was warmly supported by grand-parents steeped in the Confucian tradition that many grandchildren brought them honour, prosperity and social security.[22]

The others were for birth control but not sure if it was possible to manage it.

The gradual improvement of medical facilities has nearly eradicated venereal disease from which tens of millions of people suffered before the revolution, and made pregnancy and illness less of a nightmare. The grannies still remember the wise old woman, filthy, dirty and covered with lice, her hair falling over her face, waving her horse's tail and muttering words that no one understood, who told you to sacrifice an animal you didn't have and accept fate until whoever was doomed to die died, but the young women are familiar with doctors from the town, and health workers trained from their own village.

All these changes interact upon the position of women in the family. Indeed, it seemed at first when the communes appeared that the Chinese were creating an alternative family. During the late fifties the whole pattern of women's lives changed because of the attempt to involve them in production and the development of the communes first in the countryside and then in the towns. New communal forms of living evolved under pressure. Often these were on a small scale and very makeshift. A small group of housewives from about twelve households got together and wondered what they could do. The chairman of the local neighbourhood committee said why didn't they become a neighbourhood production team. This simply meant that they started to make cloth shoesoles and paper bags for department stores in each other's homes. As more work came in the question of how to look after the children and cook came up:

> One of the housewives said, 'If only we could have a dining-room and a nursery like the factories do!' Another woman picked up the idea and said, 'Why don't we set them up ourselves?' and before she could finish, the other women started agreeing. One of them offered a kitchen knife, others turned over pots, pans, and various utensils. One woman known for her good cooking volunteered to take over the kitchen and another said she would take responsibility for the nursery.[23]

All this was very pragmatic; communal facilities ranged from the rather grand to the very simple – sometimes they were in new buildings or converted old ones, like the dining-room which had been appropriately a temple to the god of the soil. But although many of the traditional functions of the family were socialized there was no conscious intention of creating a new basis for the family, nor was there an effort to break down the distinction between male and female roles in relation to small children.

Chinese women become indignant when the communes are said in the west to destroy the family. They claim that instead they make the relationship of the family more stable by removing the old causes of tiredness and frustration. They also like to keep the evening meal a family affair.

Nor are the Chinese forthcoming about the female orgasm. Ting Ling and Agnes Smedley were much criticized for putting forward theories of 'free' love and sexual liberation. A very strong puritan streak exists in the Chinese women's movement. However, it would be to misunderstand this to interpret it in terms of the hypocritical 'puritanism' we know as a hangover from the authoritarian repression of middle-class Victorian society. It resembles rather the earnest desire to purify the spirit felt by the seventeenth-century puritans. Bed was so much the symbol of slavery that the Chinese woman sought to escape from it as a means of asserting her emancipation. One woman commented to Simone de Beauvoir as they watched a scene at the opera in which the young heroine struggled to escape from the unwelcome embrace of the emperor: 'That's why Chinese women wanted the revolution, in order to have the right to say no to that sort of thing.'[24]

Romantic love in the accepted western sense is very strange to the Chinese, although the right to a free marriage played such an important part in the liberation struggle of girls in the towns. Because women's subservience was so completely institutionalized the young people especially in the country were and still are very reserved. Quite often boys and girls in the same village are too shy to propose. One of them, usually the boy, will go to an older person who will act as a go-between. Propaganda stories just after the revolution encouraged the young in the villages to talk to each other and to go on moonlight walks. The peasant girls choose boys who are good workers and of even temper. People do not say of girls that they are beautiful or ugly, but that 'she looks well enough in her way'. In the towns, though, the girls, regardless of their simple denim clothes, are held to be a little more knowing. 'In the towns the girls will tell you the same as those in the villages but they will only do that because it is the thing to say. In reality, town girls want smart dashing-looking boys.'[25]

The term 'Shanghai miss' still persists for town girls who put on airs and graces. The ethic of service, thrift and industry emphasizes abstinence and control. Late marriages (mid-twenties) are encouraged, and there is a general distrust of extravagance and display. This goes with the attempt to create the culture for a new work-discipline so that China can develop industrially. After the Great Leap Forward of 1958–9, when women were propelled into production, three bad harvests followed and energy was concentrated on restoring past production levels, not establishing new ones.

The cultural revolution brought a rejection of the emphasis upon motherhood which was common in the Soviet bloc. In a report on the Moscow World Congress of Women in 1963, Yang-Yun-Yu criticized a tendency to confine women's role to motherhood. 'On the surface, these views seemed to take no notice of politics, but they actually involved a very big political question. Their aim was to exclude women from political life. If these views were accepted women would never win complete emancipation.'[26] From mid-1966 these views became more common. And *China's Women* issued a

Women, Resistance and Revolution

self-criticism of its editorial policy which had 'intoxicated women with the small haven of motherhood'. This was a significant change from 1965 when embroidery and recipes were still included.

As part of the intense politicization of the cultural revolution women realized that to confine themselves simply to the home and family was to throw away equality. Yao Zi-sun, a factory worker, was happy staying at home; she didn't like going to arguments, debates and meetings, and she wasn't interested in criticizing other people. Then she became involved in the controversy which went on in her factory during the cultural revolution. This activity penetrated the other areas of her life. She made new connections. The world suddenly grew – beyond her factory, her family, her region. She understood that her actions were important: what you did in one place had its effect in another. Women couldn't leave politics to men.

The daughters of Miss Chao Wu-chieh have learned many things in the last fifty years of struggle. Yao Zi-sun's friend Wang Jui-jin says:

> I was crushed before and so my mind had to be awakened and I learned many good things. In those old days, I thought a 'good' person was an obedient person, who obeyed orders without stopping to think whether they were right or wrong; and I passively accepted the fact that some people were rich and comfortable and idle, while others lived like we did and worked so hard. Now I know different. Now we have done away with that unjust and unequal way of living, and our present cultural revolution is reminding us that we must not permit that old system to creep up on us again and catch us unawares.[27]

Along with the distrust of the elevation of motherhood goes a suspicion of romantic sexuality. This very dismissive attitude to personal emotions tends to emphasize the ascetic element in the Chinese Revolution, but it helps to discourage passivity. According to a recent article in *Eastern Horizon*, 'The Chinese girl of today disdains make-up, her clothes are loose and comfortable, her thoughts are not tied to pleasing men any more and she feels her equal responsibility with men in her work – the reconstruction of the country.'[28]

This is reflected in the changes made in popular stories like 'White-Haired Girl'. 'White-Haired Girl' was originally one of the dramas performed in the liberated areas during the Long March. It was a story of the daughter of a poor peasant who is forced to become a

194

maidservant in the home of her father's landlord. Because of his overwhelming debt to the landlord the father commits suicide. The girl is raped by the landlord and runs away to a mountain cave, to find her sweetheart. She gives birth to a still-born baby and she lives like an animal on roots and berries, stealing food sometimes from the temple. When the region is liberated by the communists she returns to her village to confront her old oppressor and find the peasant boy who loves her. Because of her suffering her hair turns completely white. In the 1970 version the girl flees from the landlord but the rape and the baby are cut out. The father dies fighting the landlord and the girl herself returns to fight him. There is much less emphasis on the suffering and more on the active resistance.

'Red Detachment of Women' is an example of a modern dance drama, which tells how Wu Ching-hua, the daughter of a poor peasant, escapes from slavery and joins the Red Army. At first she sees her commitment to the revolution as personal vengeance, but in the political classes she begins to connect her own oppression to a much wider movement. There is a hint of personal affection between her and the man who rescued her, but when he dies fighting Wu Ching-hua has to go on and organize.

The Chinese are far from complacent. The whole emphasis upon mobilization at the base, the conviction that socialism is a continuing process, which has to be consciously and actively directed by people and requires the creation of a new culture, inevitably affects women. No one has been 'given' emancipation by the revolution. They have continually to struggle for it. In the cultural revolution the question of women's participation came quickly to the fore. The relationship between women's liberation and self-government appears clearly in the street committees. In outer Shanghai for instance the street committee consists of twenty-two people representing various districts and political organizations. Women form a high proportion of its members – sixteen out of twenty-two. It organizes nurseries, kindergartens, non-profit-making dining halls, service centres and small factories in which women who can't work at a distance or full time are employed. Conditions are often better in places of work organized in this way because suggestions and complaints can be immediately expressed and implemented.[29]

The cultural revolution has had an impact on the family. Typical is the experience of Ding Hai-yu, who is a barber in Lunghua

Province Production Brigade. He came home from a political study class full of enthusiasm, eager to discuss the new ideas in his own family. His wife, who works in the commune tailoring shop, was unimpressed. She couldn't read or write very well, she was a mother, she felt politics was nothing to do with her. But the older daughters supported their father and managed to persuade her. Instead of simply reading Mao's works, the girls started to make up songs and dances and plays to illustrate what they read. Soon Ding Hai-yu's wife became involved and the whole family were acting out the new ideas for the neighbours.[30]

Members of the Society for Anglo-Chinese Understanding who visited China in October 1970 found that the complete communalization of family life which appeared at the end of the fifties was not so evident. The dining-rooms and nurseries continue but not on such a scale. This is probably partly for economic reasons but the peasant women particularly seem to prefer their individual families to communal facilities. They visited a very simple crèche attached to a factory. There were colourful pictures round the walls. Women looked after the children, but fathers as well as mothers collected them. The children danced and sang together but the girls seemed to do this more naturally than boys.

The tendency of the cultural revolution seems to have been to include the specific oppression of women within the general attempt to encourage all the underprivileged to throw off the old authorities. Consequently it is argued that there are no longer men's or women's jobs. It is true that women are doing jobs they have never done before but some of the old distinctions still exist in traditional trades. The S.A.C.U. members visited an embroidery factory which used nearly all women workers, with only a few men. But these men were mainly doing the very skilled design work, and most of the women were either doing hand embroidery or working on the machines, though among the apprentices in design there were many young women. The man who showed them round said that rather than making particular efforts to alter the sexual division of labour they were breaking down the distinction between skilled and unskilled by interchanging all the workers and teaching all the women to design, and the men to embroider and work the machines. When he was asked about the composition of the revolutionary committee he replied with a twinkle in his eye that he was the only man on it. The committee had the job not only of running the factory but of judging the designs and deciding which ones could be sent out. Although the women spoke he was obviously more confident and articulate than they were.

In the attempt to eradicate the legacy of the past there is the constant emphasis on the need to encourage all the people who normally would be silent to speak up. Joshua Horn in *Away With All Pests* describes the way in which the cultural revolution shatters the hierarchical structure of the medical profession. As women have traditionally been at the bottom of all authority hierarchies they are radically affected. Nurses criticize the doctors. Equally, in the schools, by encouraging students to challenge their teachers, young girls have been hurtled out of passivity. They often leave their parents for a long time to work in the country. The difficulty has been in containing the resentment of the young rebelling in a society which retains a deep-rooted respect for authority, and veneration for the old. A fifteen-year-old girl who struck her teacher for reactionary ideas after much discussion with Red Guards in Peking returned home convinced that 'when you use force it only makes people resist, but if you use reason you might convince them.'[31]

Politically, all this has had a great effect at a local level but at the centre of power women are still under-represented, although a few women like Mao's wife have emerged through the cultural revolution into positions of great significance. This is part of the more general problem of revolutionary democracy. Moreover, it is apparent that the old ideas of women's place still persist. Some young girl graduates from a junior middle school who went off into the country in the summer of 1969 found they were still regarded with scepticism by the comrades there when they announced they were going to be a herding team. 'In all my years here,' one peasant said, 'I've never seen a herdswoman. These girls don't even come up to the stirrups. How can they herd horses?' Another comrade was of the opinion that 'If they can herd horses then the sand-grouse can fly up to heaven.' The girls retorted, 'Women have flown planes. . . . Why can't we herd horses?' They kept falling off and were laughed at a great deal but they persisted.[32]

A report from an old poor peasant in Chungsan County, Kwantung, indicates that support for the 'buying-and-selling type of matrimony' continues:

In our commune, an unreformed landlord has spread openly such reactionary nonsense as 'parental care is like the grace of heaven', and 'giving away your daughter without asking for money is valuing a human being as cheap as mud.' He instigated those who gave away their daughters by marriage to ask for so-called 'gift-money' and 'silver for her person'. This is the new trend of the class struggle. We must heighten our vigilance.[33]

Chinese vigilance has found dramatic expression but many problems remain unresolved. It is not clear whether it will be necessary for women again to emphasize their specific oppression before a completely different sense of value can emerge, nor whether self-activity at the base can be reconciled with the magnified figure of Chairman Mao directing from the top. It is difficult to estimate now how far it is possible to achieve human liberation when the margins between socialist reconstruction and starvation are still all too close. How far the emphasis on women's general involvement in revolutionary politics can be separated from an interchange in male/female roles, changes in the family and a conscious attempt to relate sexual liberation to the new society stays an open question, but the contrast between the old world before liberation and China now is undeniable.

Han Suyin is not uncritical of some aspects of the cultural revolution. She shrinks from its self-righteousness, which resembles Confucian moralizing; its extremes are alien to her. But she understands the depths of subjection suffered previously by the Chinese people, and particularly the oppression of women, which demand the profoundest cultural re-creation. Female subordination is inscribed in the letters of the language:

The very ideogram for 'woman' denoted subjection, the bar across, horizontal burden of her heavy breasts, the protuberant hips and the crossed bow legs, not quite quadrupedal, but almost. Since then I have often thought that in today's China, with the cultural revolution which compels all to weigh in the light of reason our secret clingings to primeval devices of subjection, the first thing that should be done is to eradicate totally, to change totally, some of those odious ideograms which are exact pictures of two millennia of feudal oligarchy, four millennia of woman's inferiority.[34]

In considering this extremely fundamental relationship of women with our own past, and ultimately of all human beings with all history as part of the scope of continuing revolution, the Chinese ask a question we can't afford to ignore – why do we cling to subjection?

To say there are still definite limits to the liberation of women after the Chinese Revolution is not to dismiss what has been achieved. Indeed, the attempt to understand historically the point from which women emerged helps us not only to appreciate what has happened in real terms, but also prevents us from lifting their experience mechanically onto ours. We come from different pasts, and the kind of socialism and liberation that we can conceive and create differs greatly. The emphasis on the work situation, the puritanism in sexual matters which appears in the emancipation of Chinese women, is not some formula for western capitalism, or the other socialist countries for that matter, but should be understood as part of a particular process of development. But while we make our own liberation the experience of other revolutions shows how from the most wretched of beginnings the impossible can happen. The sand-grouse is on its way to heaven.

## CHAPTER 8

# Colony
# Within the
# Colony

Ultimately, we live in a kind of international caste system with the white western ruling-class male at the top and the non-white female of the colonized world at the bottom.

Mary Kelly, National Liberation Movements and Women's Liberation, in *Shrew*, Women's Liberation Workshop, December 1970

My mother, whose feet, daily and nightly, pedal, pedal, for our never-tiring hunger, I am even woken by those never tiring feet pedalling by night and the Singer which my mother pedals, pedals for our hunger, night and day. . . . And the bed of planks on its legs of kerosene drums, a bed with elephantiasis, my grandmother's bed with its goatskin and its dried banana leaves and its rags, a bed with nostalgia as a mattress and above it a bowl full of oil, a candle-end with a dancing flame and on the bowl, in golden letters, the word MERCY! A disgrace Paille Street.

Aimé Césaire, *Return to my Native Land* (Martinique)

The mothers of the Mulattoes were in the slave-gangs, they had half-brothers there, and however much the Mulattoe himself might despise this half of his origin, he was at home among the slaves and, in addition to his wealth and education, could have an influence among them which a white man could never have. Furthermore apart from physical terror, the slaves were to be kept in subjection by associating inferiority and degradation with the most obvious distinguishing mark of the slave – the black skin.

C. L. R. James, *The Black Jacobins* (West Indies)

Where are you now, O Shango?
Two-headed, powerful
Man and woman, hermaphrodite
Holding your quivering thunderbolts
With quiet savage malice;
Africa, Cuba, Haiti, Brazil,
Slavery of mind is unabolished.
Always wanting to punish, never to love.

Abioseh Nicol, *African Easter* (Sierra Leone)

Certain similarities exist between the colonization of the under-developed country and female oppression within capitalism. There is the economic dependence, the cultural take-over, the identification of dignity with resemblance to the oppressor. There is also the trap which consists in making a cult of a particular form of primitiveness designed and constructed from the romantic conceit of the oppressor. The 'noble savage' and the 'earth-mother' become impotent self-binding symbols of the qualities the white man in capitalism has destroyed for himself. Nostalgia lingers delicately round an advanced technology. Paternalism has many forms, but the line is essentially the same. The slave-owner is the affectionate father until the slaves rebel. The victim of colonization is allowed to develop, but according to a particular pattern of underdevelopment. The master urges equality and then bites back his words with the lash. The colonized, like Caliban, find themselves trained for dependence, then finally rejected as equals:

> You taught me language, and my profit on't
> Is, I know how to curse.[1]

From this first curse with the master's language comes the movement for liberation. There is a delicious relief in the first act of ingratitude.

Here the analogy between sexual and racial imperialism stops, partly because the colonizer's women have themselves enjoyed the spoils of imperial domination. Sometimes they have been its most vehement and cruel defenders. Because their own superiority was insecure they have turned on the native women with a bitterness in which sexual and racial jealousy combine. When colonization included slavery as in the West Indies this was particularly intense. The wives of the slave-owners dwelt upon the obvious preference their men showed for the black bodies of their female slaves. The men returned to the black women who had suckled them for orgasm. The appearance of mulatto children, taught to despise their own mothers, was the ironic testament of the white woman's rivals. Occasionally, when her man was away she would break out into acts of terrible vengeance upon the slave.

In industry in the towns a complicated series of racial and sexual hierarchies develops along with the formation of a working class. Esther Boserup comments:

It is normal in European-owned industrial establishments in developing countries to find a division of labour along both the race and sex dimension, with European men at the top of the hierarchy, in the most responsible jobs with the highest incomes, and indigenous African or Asian women at the bottom doing the least responsible and lowest paid.[2]

In white-collar jobs – clerical and supervisory – Chinese or Indian men are found along with European women: here the ranking of race and sex is less determined. But within the indigenous elite even the small minority of privileged women tend to work as nurses or teachers, which are extensions of the family role. Their privileged occupations are thus structurally distinct from the men's. Women moreover form a relatively small percentage of the elite group in all developing countries in terms of educational and job opportunity.

Imperialism has served to generalize discontent. Dissatisfactions have ceased to be particular and local; they have become national. The national liberation movements act as the focus for these. Demands like monogamy, birth control, education, the right to organize, borrowed from western capitalism, combine with the desire for economic security, right to the land, control of the markets, expulsion of the foreigners, which come from the direct experience of the wretched of the earth. When a section of the urban intelligentsia breaks with their class to argue for social revolution this combination finds a theoretical shape. Feminism has followed this process, though it has only been a faint echo of the male-dominated movements.

In the 1920s and 1930s an incipient feminism emerged in developing countries which resembled the early 'equal rights' feminism of middle-class women in capitalist societies. However, the lack of a strong bourgeoisie meant that it rarely became significant. Sometimes this was imposed by the state in an attempt to westernize. In Turkey Mustafa Kemal ended the veil and banned polygamy. In other cases it came out of movements of the more privileged women and carried a note of radical humanism and faith in individual potential. The novel was always an important vehicle of propaganda. In Indonesia for example Takdir-Alis Jahbana wrote *Under Full Sail* in the 1930s. She discussed the difficulties faced by emancipated women. The heroine Tati breaks off her engagement so she can participate fully in the feminist movement. She makes a speech at a women's congress which is typical of the ideas of this kind of feminism:

For the man she was no more than a toy, a doll pampered while it is loved but cast aside and replaced once it has lost its attraction. A slave, she has no will of her own but obeys those whose servant she is. Up to the present day our people do not regard a woman as a human being with a life of her own. She is only a part of the man's life . . . and in order to prevent her becoming conscious of her humiliation, she is caged in her house until it is time for her to marry. Why send her to school if afterwards she is to be confined to the kitchen?

Later in the book she adds: 'We must point the way in order that the new woman may be born, a freed woman who will have the courage to stand up for all she does and all she thinks.'[3]

Such a woman would not think in terms of the house but of the world; she would not just marry but have a career. She would be 'no longer the man's slave but his equal; no longer fearing him or appealing to his feelings of pity'. This kind of moral radicalism was very important in creating a new consciousness in women but such an approach necessarily excluded all women who weren't from rich families. Education is assumed to be available and presumably there is someone to look after the children while the emancipated woman gets on with her career.

The film *Les Ramparts d'Argile* shows the impossible struggle of a young girl in a village in North Africa. She is restless, she watches the men, she learns reading from her little brother hanging around the schoolhouse, she gazes enviously at the chic health visitor from the town. When a sit-down strike starts among the men in the village because they question the rates allowed for their stone-cutting, and the soldiers come to prevent them being given food or drink, she hides the bucket from the well and forces the soldiers to go away because then they can't drink either. After this she shows open rebellion to her father and the old women humiliate her, smearing blood on her face and hair, twisting and pulling her hair before they cast her out into the desert. The situation of women in such a society is completely fixed in a network of traditional social relationships which make individual resistance almost impossible for the majority of women. They can only become outcasts. The alternative has been revolts about consumption, for instance the organizing of African market women to defend their monopoly and rights. Their revolt appears legitimate because it is defending what existed before.

It is only in the abnormal circumstances of political revolt that it is possible for women to take uncustomary actions. It has been the national independence movements which have created the impetus for the active involvement of women outside the small social elite. Invariably this has been a result of initiative taken by the privileged women first. But this has meant that the political choices open to women have been determined by the nature of the movements for national independence. For example, in the course of Arab resistance to the British support for the Zionists, Arab women organized a congress in Palestine in 1929. Two hundred women delegates attended, among them the wives of prominent Arab leaders. Not only was this the first ever women's congress in Palestine, but all the women attended unveiled. The women's movement was completely identified with Arab nationalism; they worked for the mitigation of political sentences, protested against the import of firearms into Palestine to be used by the Jews. After Lord Allenby's visit to Jerusalem in 1932 the women had extended outwards and organized mass demonstrations. But with this identification came collapse. The women's movement failed along with the general movement which tried to prevent the creation of a state of Israel. Not only were the national political objectives not achieved but Palestinian women were not able to establish any social basis for the liberation of Arab women.

In India women played a prominent role in resisting the British. Even in the mutiny of 1857–8 women of the bazaar are reported as taunting the men to rise. Rather later in the early 1900s educated women became involved in religious groups and organizations which met as a focus for discontent and voiced forms of feminism, like the Theosophical Society founded by the woman who had organized the London matchgirls, Annie Besant. As the nationalist movement spread in the 1920s and 1930s women became active on a larger scale. Despite Gandhi's suspicions about women participating, they demonstrated, picketed shops, were imprisoned and faced police charges with great courage. In the Punjab women workers were drawn in. A left wing within the feminist-nationalist movement was as critical of exploitation by Indians as by the British, but this was submerged in the general right-wing current of the independence struggle. 'Emancipation' now in India is reserved for the most privileged – and even for them the limits of what can be done are severely circumscribed.

Bourgeois nationalism has proved consistently incapable of answering the needs of the poor in the Third World. This is particularly true of the needs of poor Third World *women*. It is only when national liberation struggles have become revolutionary movements that the real problems of women's liberation have even begun to be considered.

However, there are many complications even at this stage for women because they often face the hostility of men in the male-dominated revolutionary organization. Perhaps they accept the participation of women actually while they are fighting imperialism, but they tend to see the future society as one in which women are put back firmly in their place. Women are made to carry babies. These alien ideas of 'emancipation' came with the white man. They were the justification apparently of the arrogance which white women often showed to the colonized men. This presents a dilemma for those women who realize that their only hope is through the success of the revolutionary movement. It is difficult for them to know what to do. They realize that the men's reaction is partly the age-old response of the male oppressor, but it is also something else. The white imperialists did not only colonize economically but psychologically. They usurped the men from their 'manhood', they took over from the colonized men control of their women.

Fanon describes the frequency with which the unveiling of Algerian women appeared as a theme in the dreams of French males as a symbol of rape. The passivity and complete subordination of the colonized woman fascinated the white imperialists; with her they could act out the fantasies of domination they were forced to suppress with their own women. The right to possess his own woman thus becomes a kind of madness in the mind of the colonized man as he takes off the white mask. With it develops the idea of invading and desecrating the white man's women. These are the means out of humiliation. He wants to act out the domination he has been made to suffer by imperialism. He has taken over the same structure of sexual fantasy as the white man. He is still trapped within the white mask; he has simply inverted its facial characteristics. The white woman is in an ambiguous position. She comes from among the powerful but she finds herself at once humiliated and reverenced by the men she was taught to regard as both forbidden and inferior. In going towards the colonized man she implicitly rejects the male of the dominant race, but she keeps her own skin, the passport back into imperial protection. She is looked down upon and secretly envied by women of her own kind, while colonized women resent her as encroaching on their own underprivilege.

Though solidarity between the women can help it must be the colonized women who shatter this legacy of humiliation and domination. Here a male-defined movement regardless of its social aims is not sufficient. The liberation of women in developing countries required the revolutionary emergence of the colony within the colony. Without this not only will one section of society continue to be despised, but the creation of Che Guevara's new 'man' will prove impossible because revolutionary men will only understand liberation as their power to control other human beings. When women in the colonized countries articulate a revolutionary feminist consciousness, it becomes possible to see their previous situation and conception of the world in a different way. We are only just now recognizing the embryo. The whole human being has yet to be born.

## Vietnam

When citadel walls collapse, it's the business of the king. There is no reason for the widow to worry about it day and night.

Vietnamese proverb

How tragic is the destiny of women,
How sad is their fate,
Creator why are you so cruel to us?

Wasted are our green years, withered our pink cheeks.
The woman who lies here was in her lifetime the wife of all.
Yet after her death, her soul wanders in loneliness.
                    Kiêu; eighteenth-century poem about a courtesan

Guerrilla Woman:

   The night is shorter than the road
   its path more intricate than the tiny lanes
   that curve the surface of my baby daughter's palm.
   Yet I will wound this land, our own, with trenches,
   With pits for the French when they march this path,
   beds for the French to sleep in,
   groves in the land for the enemy of the land.
   The ditches must go deeper than my hatred.
   The work must fly faster than my tears . . .

   You can drown the calls of my children,
   but you can never hush the rhythm of my naked hands
   clawing the frozen mud that will contain you.
                    After To Huu 1948, translated by Robin Morgan

The Vigil:

   She should write him, perhaps that she is pregnant,
   What to name this child with his almost forgotten face?
   If it is a girl, Napalm.
   If it is a boy, M-14 or Shrapnel,
   so as not to forget, never to forget
   that he is fighting for the land –
   twenty years of war minus twenty years of suffering
   equals nothing.
   Each evening she waits for sleep until dawn.
   She should write him, perhaps
   but watches him, instead, behind closed eyes,
   seeing him high in the wooded mountains happy enough
   to display the unwritten letter to his comrades.

When women massively become political the revolution has moved
to a new stage.
                    Vietnamese women at a conference of the Women's
                    International Democratic Federation, Off Our Backs,
                              14 December 1970

We are all Vietnamese.
Line from the poem of 'The one who burns herself for Peace',
Phan Thi Mai, May 1967.
Buddhist student leader

In many ways the oppression of women in Vietnam resembled that in China. There was the same system of forced marriages, women could not inherit, and owed complete obedience to their fathers, their husbands and finally to their eldest son. Confucian ethics supported male authority and condoned the subordination of women. According to the Book of Rites, 'Morals forbid her to step out of her room. Her only business is the kitchen.' Rebellion should be severely suppressed. 'The populace and women,' said Confucius, 'are ignorant, filled with bad instincts, and hard to educate.'⁴ At the bottom of the scale were concubines, like the girl in the poem Kiêu, whose soul wandered in loneliness after her death. During her lifetime a girl who was a concubine held the same rank as the first wife's children. Peasant women maintained an undercurrent of resistance, possibly because they toiled with their men in the fields and were less enclosed than upper-class women. Folk songs record a common resistance to oppression. More than a thousand years ago a twenty-three-year-old girl from a peasant family in Tranhoa called Trieu Thi Thrinh dreamed of a different world. She told her brother: 'My wish is to ride the tempest, tame the waves, kill the sharks, I want to drive the enemy away to save our people. I will not resign myself to the usual lot of women who bow their heads and become concubines.'⁵ Together with her brother she led a peasant uprising against the Chinese feudal lords and when this failed took her own life rather than submit to serfdom. Sometimes folk songs carried an alternative idea of women's importance, or they hinted at the right of the young to love by choice rather than arrangement. When the French invaded Vietnam in the nineteenth century many women joined the fight against them.

With colonialism came poverty and famine. Peasants left the villages and went into the towns or into mines and weaving mills. As always, women experienced not just economic exploitation but their own specific oppression. When they were pregnant they tightened their belts so much that their children were often stillborn. Unmarried mothers and their children were rejected and despised by everyone. They were outside all legal protection. In the towns brothels sprang up. A double standard of sexual morality pervaded. There was no mercy for 'fallen' women but the colonialists expected to make any woman they wanted whore for them. The upper-class Vietnamese colluded in this, ready to offer their wives to the French for the chance of promotion. Rape was barely an offence if the victim was Vietnamese. The sexual violation of a woman seemed nothing amidst the violation of a whole people.

In such circumstances it was impossible really to isolate the 'woman problem' from the expulsion of the French invaders. Small groups of women in the town tried to argue for equal rights in a moderate and reformist sense but they met too many impossible contradictions for such demands to develop into a strong movement. The Indochinese Communist Party, founded in 1930 (renamed Vietnamese Workers' Party in 1951), made it possible to integrate the emancipation of women with class emancipation and the national liberation movement. The 'woman problem' was central from the start. A resolution at the party plenum in 1931 recognized the Vietnamese woman as the 'most persecuted element in society'.[6] The equality of the sexes was seen as among the principal tasks of the revolution. Women who had so little to lose and so much to gain entered the women's organization of the party and resisted first the French, later the Americans. At first they worked underground, infiltrating factories, markets and workers' areas, talking to people about the French and organizing sabotage. Many were killed. One woman who was tortured left a poem written in her own blood on the prison cell before she died:

A rosy-cheeked woman here I am fighting side by side with you men!
On my shoulders weighs the hatred which is common to us.
The prison is my school, its inmates my friends.
The sword is my child, the gun my husband![7]

The unnatural circumstances of the unending war binds people together. The Vietnamese have a long tradition of resistance. Their history is one of continuing colonization and continuing rebellion in which suffering and martyrdom recur with an aching regularity and pain shuffles endlessly back and forth through forgotten time. The pain of the past is before them, the pain of the future is behind them.

Pain is the legacy of the parents to their children. One day a French patrol in the Mekong Delta came upon an old woman who was trying to hide a large pot of rice. They demanded to know where the guerrillas were, hitting her with their rifle butts. The old woman raised her head proudly. "I am old," she said, "and cannot carry a gun. But my children, and there are hundreds of them, all over the country, will kill you all, pirates. I am not afraid of dying." [8] The French, who could carry a gun, killed her, but the old woman was right; they drove out the French pirates only to find an even greater gang arrived: the Americans.

The course of the war has directly affected the lives of the women just as much as the men. Gradually women have been drawn into a situation of complete equality in suffering, and with them have come their children. Such developments did not occur all at once; they have depended upon the nature of warfare and there are obvious differences between the north and the south. During the guerrilla warfare against the French thousands of women in the north took part, but still in roles which were extensions of normal female activities. For example, mothers and wives blocked roads to stop lorries in which the French were taking their men away. They were in charge of supplies to the front and transported ammunition and food. They repaired roads and looked after the wounded, carried messages and provided hide-outs. These were all vital tasks and many women found themselves for the first time responsible for the citadel; but they were not exactly equivalent to the part the men played in terms of strategy and leadership at the front. In the south, probably because there is a less clear distinction between a military front and the rearguard, women have slowly moved into a position of outstanding significance.

The stages in the emergence of women in the south is well illustrated by Mme Binh's own life. When she was eighteen the Second World War ended and the Japanese were expelled. She had vague patriotic ideals. She saw how her people were despised by the French. She was hopeful of independence. When the French came back in 1945 her father took up arms against them. It seemed too bitter now simply to submit again. She herself worked in the resistance movement first as a student and then with the women's organizations and later with groups of intellectuals. No one was clear what to do, they had to learn from experience. Their political activity was non-violent and within the bounds of the law.

'We organized protest marches against the arrest of patriots, we distributed leaflets, we met and discussed.' Within the context of colonial occupation however this was enough to produce violent repression. When she was twenty-four she was imprisoned and tortured by the South Vietnamese under French direction: 'mercenaries who torture their own for money'.[9] In prison she found that 'there were hundreds and hundreds of women with me who did not even know why they were there. They asked what have we done. They did not know when they came but when they left they knew. They left as patriots.'[10] Imperialism is a great educator.

Released at the time of the General Agreement in 1954, she was part of the crowds celebrating freedom when Dien's police opened fire and killed one of her girl friends. In the fifties she and other women still tried to organize peaceful protests, but these became increasingly impossible because marches and protest became simply a guarantee of certain arrest. In 1957 Mme Binh left Saigon and went into the country to live quite literally underground, coming up for air only at night. Under these conditions she bore her first child, while organizing villagers to fight. In the towns women continued to demonstrate:

On 17 December 1960 in Mython sixteen-year-old Truong Thi Bay, carrying a banner, marched at the head of a demonstration. Police shot her dead. Her place was immediately taken by eighteen-year-old Nguyen Thi Be who in her turn was mortally wounded. A third young girl took the lead and was killed. But the demonstrators continued to surge forward; the soldiers lowered their weapons.[11]

The following year the Union of Women for the Liberation of South Vietnam was formed and schoolgirls, college students, along with women workers and intellectuals, joined. Not only have women been fighting alongside men, they themselves have been responsible for liberating villages and setting up new administrations in border areas. Some women have also taken on the leadership of mixed units. For example Nguyen Thi Dinh is the first woman deputy commander-in-chief of the army, as well as president of the Women's Union. Mme Binh is not just an exception.

The totalizing effects of the war continue to make it impossible to distinguish the liberation of women from national liberation. The long-haired army experiences the American presence most intimately. In a population of five million women, 400,000 are now prostitutes, and young girls between 12 and 14 are quite commonly raped. South Vietnamese women learn about the value which western capitalism sets on human life, not only from the bombs that fall on their children at school, from the massacres in which none are spared, but from the toxic gases which wipe out vegetation, and have caused since 1961 an abnormally high percentage of miscarriages, stillbirths and deformed children, born with large heads and small brains. When you carry your child nine months in your womb, bear it in labour with death all around you, only to find the monstrous weapons of imperial technology have assaulted you even there, you carry the war deep inside you.

At a meeting with members of the women's liberation movement in December 1970, Ma Thi-Chu, an executive member of the National Liberation Front of South Vietnam, described various ways in which women became identified with the national liberation struggle.[12] They are involved as guerrillas in sabotage and ambush as well as liaison work. Members of the Women's Union go into areas when the enemy is advancing to get young women to form units to fight. Although the young women take the uniforms away it is invariably old women who return wearing them. They say: 'Why should our daughters be raped by American soldiers; let us old women have a go.' The political side of the liberation movement is also important. Many previously uncommitted women have joined in as the horrors of the war have escalated. Recently women took the bodies of people killed by bombing and chemicals to the heads of provinces. One man became very embarrassed and said it was the fault of the Americans. When one of the women asked him who gave them the right to be there, he had no answer.

In 1970 a particularly flagrant and horrible case of rape drove a group of women in Saigon, who had not been part of the national liberation struggle, to form a Committee of Women fighting for the right to live and the dignity of Vietnamese women. The assertion of the Saigon authorities that the women (a mother and daughter-in-law attacked by American soldiers while they were working in the fields) had died of exhaustion, infuriated the women. As a result they organized a conference demanding the withdrawal of American troops. These are both relatively immediate and spontaneous responses, but the peasant women have an ingenious underground system of long-term organizing.

Ma Thi-Chu told us how they come into town expecting to demonstrate. They arrive imperceptibly in little groups as if they were going to markets, with their scarves round their heads and the older women hobbling along with sticks. Then suddenly they all converge on one spot. In an instant their scarves turn into banners and reveal slogans like 'American Imperialist out of South Vietnam'. The old women's sticks serve as poles. The women divide quickly into groups; one goes to the Head of the Province, another to government representatives, others to various heads of religious bodies. If one group gets their petition through they have to collect all the others. Frequently large numbers of women are arrested and secretly the town population has to be alerted and reinforcements of women brought in from the countryside. If the women aren't released, great crowds of women just stay in the town for days and days. They bring their babies and children and camp outside official buildings making almost continuous noise and chaos – a combination of slogan-chanting and howling children. The South Vietnamese officials quite often give in, receive their petitions and release the prisoners because they don't know how to deal with all these angry women and children.

The Women's Union unites women of quite varied political and religious views and acts as a means of coordinating this kind of political demonstration, though the initiative remains with the women locally. It also tackles 'problems which specifically affect women, like how to build up confidence and initiative when you have been taught to be diffident and submissive'.[13] It also organizes help for those whom the war has left without relations or resources. Its members are very conscious that the kind of liberation which comes through the war is important, but that the task of liberating women once the Americans have gone is an immense and quite different problem. Ma Thi-Chu said that:

> At the last congress members of the Women's Union discussed the importance of making sure that women did fully benefit when victory is eventually won; and the congress determined to avoid the unfortunate experience of Algerian women, who helped in the fight for independence from the French but were unable to achieve their own emancipation.[14]

One of the women delegates in Paris with Mme Binh expressed a similar position to American members of women's liberation:

She said she was sorry that we did not have time to talk about the United States' 'women's struggle'. She went on to say that women in the South had been taking power, and that they know that there is another struggle when the war is over and are quite prepared for it. She expressed great solidarity with the women in the U.S. in their struggles.[15]

The American women did not find that women in the north felt conscious of the need for women to struggle as women after the war was won. This is probably partly because of the nature of the war: women have taken over the administration of the villages, but they don't fight at the front; partly because the party organization is more cohesive and women have therefore taken action through it; and finally because the Communist Party has achieved very substantial improvements in women's conditions, so the women feel a general commitment to the party, although they are not prominent in leadership positions.

As in China land reform was very important. From 1950 women could own equal allotments of land and receive equal wages paid to them rather than to the head of the family. The Constitution guarantees equal rights and equal pay, and maternity leave. The Labour Insurance regulations and other trade union laws provide further protection for women at work. But in practice great problems have arisen in securing the most basic equality for women. Despite official support women were hampered by their own lack of education and their own sense of inferiority and inadequacy. Regardless of party directives women continued to participate in work and politics in a secondary capacity. A few taught in the schools, but they did not run them. In the early fifties, it was still thought that education was actually harmful for a young girl. People said that if young girls learned to write they would spend the time making up love letters. Now, however, nearly all the women can at least read and write and since 1960 there has been an emphasis on higher education. It was very difficult for the older women, some of whom had nine children, to benefit from this, but the young girls have gone on and become trained in engineering and other technical subjects as well as the arts. Factories sometimes have their own song and dance troupes. A young spinner, Tran Bich Dao, after attending a course at the school of Theatrical Arts in Hanoi in 1963, returned to produce a play for the workers in her factory about the first textile strike in 1930. She is interested in Stanislavsky, Brecht and Shakespeare. In the old days people looked down on actresses as immoral; now this has completely changed. Girls like Tran Bich Dao are seen simply as workers with a special skill.

The appearance of skilled women workers is relatively new. In 1954 there were only a few hundred women in industry and all of them unskilled. There were no forewomen or managers. The older women had been in the factories since they were twelve; their health impaired by bad conditions, they found it difficult to learn because their eyes were weak and they were not very strong, and their spirits were very crushed. Now women make up fifty per cent of the labour force but are still behind men in terms of skills. Gradually, as more of the young girls come into industry with a much better education this is evening out.

Within the structure of the party the same problems are reflected. Sometimes women who were appointed to responsible positions resigned because they were overwhelmed with the strain of the new tasks on top of housework and looking after children. In some cases their lack of confidence was not helped by men who made up the leading cadres in the area. They looked on the appointment of women as a threat and were scornful of their ability. The continuation of the war, however, forced even diehards to recognize the necessity for women taking over from the men who were away fighting. By 1960 it was apparent that the 'Five Equals Plan' – equality in fighting, in labour, in party leadership and administration, in management of the society, and in the family – needed to be made more practical. Women's liberation was stressed at the Party Congress in September 1960, as was the need to 'wage a persistent struggle against oppression of and contempt for women which are the last vestiges of the old ideology'.[16]

Last vestiges cling tenaciously however and there was opposition to the formation of special women's groups because the men did not like the idea of women meeting on any terms. In one district called Thanhthuy, to counter the scorn of the men it was suggested that there should be an investigation of the work women were doing in various communes. This inquiry revealed that the women did more work days than men, knew as much about the situation in the fields, received less help, and had much less chance to learn. Then the real reasons for the men's opposition came out into the open. 'With the women at the helm it will be the end of everything,'[17] one party member complained. Resistance was only overcome by a great upheaval in local party democracy. A meeting was held which 540 women attended to describe their difficulties. In the course of this they criticized some leading party officials who had set ideas about the role of women. As a result many women were elected to run co-ops and communes, and self-criticism meetings were held in which the women voiced their complaints.

It is apparent that the combined force of the military situation and the commitment of the Communist Party have both pushed emancipation further, but that much has still to be done. Members of the Women's Union in the north told Charlotte Bunch-Weeks that there were three areas in which they felt the women's revolution was not yet complete: self-image (many women still felt themselves to be inferior to men); participation in politics (positions of responsibility in the government and administration are predominantly held by men); and finally equality in the family. The nuclear family characteristic of western capitalism has never existed in Vietnam, but polygamy was only outlawed by the marriage law of 1960. Until then in the countryside polygamy and child marriage were quite accepted and women weren't allowed to divorce men. Not surprisingly the old attitudes linger on.

Ho Chi Minh introduced the law cautiously and explained its aims in a careful homely way:

> There are people who think that as a bachelor I may not have a perfect knowledge of this question. Though I have no family of my own, yet I have a very big family – the working class throughout the world and the Vietnamese people. From that broad family I can judge and imagine the small one.[18]

He justified the new law on several grounds: the need to involve women in production, the need for harmony between husbands and wives, the need to liberate 'half of society', in order to build socialism. He was obviously wary of alienating the men but committed to women carrying out their own liberation. 'The emancipation of the women must be carried out simultaneously with the extirpation of feudal and bourgeois thinking in men. As for themselves, women should not wait until the directives of the Government and the Party free them but they must rely upon themselves and struggle.'

In some ways the war has created a basis for women's liberation, but in other ways it acts as a limit on what can be achieved. This is well illustrated in welfare facilities which affect women. Possibilities for communal canteens, child care, home services, and nurseries are restricted because military needs have to take priority. But even so under continual bombing nursery facilities exist for fifty per cent of the children in the north, and voluntary cooperative groups called the 'three look-afters' care for the children, cook the rice and shop for other women. In the towns service teams help working women with cooking and sewing. It is difficult to develop these nurseries and kindergartens educationally because they have to be evacuated and moved around all the time to avoid the bombs. It is also impossible for the young men to share this work with the women because they are needed at the front.

Scarcity affects medical services and birth-control methods available. There are very few mechanical devices like diaphragms and the coil, the pill is not available, and though the Women's Union gives out information, the rhythm method is still the most common. Moral persuasion has to be the substitute for contraception. Members of the Women's Union urge girls not to marry until the mid-twenties, and not to have more than five children, though traditional ideas about the value of large families, and concern to keep the population up because of the war, combine to undermine the full force of this propaganda. In the north the women do not seem to feel it necessary to try to break down sexual role distinction. They expect that after the war women will return to light work; in the kindergarten they are unconcerned that the girls sing and dance and the boys fight. Quite often in posters and films women are presented in supportive roles, doing embroidery for their husbands at the front. The contradiction does not seem to be apparent to them.

There is a strong strand of self-denial in Vietnamese culture which has been undoubtedly strengthened by the years of fighting. Like all northerners the North Vietnamese claim the southerners are less hard-working and more lax sexually, but in fact both cultures stress decorum, abstinence, formality and cleanliness. Buddhist respect for transcendence of self combines with a Confucian emphasis on cultivating the rules of appropriate and just behaviour, and the Communist Party's ethics of struggle, sacrifice and social commitment. The Vietnamese possess a great admiration for sexual self-control but are not remotely prudish. Male revolutionaries visiting North Vietnam found that when they tried to get off with Vietnamese girls they met with fits of giggles and the remark that they were too busy building socialism to make love. 'Come back after liberation,' they told them. Susan Sontag in *Trip to Hanoi* describes how men and women work, eat, fight and sleep together without any suggestion of sex. Separate accommodation was provided for her and her male travelling companions, but when one of the American men was ill the young pretty nurse slept in the same room as the guides and drivers, who were all men.

The Vietnamese have learned painfully that other countries have different customs. Susan Sontag's North Vietnamese interpreter told her how shocked he was when he went to Russia and heard people telling dirty jokes. He understood that 'marital fidelity' is not common in the west. Vietnamese observations on foreign sexual customs have rather the quality of the Little Prince arriving on an alien planet. Again it is not possible to see yet whether the ethic of abstinence and fidelity will survive after the war. As it is it is obviously an integral part of the military morale, and provides a needed contrast to the degradation of the brothels for the U.S. troops in the south. In this context ideas of sexual liberation are somehow incongruous.

It would be rash to conclude from this that the Vietnamese are different from all other human beings, and adapt naturally and without suffering to sexual repression and separation from people they love. Mme Binh told Martha Gellhorn:

I can count the days – not weeks, not months – in all these years that I have seen my husband. My children count the time they have seen me or their father in days. People say we are accustomed to this life. But we have the same desires and wants as everyone else. It is difficult to live as we do.[19]

At a meeting of the Women's International Democratic Federation in October 1970 in Budapest, women from America started to talk personally with the Vietnamese delegates:

Out came everyone's pictures of children, grandchildren, husbands, friends, and also the stories. Almost all of them have at least one child who is missing. The Cambodian woman who has not heard from her five children for over three months began to cry. All have children who are guerrillas.[20]

The Vietnamese women were careful to distinguish between American imperialism and 'their friends'. Alice Wolfson kept wanting to cry whenever she was with them. She wanted to just say 'I'm sorry, I'm sorry, I'm sorry.' When she told one of the women from South Vietnam, 'she took me in her arms and said, "This is not a time for tears, this is a time to rejoice because we are together and we are sisters." '21

The Vietnamese women have the sensitivity and kindness which women in women's liberation are trying to discover. In various small ways – offering the American girls their embroidered dresses when they had nothing to wear for a ceremony, offering to share their beds, quite simply and without embarrassment, holding their arm or kissing them with real affection – they expressed their own form of sisterhood. 'Somehow, the ability to show warmth and touch which our culture has crushed in us, is alive and beautiful in them and makes me feel free to respond. . . . They have never . . . lost touch with their humanness.'22

They continue to believe in the capacity of men and women to respond to reason and love, long after such a belief has been made unreasonable by their own experience. A Buddhist nun in Vinh City told American girls from women's liberation that 'She was sure that if women in the U.S. understood what was happening in Vietnam, they would stop it; they would find a way to stop the madness of their country throughout the world.'23 Sadly we have not yet reached such a consciousness among women in western capitalism.

The American girls in Budapest noticed that they were open to but thoughtfully critical of ways of organizing which differed from their own. Alice Wolfson explained the lack of leadership in the women's liberation movement in terms of American individualism and the feeling that collectivity was an important and necessary stage. 'Madame Cao thought for a minute and then said, "Yes, but collectivity which destroys the potential of the individual is not good collectivity. It is necessary to reach a compromise." '24 It is rather as if we were standing at two sides of a mirror.

The Vietnamese representatives in London politely call women's liberation 'the beginnings of thought'. To them we don't go far enough, while to us it seems that their definition of women's liberation is too narrow and does not touch many areas of consciousness which appear to us as integral parts of our subjection. We cannot believe that they don't feel as we do. Alice Wolfson is puzzled and honest:

> My fears about speaking have lessened. The Vietnamese are so helpful and they are so willing to accept that struggle . . . on any level . . . is good . . . that they have made us feel as though we are their equals. In comparison I am struck by the arrogance and imperialism of our movement. We are so quick to condemn people if their consciousness is not where ours is. We assume that the American reality . . . exists in some form everywhere, and this simply is not true. I must think more about this.[25]

So must we all.

## Cuba

> If we were asked what the most revolutionary thing is that the Revolution is doing, we would answer that it is precisely this – the revolution that is occurring among the women of our country. . . . If anyone had ever asked me if I considered myself prejudiced in regard to women, I would have said absolutely not. . . . I believed myself to be quite the opposite. . . . We are finding that . . . this potential force is superior to anything that the most optimistic of us ever dreamed of; we say that perhaps at heart, unconsciously, something of bias or underestimation existed.
>
> Fidel Castro, The Santa Clara Speech,
> 9 December 1966

> We know that it is not enough to transform the production relations that in ideology, customs in the superstructure, we can go on being bourgeois and reactionary . . . and in our case underdeveloped.
>
> Edmundo Desnoes

In the 1960s the Cuban film *Lucia* was made. It tells the story of three different 'Lucias' struggling for liberation in very different historical circumstances. While her brother fights Spanish colonialism, Lucia in 1868 is courted by a Spanish gentleman during the war of independence. Even though he has deceived her, as he already has a wife in Spain, she rebels against the life of tea parties, church going and false respectability of the Cuban upper-class girls and runs away to join him. But when she takes her lover to her brother's hideout the Spaniard betrays them both and in the battle that follows her brother is killed. As she is dragged away a poor old woman comforts her. Tears stream down both their faces. The fate of the first Lucia is one of individual tragedy. She is very much a helpless pawn and it is the men who fight.

In the 1930s, the second Lucia, in contrast, herself participates in the movement against the Machado dictatorship. When Batista takes over, most of her companions settle easily into the bureaucracy – but her lover goes on fighting and is killed finally by the police. She is left to wander hopelessly in the street, pregnant, with nowhere to live, carrying a suitcase. Though she can participate there is no place for her own specific needs and the hope of liberation fades with Batista in power.

The third Lucia is, significantly, a black woman living in the country, married to a young white farm worker who drives a lorry. The focus of conflict has shifted. This Lucia does not have to struggle to be allowed to love, she has to confront the contradiction between her own sexuality and the attitudes of the man she loves. Their love is gay, passionate, and at first carefree but it is overshadowed by his almost pathological jealousy. This jealousy is part of the machismo of the Latin male and is deeply hostile to the smallest sign of female independence. He locks her in the house to prevent her from learning to read and write from a boy of fourteen. She goes finally to one of the women leaders in the village and explains tearfully that she loves her husband but can't go on living this way. She leaves him with a note in her newly learned handwriting: 'I am not a slave.' Separate they are both miserable and long for each other. She returns and explains that she wants him but wants her freedom too. Though he is overjoyed to see her he still has to try to possess her. They start fighting again almost immediately. A little girl watches from a distance, not comprehending at first, and then, slowly realizing what is happening, bursts into laughter. The third Lucia has not won, but she is fighting in areas the others never even entered. The film hints that the fourth Lucia will not encounter such problems.

The film not only raises questions about the nature of women's liberation in Cuba now, it indicates something of the narrow alternatives women faced before the revolution. There were really only three possibilities for women: to be a slave to a man in the house, become a mother, or be an object of pleasure. When the middle-class girl was handed over from father to husband, her virginity was part of the contract; an already used object was of no value to her purchaser. The other side of the coin was the poor women touting for trade in Old Havana or along the waterfront in Santiago. In the countryside the women of the camps toiled in the fields as well as at home, bearing endless children and looking fifty when they were twenty-five.

Cuba was a deeply divided society. There was a great split between rich and poor, between Havana and the rest of Cuba, between black and white, between men and women. There were a whole series of little colonies within the colony, strata upon strata fattening upon one another, and on top the ruling minority of government officials, army officers, mill- and plantation-owners and large businessmen, who were bound together as an elite by family tradition and a semi-feudal mentality. In Havana the poor lived in ramshackle slums, with no running water or lavatories, with terrible overcrowding and high rents. Many of the men were permanently underemployed, the women struggling to make do, with vast families of eighteen sometimes in tiny units divided by thin partitions, so that sometimes they were even cooking in the yard. Working-class women were despised even by their own men: 'Even her own class looked down on her and under-rated her. Not only was she underestimated, exploited and looked down upon by the exploiting classes but even within her own class she was the object of numerous prejudices.'[26]

If anything the peasants lived somewhere below them in palm tree huts and the earth for a floor. Disease, malnutrition and a high mortality rate were common. The poorest of the poor '*desalajos*' squatted homeless by the highway. Blacks and mulattoes were invariably among the poorest. Even here there was a hierarchy according to skin colour, with Haitians and Jamaicans at the bottom. As for the women, they suffered the combined oppressions of class, sex and race. A young black woman might be in high demand as a prostitute or a cabaret dancer but she rated for little else.

Nonetheless, in all the rebellions against slavery and against Spanish colonialism women took part. Maceo's mother and wife were active. 'Canducha', daughter of the man who wrote the Cuban national anthem, rode proudly through the streets of Bayamo in 1868 carrying the patriots' banner. A slave, Rosa Castellanos – 'La Bayavese' – joined her husband in the 1868 insurrection. There is a long tradition of the heroic, long-suffering woman in Cuba. Catholicism and machismo from the Spanish colonizers combined with slavery to produce a kind of matriarchy in which the older women were responsible for holding things together. Afro-Spanish culture never succeeded in internalizing sexual guilt and the corollary of the stereotyped feckless male and the cult of the noble tragedy of mother and grandmother meant that a particular kind of female assertion was acceptable. However, this has meant that the resistance to feminism has taken specific forms which are by no means identical with the responses in European protestant countries and in North America. Slavery and the interaction between sexual and racial dominance has further complicated the manner in which ideas about the liberation of women have emerged.

The demand for equal rights came with the war against Spain in the 1860s, when a woman called Ana Betancourt demanded equality for women at an assembly of leaders of the independence movement. In the early twentieth century a suffragette style feminist movement arose; in 1934 Cuban women got the vote, and other formal equalities followed. These served really to highlight the contrast between legal equality and economic and cultural subordination. The insurrection against Batista brought women who were active into situations in which a machismo-defined femininity appeared absurd and irrelevant. Haydée Santamaria was among the group who attacked the Moncada barracks in 1953. After she had been captured her brother's eyes and her fiancé's testicles were brought to her in a box by Batista's police to get information from her. Her response was, 'If you have done this to them and they haven't spoken, how can I?' On her release she fought with the rebel forces in the Sierra Maestre.[27]

Although a women's Red Army battalion was formed, named after the mother of the famous nineteenth-century independence fighter, Maceo, the conditions of guerrilla fighting did not encourage the emergence of women. Among the guerrillas the female minority mainly did traditional tasks like cooking and nursing. It was something of an issue how far they were equal members. In his autobiography Che recalls a young girl called Oniria asking in an anguished voice if she could vote when a man was being tried for killing another accidentally. The rough and ready democracy of a guerrilla military unit in Cuban conditions inevitably meant almost complete male control. This particular aspect of the present remained unfreed from the past. There were a few individual exceptions like

Lydia and Clodmira whom Guevara mentions specially as messengers. They obviously knew themselves as exceptions: there was a kind of boastfulness in Lydia's defiant courage, a high-handedness typical of those who become successful and distinguished themselves as individuals from oppressed groups. Like other women who have operated in a completely male world she felt the need to prove herself continuously. Guevara describes the complicated reactions of the men:

Cubans were not accustomed to taking orders from a woman. . . . Her infinite courage was such that male couriers avoided her. I remember very well the opinion – a mixture of admiration and resentment – of one of them, who told me: 'That women has more [balls] than Maceo but she's going to get us all killed. The things she does are mad. This is no time for games.'[28]

Both Lydia and Clodmira died fighting. Their only possibility for liberation in such a context was to become more manly than the men. In the towns, under normal living conditions the men were less suspicious and women became involved rather more, acting again as messengers because they were less suspect, and as saboteurs.

Though these individual women obviously shook the traditional concepts of femininity to which the men in the movement still adhered, it was very easy to distinguish them from other women who continued to live in the old way. It is quite easy for men to respect and grudgingly admire particular women who achieve a kind of sub-male status in exceptional conditions. It is a different matter for men to reorientate their ideas about all women, and question the world as seen only through men's eyes.

As a first step the Federation of Cuban Women, set up in 1960 after the revolution, began a drive against illiteracy, partly so that women could enter in production and partly to enable them to participate fully in political and social life. The federation was not formed as a result of a strong women's movement and consequently very elaborate attempts have been made to ensure that ideas about what should be done come from the bottom as well as the top. Irina Trapote and Ana Ma Navarro, two young members of the federation, described its organization to members of women's liberation in London in October 1970.[29]

The federation has a million members and is led by a woman called Vilma Espin who played an active part in the struggle against

Batista. There are several layers of committees, a national central committee, six provincial committees, as well as regional, municipal and 'block' committees. Each level elects representatives for the plenary session where the work for the year is decided upon. Each local leader or '*dirigente*' is elected by about fifty women and has a commission of about five women to plan work in specific areas like education or social work. Despite this constitution however the federation undoubtedly shares the problem of all political structures in Cuba in effecting communication from the base to the centre in practice, because a large-scale popular movement has been a post-revolutionary creation. The federation tries to involve women at first in practical work, organizing child-care facilities or some other locally needed amenity, because they won't go to political meetings. Slowly the attempt is made to develop a revolutionary political consciousness among the women who take part. This goes along with measures like the same military training for boys and girls. At school girls do guard duty as well as the boys and there are women officers in the army. The aim is to involve women in the world outside the home.

The desperate needs of the Cuban economy mean that the emphasis on women taking part in production is as much because their labour is needed as it is part of the liberation of women. The familiar problem of male/female segregation at work arises here again. Though there are women in every branch of the economy, the largest number are in light industry, education, day nurseries and the food industry, which are generally accepted as women's work. There are, too, areas in which only women are employed – child-care work and primary-school teaching. The Cuban girls interviewed in London were not particularly concerned about this. The continuing existence of jobs which are extensions of women's traditional role in the family presents a problem which is distinct from the other related question about the extent to which emancipation means doing heavy and hard work. It seems to me that such work is not always skilled, and it is absurd that human beings who are physically weaker should exhaust themselves proportionally more than others who are stronger physically. Physique rather than gender should be the criterion. However, in other cases work which is heavy *and* skilled should not necessarily be exclusive to men, because if women are not free to choose, male superiority will be then reinforced.

American women members of the Venceremos brigade were insulted because they weren't allocated to cutting cane. The Cuban girls were amused by this kind of feminism because they know what hard work it is and are relieved to collect rather than cut. But they admitted that although most of them collapsed exhausted, a few continued. Cane-cutting, like some other jobs, carries a strong male-orientated sense of value. This could be overcome in a wealthier society than Cuba which did not need to keep in mind the immediate need always to increase production, by alternating male/female roles and accepting inefficiency and a slower working rate. In the short term in Cuba this isn't possible so they accept that men carry on working at heavy physical tasks. Underdevelopment limits the possibilities of social experimenting in small and particular practical ways.

In other forms of skilled work however there is officially no problem about women participating and the Cubans are justifiably proud of what has been achieved so far. There have been several federation campaigns to break down old ideas of what it is suitable for women to do. Now in practice there are women technicians, motor-car mechanics, refrigerator-engineers, tractor-drivers, city-planners, dentists, doctors, reporters, publishers. But there is still resistance from male workers and officials to women in industry, or in key posts of responsibility. Sometimes women are simply rejected in jobs for other reasons or they get work nobody else wants. Forced to employ women, male supervisors can take it out on them by trying to humiliate them with particularly arduous work which they won't do very well, while boasting that this will 'give them a chance to find out what hard work really is'.[30]

In other cases the resistance comes from families or husbands, who are opposed to young women going off to train. It is of the utmost importance in all these conflicts that the women have the authority of the revolution behind them. Elizabeth Sutherland in *The Youngest Revolution* quotes a young painter called Tomas as saying, 'The changes have been traumatic for Cuban men. The hard thing is that they cannot legitimately oppose the changes. A woman who goes to work or on guard-duty is doing it for the Revolution. The men would have to be counter-revolutionaries to oppose it.'[31]

This means that within the bounds of economic underdevelopment and Marxist traditions of female emancipation there is a clear commitment to the liberation of women. Castro believes that while sexual and racial oppression cannot be ended within capitalism, the existence of a socialist ownership of the means of production does not automatically secure their abolition. These groups have a further struggle against their specific oppression, a revolution within the revolution:

> Among the functions considered to belong to women was – almost exclusively – that of having children. Naturally reproduction is one of the most important of women's functions in human society. But it is precisely this function, relegated by nature to women, which has enslaved them to a series of chores within the home.[32]

Thus the Cubans, like the Russians in the 1920s and the Chinese today, are committed to trying to socialize the household tasks, and attempting to stop individual women being exclusively responsible for their own children. Immediately though there is an economic contradiction. Women's labour is needed in production; it is politically desirable to free women from the home. Who, then, is to do their domestic work and care for the children, and how is money to be found for communal facilities? Here material circumstances are interlocked with traditional reactionary ideas of the woman's place being in the home. Vilma Espin has commented on this dilemma:

> Obtaining the participation of women in work requires overcoming numerous obstacles . . . of a material nature such as day nurseries, workers' dining-rooms, student dining-rooms, semi-boarding schools, laundries and other social services which would make it easier for the housewife to work.[33]

Lack of such facilities can mean that women are trained and then can't work. As a short-term measure the Women's Federation is thinking of part-time work. Meanwhile, slowly the conditions are being created which will make this only a stop-gap measure. A woman automatically gets paid for a maternity leave of six weeks before and six weeks after delivery, and for the first year of her child's life, if she wants to work, her hours are reduced. Most towns now have free nursery facilities for children from six weeks to school age. Every new housing community is built with well equipped centres and there are nursery schools in factories and work camps. Besides play and education the children also receive three meals and snacks and medical and dental care. The attempt is also being made to involve school-aged children in education away from home to relieve the mothers. Besides boarding schools, usually on a weekly basis, there are semi-live-in situations where children are involved in their own activities away from home most of the day. In the Youth Organization, 12–17-year-olds combine study, work and community living on a project basis which leaves them quite independent of the family.

In this way some of the mothers' traditional tasks are taken over by various agencies. In other ways too the revolution has changed people's attitudes to the family. Divorce is now a much more casual matter than before. Couples are often separated from each other for quite long periods because of work or studying, or visits to the camps in the country. But on the other hand women still accept the idea that they are responsible for the housework. Nor are the Cubans consciously trying to create new forms of the family. The girls who spoke to the members of women's liberation said the group-living on the Isle of Pines was not regarded as experimental social living but as a practical way of increasing production. When they were asked what they thought of the idea of living in communes they giggled at first and implied it was not among their priorities. Then they answered very seriously that it was not because they did not think that living in a communal way did not help the revolution. They said they thought small family-type communes were unnecessary. Since the revolution, villages and towns had become real communities – there was no need to create artificially lots of little communes within them. They saw the sense of community coming from sharing common aims and work rather than growing out of numerous mini-social units. They believed it was the general needs of revolutionary society which should define personal living-styles, not the other way round.

Insistence on small communes might well be an obsession peculiar to the isolated urban living conditions of advanced capitalism, but they were simply dismissive of the practical question of how to distribute household tasks equitably. Despite the facilities for children these still fall on Cuban women. The Cuban girls stressed that people were thinking in much wider terms than their own family; they weren't dominated by old ties from working for people outside their own circle. This attempt to direct the inner personal units of living outwards is obviously important. The question is really whether it is sufficient without some attempt to transform the manner in which men, women and children interlock in the family. The traditional family acts as a socializing agency and carries the values of the pre-revolutionary society, not so much by what is explicitly said but by what is implicitly practised. A small girl at school may learn that women must enter social and political life on the same basis as men, but at home without question mother cooks and stays with her and father goes out. A woman may hear Castro's speech on the struggle of women at the point of reproduction, but deep inside her she knows she is attractive to her man when he controls her.

One of the most exciting features of the Cuban Revolution is the manner in which the demands of active female sexuality are being raised, and with them the subterranean formations of consciousness which remain untouched by Marxist theory. The painter Tomas, who would seem to have a shrewd eye for these matters, told Elizabeth Sutherland that he thought 'the most interesting question in Cuba today is the new relationship of men and women.'[34] Abortions are free on demand as long as you report to a hospital within a month of becoming pregnant. But the fact that the family is notified deters some girls. Contraceptives are easily available. Women use diaphragms and an intra-uterine loop called 'anillo'. The pill is still regarded as dangerous. Most women still don't use contraceptives, however, and suspicion runs deep. The party line wavers – *Granma* has carried birth control information but they don't actively disseminate it, partly because they don't want to upset old prejudices, but also because population control is seen as an issue used by overdeveloped countries to continue their control over poorer under-developed places, to prevent social redistribution. Fundamentally people's resistance to contraceptives comes from opposition to women controlling their own bodies and minds. Women themselves fear the responsibility of such intervention in their own natures.

Old ideas of masculinity can mean that a man feels threatened by any extension of female control which he can only see in terms of his own loss. In Cuba babies are still the proof of 'manhood'. When a wife gets the 'anillo', the man may say 'Me molesta', although he can't feel it physically, and get her to take it out. But these matters are beyond the bounds of the party line. Castro told Lee Lockwood in 1965:

Traditions and customs can clash somewhat with new social realities, and the problem of sexual relations in youth will require more scientific attention. But the discussion of that problem has not yet been made the order of the day. Neither customs nor traditions can be changed easily, nor can they be dealt with superficially. I believe that new realities, social, economic, and cultural, will determine new conditions and new concepts of human relations.[35]

This is all very true in the long term but in the short term we can all get pregnant. Immediate attitudes are pragmatic and varied. The Federation of Cuban Women predictably go cautiously. For this reason some people told Elizabeth Sutherland: 'The federation isn't on the same wavelength as the younger generation.' The young Cuban women who came to London in autumn 1970 were troubled about how to present sex education in the schools. They asked us for 'serious' books or pamphlets on the subject. There are so many different levels of sexual moralities, from the old peasant women who still don't like their daughters going out, to young girls from workers' families in Havana who are concerned that they get their allowances as wives, to young militants on the Isle of Pines who are against casual sex and for serious relationships, to sophisticated black intellectuals conscious of the interactions between sexuality and racism.[36]

But behind all these levels there is machismo which continually sets the limits for female sexual liberation. For example, in 1960–61 there was tremendous propaganda made of communist boarding schools for school-children where the girls' virginity was to be sacrificed in an orgy of red free love. This accounts for the sexual segregation in the 'becados' which made Allen Ginsberg explode in incomprehension in 1966: 'What's your program for these kids – masturbation?'[37] But the reality of machismo is a tradition of the predatory male without ties who uses women sexually and the Cubans are afraid that 'free love' will only be interpreted as freedom for the men to return to their own habits. Castro personally has kept the situation very open. He's well known for jokes about marriage and his personal opinions carry a lot of weight. On one issue at least machismo and the official attitudes are in agreement: homosexuality is an offence in Cuba. It occupies a special horror spot in the psyches of Cuban males. Castro tries nobly. He admitted a great lack of knowledge, that it would be unfair to treat anyone badly for something they couldn't control, that some homosexuals might accept revolutionary ideas; but he shares the common prejudice. He said to Lockwood:

And yet we would never come to believe that a homosexual could embody the conditions and requirements of conduct that would enable us to consider him a true Revolutionary, a true Communist militant. A deviation of that nature clashes with the concept we have of what a militant communist must be. . . . In the conditions under which we live, because of the problems which our country is facing, we must inculcate our youth with the spirit of discipline, of struggle, of work. . . . This attitude may or may not be correct, but it is our honest feeling.[38]

This passage carries one hope – his obvious honesty. He makes it clear that his approach to the question comes from his own perspective and from the immediate needs of the Cuban economy for repression of eros. The dangers, though, are all too evident. Because of their practical problems, the lack of a revolutionary theoretical tradition and the force of old ideas which were intensely suspicious of pleasure in sex without reproduction, the Cubans slip often into an exhortatory moralism in official statements which is not reflected in personal conversation or in personal life.

Both revolutionary homosexuality and active female heterosexuality imply the redefinition of masculinity – 'revolutionary' masculinity included. At this point the most revolutionary of comrades become paternalist. Women told Elizabeth Sutherland: 'The idea that sex is for the woman's pleasure as well as the man's – that is the taboo of taboos. . . . Less change has taken place in this area than any other.'[39] A few men were beginning to recognize the political implications of this for men as well as women – Tomas, for instance: 'Cuban men will have to find new ways in which to be men.'[40]

None of us know how this is to be done. The Cubans face such rapid and uneven development it is hard for them to decide what to accept or reject. A most complicated example of this is the battle of the mini-skirt in Cuba. This was waged at several levels, from the apolitical conventional girl who thought they were immoral, and wouldn't wear one until the revolution told her to, to a tendency in the party, which was point-blank opposed to anything western, to old ideas of modesty. There is not the same confusion about other aspects of the fashion and beauty industry. There are beauty shops even in the mountains on the Isle of Youth, though their presence is still not as ubiquitous as in western capitalism. The official attitude is: 'We want all our women to be beautiful. Before the revolution only the rich had the time or money to go to beauty shops. The revolution gives everyone the advantage of having this opportunity.'[41]

Indeed, make-up for young Cuban women is often the symbol of defiant liberation from the traditional control of parents and the home, in contrast to its role as an integrator into passivity in capitalist countries. However, in another sense female decoration continues to be ambiguous because for centuries women have been dependent on men choosing them. And in Cuba male decoration, long hair and modern clothes are frowned upon as decadent.

There is a welter of contradictions here. Elizabeth Sutherland summarizes:

All in all, the status of women and sexual relations in Cuba was a curious but not so surprising mixture of past and present, and future; of Revolution and conservatism; of the situation in some highly industrialized countries and the situation in some very undeveloped ones. Giant steps had been taken and were being taken towards the liberation of women. But if that liberation is defined as freedom from old roles and definitions, with full availability of alternative life patterns, then it would be more accurate to define the changes which have taken place thus far as the basis for a total revolution rather than the revolution itself . . .[42]

. . . Even if the men who ran the country were willing, Cuba's economic and political needs inhibited a revolution in certain areas, mostly outside work. The conquest of material underdevelopment had top priority; politically, people had enough gripes about things like rations for the regime not to take an unpopular position on gut issues like femininity and masculinity.[43]

However, it would be a mistake to think that no women were critical or attempting to create positive alternatives now in Cuba. Not surprisingly it tends to be the more privileged, like the university students whom Elizabeth Sutherland met in Havana, who are most exposed to the clash of incongruities, like the coexistence of 'free love' with semi-primitive ignorance, and the vacuum in official theory before matters which concern them profoundly. In 1967 a document circulated in Havana University which carries a note reminiscent of the revolutionary discussions in the Soviet Union in the twenties, and also relates very closely to the demands of women's liberation in the western capitalist countries:

Economic independence is not enough. It is not a matter of a woman being able to pay her way but . . . of being able to transform her attitude toward life . . . the problem will not be solved simply by the incorporation of the woman in work. Extracting her from the role of housewife will not automatically change her attitude toward life. A woman working for the collectivity can continue to view problems through the prism of subordination and passivity. Change of occupation is only the basis for the transformation of women . . . her whole attitude must change. It is a process of personal realization, which does not lie merely in dedicating herself to a creative task but in shifting the centre of interest from the limits of one's emotional life and events within the nuclear family, to a much broader area . . . which goes beyond individual interest, the interest centred in social activity. A woman realizes herself as a person when her viewpoint transcends egoistic interest.

The true feminine struggle is the rejection of all those childhood teachings, all those family pressures during adolescence, and even the dominant social thinking which affects her as an adult . . . the idea of femininity, of womanhood, as meaning the dedication of one's life to finding and keeping a companion generally, at the price of being his satellite.[44]

Like the black people in Cuba, women face the particular subjection of a group colonized within a colony. The forms of possession vary but in essence they remain the same. The revolution within the revolution means seeing through your own eyes, learning to touch the external world with your own hands, translating experience in your own mind, shaping sounds, making your own words and dissolving the mask which is not just imposed but has grown into your own skin through centuries of being directed by someone else.

It requires a great act of revolutionary cultural creation – which is only possible through the possibility for human growth which comes through conscious combination.

## Algeria

They will ask you about menstruation: say it is a hurt. So keep apart from women in their menstruation, and go not near them till they be cleansed. . . . Your women are your tilth so come into your tillage how you choose. . . . The men should have precedence over them. When you divorce women, and they have reached their prescribed time, then keep them kindly, or let them go in reason, but do not keep them by force to transgress.

The Chapter of the Heifer, The Koran

The woman who sees without being seen frustrates the colonizer. The men's words were no longer law. The women were no longer silent.

Frantz Fanon, A Dying Colonialism

One of the trench-coated young men had taken charge of the column; there was blood on his trenchcoat: he had been carrying the deputy leader. He was giving orders to two other young men who wore the civilian blue trenchcoat that was a uniform of the F.L.N. hierarchy . . .

'Get the women and children to the Métro at Sevre-Babylone. We'll double back into the Boulevard Saint-Germain and draw them after us.' He was speaking in French. Then he gave them his blessing in Arabic: 'Barake.'

The parties divided but Nefissa marched with the men.

'You should go with the women,' Hanna said. 'I'll take you to them.'

'I won't go with them. They are just wives. I'm a militant.'

The new leader turned to ask what was the matter. He had a young face, pock-pitted and sad.

'This girl refuses to go with the women,' Hanna told him.

'How dare you speak of me like that?' asked Nefissa. 'You who are not even one of us. I am a militant of the F.L.N. and my place is with the column.'

'Go with the women,' the leader told Nefissa.

'No,' she said. 'I'm a militant. My place is with the column.'

'Your place is to obey orders,' said the leader.

'You are not of my cell,' Nefissa said. 'I don't take orders from strangers.'

'I can't force you to leave,' the leader said. 'You will have to look after her,' he added, speaking directly to Hanna. 'Barake.'

'I'll do my best,' Hanna promised.

'I can look after myself,' Nefissa said. 'I am a militant of my cell.' But the leader had turned away . . .

. . . 'This is a regulation search,' the commandant said. 'Made before witnesses. It must be thorough.'

When he raised Nefissa's skirt above the tops of her stockings, Hanna started forward and felt a hand upon his shoulder. There were two flics standing behind him. They were laughing, but they had drawn pistols.

'Remember that you are almost a French citizen now,' said one of them, a brigadier. 'You can watch if you haven't seen it all before, but don't move.'

'But it's disgusting,' Hanna said. 'Disgusting and degrading.'

'Don't move,' the brigadier said.

Nefissa screamed once; she was straining to keep her thighs closed as the commandant's hand quested beneath her buttocks. The commandant stepped back and hit her twice between the knees with the heel of his hand. When her legs gave he thrust his right hand into her crutch. Nefissa squirmed, then whimpered.

'There's something hard there,' the commandant said. 'And this time it isn't a penis. I know you Muslim virgins. It makes a convenient receptacle for everything – isn't that so, mademoiselle?'

Nefissa said something into the wall and cried out and said something more.

'Don't give me that, dear,' the commandant said. 'I was acquainted with the facts of life before you were born.'

The commandant removed his hand for an instant and tugged: Nefissa's briefs fell about her ankles: they were white, as though in token of surrender.

'Now we can resume the search,' the commandant said.

Then Nefissa stepped free of the restricting nylon and elastic; she kicked backwards and caught the commandant on the shin with her sharp leather heel; the inspector said 'Merde' and caught her by the ankle: his unfettered right hand thrust upwards between her legs.

The commandant grunted and extracted something from between Nefissa's legs: he allowed the bloody cylinder of cotton wool to fall to the pavement.

'The investigation is completed,' the commandant announced. He took the handkerchief from his right sleeve and wiped his fingers; then he returned it to his sleeve.

'You may go now, children,' he told them. 'You see that you have nothing to fear from French justice as long as you are innocent.'

> Francis Fytton, Excerpts from 'Manifestation', a short
> story based on the demonstration for an independent Algeria,
> *Stand*, vol. 6, no. 3

Nefissa's encounter with the forces of order took place in the context of a larger demonstration which Francis Fytton reports in his story 'Manifestation'. It occurred on the evening of 17 October 1961 and was part of a whole series of violent instances which marked the course of the war in France. More generally it is a metaphor of the way in which Algerian women in the F.L.N. encountered their colonizers. Nefissa distinguishes herself from the 'wives'; she rejects womanhood because this implies passivity. Her consciousness comes as a militant, by identifying with the liberation movement, not from her femaleness. To the men though she remains a woman. With the 'flics' her submission is brought home to her. Under cover of routine and legality they humiliate her racially as an Algerian and sexually as a woman. She is completely helpless. Her only act of aggression is the traditionally feminine gesture with her shoe. Hanna is impotent. He cannot protect her as a 'man' by his own definition. Emasculated by the white men he is forced to collude with them in viewing her humiliation. He is included among the other men – he observes. He is congratulated on his desire to be French – he collaborates. Commitment to the F.L.N. is the only way in which he can regain dignity and self-respect. But Nefissa is stranded by her sex. Even if Hanna had been of her cell he would not have menstruated. Her sex, her thighs, the hand of the flic thrusting inside, the tampax, her whimper. 'They will ask you about menstruation – say it is a hurt.' It is her hurt – a hurt she holds between her legs, hobbling down the road while the flic wipes the blood from his hand.

The French colonization of Algeria held many ambiguities. The colonizers had many faces. The official façade was of progress, enlightenment, western culture. Official colonialism was shocked by the situation of Algerian women – veiled, confined in the home, without any say in whom they would marry, completely subordinate to men. The French made laws against polygamy and child marriages, campaigned against the veil and said girls should go to school. They started to erode with these western liberal concepts of emancipation certain points in traditional Algerian culture which had kept women completely subordinate. 'Emancipation', however, was completely imposed from outside – it was part of the take-over bid, part of the modernization of the firm.

Fanon describes how European employers put pressure on the man in industry. They were not content to own him at work, they extended their occupation into his home. They asked him if his wife wore the veil, if he took her out. Finally they suggested that he should bring her to the office or factory party:

The firm being one big family, it would be unseemly for some to come without their wives, you understand? Before this formal summons, the Algerian sometimes experiences moments of difficulty. If he comes with his wife, it means admitting defeat, it means 'prostituting' his wife, exhibiting her, abandoning a mode of resistance. On the other hand, going alone means refusing to give satisfaction to the boss; it means running the risk of being out of a job.[45]

There is something at once infuriating and enticing about the passivity and fatalism of the Algerian woman for the colonizer. They recognized that the older women possessed a particular kind of power to keep things as they were, and that the younger women's acceptance of their men as masters prevented Algerian men from really bowing to their colonizers. The Algerian man remained sure of his manhood because he controlled his own women so completely. Fanon describes the significance of the veil in the psyche of the colonizers. Here the hidden reality of exploitation and domination appears. The veil persistently appears as a symbol of rape. 'Emancipation' to the European male meant the possession by western culture of the Algerian woman. He wanted her to see herself through his eyes, to decorate herself according to his standards. He wanted to give her the facial movements, the language, the façade of his own women. Then he wanted to take her. In the private world of sexuality she became again one of the subjected – Algerian. The European women connived indirectly in this, because while the Algerian aspired to be like them their superiority was confirmed. For the Algerian girl to become Europeanized meant sometimes a relative freedom. She moved into a territory marked by different boundaries. But essentially she exchanged one subordination for another and colonization scored a tiny but significant victory:

Every new Algerian woman unveiled announced to the occupier an Algerian society whose systems of defence were in the process of dislocation, open and breached. Every veil that fell, every body that became liberated from the traditional embrace of the haik, every face that offered itself to the bold and impatient glance of the occupier, was a negative expression of the fact that Algeria was beginning to deny herself and was accepting the rape of the colonizer.[46]

The Algerian man, regardless of his political sympathies, sensed this. Cut off from the normal ties of the traditional family the

237

Algerian workers in France represented the profound uprooting of colonialism. At home the women were left to hold things together. The colonized man became somehow extraneous. The Algerian in Paris, rather like the Irish immigrant in London, was living in predominantly masculine company and in an alien culture. He lived in poor parts of the town or in the corrugated iron shacks which developed around building sites in the suburbs. He was restless, aggressive, easily insulted. He was filled with self-hatred in a society where superiority and dignity belonged to his colonizers.

The Algerian in his fantasy became a thief at night. He tried to steal back his manhood from the European woman because he was not able to confront her man. He was obsessed with revenge. He tantalized himself with sneaking encounters on the street at night, enjoying her fear as he closed the gap between them, walking faster with her sliding into the wall. He enjoyed too the vehemence of her rejection. He felt a momentary elusive sense of power as he cornered her and forced her loathing and contempt into his face. He waited patiently for consummation, when he could hold a white woman down as object, reduce her far below any Algerian woman, when his hands on her neck and mouth stifled her screams, and his hands forced her legs apart and her justice was powerless to save her. But this stolen sexual vengeance cheated the colonized man terribly. He realized he was becoming even more enmeshed in the structure of his oppressors. He was a cultural parasite. As the movement against the French became more violent, his allegiance became clearly polarized. His conception of revenge became politicized. The liberation movement was intimately related to hope of self-esteem and the qualities he identified with his manhood. The role of Algerian woman was most ambiguous. He wanted to reclaim her rather than liberate her.

The decision to involve women in 1955 was not taken easily. It was a product rather of urgency and necessity. They had helped the guerrillas in the mountains, but they had not borne real responsibility themselves. At first the wives of militants were approached, then widows or divorced women. Then young unmarried girls persisted in volunteering and finally forced the F.L.N. to accept support from all women. The women, still veiled, operated as messengers within the Kasbah, but as activities shifted into the European part of the town the veil made her conspicuous. It was unusual for a young veiled Algerian woman to leave the Kasbah. Because of political commitment she started to go unveiled. She appeared as a European, flirting with the French soldiers and facing the insults and obscenities of Algerian men as she stood watch outside a meeting. From 1956 she was carrying bombs, revolvers, grenades. She had a false identity, and was responsible for people's lives. Her actions and bearing mattered vitally. She was thrown out of her normal enclosures.

Fanon describes how her relationship to her own body changes. She walked differently now she was no longer contained and effaced by traditional clothing. But it has been by her own choice. It is frightening but it is not rape:

> She has the anxious feeling that something is unfinished, and along with this a frightful sensation of disintegrating. The absence of the veil distorts the Algerian woman's corporal pattern. She quickly has to invent new dimensions for her body, new means of muscular control. She has to create for herself an attitude of unveiled-woman-outside. She must overcome all timidity, all awkwardness (for she must pass for a European) and at the same time be careful not to overdo it, not to attract notice to herself. The Algerian woman who walks stark naked into the European city relearns her body, re-establishes it in a totally revolutionary fashion.[47]

When the authorities started to search women without veils, the women wore veils again as a conscious political step. The symbolism of the veil was transformed. Originally the distinguishing mark between wives and concubines in the towns, it became the emblem of the Algerian woman's confinement, and finally a revolutionary instrument.

Political activity changed the woman's relationship to her family. She was forced to travel to other towns, sleep in strange places. It was only because of the urgency of the political situation that fathers and husbands were not overcome with shame. They knew that their acquaintances were sharing a similar experience. Young girls started to admire the women who suffered death and who were imprisoned for the liberation movement. They not only took off their veils and put on make-up, they joined the maquis living in the mountains with the men. They returned with new identities, full of ideas and arguments; and as for their virginity, how could their father question them about that when their very lives were in danger and they risked more than he did. Gradually during the war the father's control slipped. Marriages were no longer arranged. A new mode of women's liberation evolved out of the national liberation front. This was not imposed like the colonizers' emancipation; it came out of a situation which men and women made together and in which they needed and depended upon one another in new ways.

Militancy was not without pain, psychological and physical. Fanon mentions puerperal psychoses, particularly in the refugee camps. In the report of French atrocities in Algeria, published under the title *Gangrene*, the torture women were subjected to is described. Pain came also between men and women. Fanon describes the case of one of his patients whose wife was raped by the French. He had never really loved her, and he knew such violations were common. He'd seen peasants drying the tears of their wives after they'd been raped before their eyes. He knew too that she had protected him and his organization; she hadn't talked. It had been his political involvement which had implicated her:

> And yet she didn't say to me, 'Look at all I've had to bear for you.' On the contrary, she said, 'Forget about me; begin your life over again, for I have been dishonoured.' And really he felt he had been dishonoured, but experienced guilt because he felt this way. His wife and child seemed rotten to him, he could not have intercourse with other women without being repulsed by the thought, 'She's tasted the French.'[48]

Conflict which is out in the open can at least be resolved. This inner conflict and pain consumed people in a different way. It was not observable on the surface; it effected an interior war of consciousness. It is not surprising that after independence the women militants received contradictory messages from the party. The party after all was predominantly masculine and the men did not stop feeling as men because they became militants. The inner structure of consciousness remained profoundly hostile to the liberation of women regardless of official pronouncements. Ben Bella might maintain that women's liberation was not a secondary aim, that the solution to women's oppression was a precondition for socialism. But the practical world of the Algerian woman presented a very different reality. She operated in an atmosphere which was completely defined and controlled by men. She was subjected continuously to sexual jokes, paternalism and polite indifference. If she spoke in front of a room full of men on the suppression of polygamy there were likely to be roars of laughter. The temptation to glide back behind her veil, to hold herself back, not to push herself into the hostile barrage of male revolution, was intense. This was of course self-reinforcing. Although the party piously promised women posts, when each instance arose the men automatically decided the women were still too backward, too inexperienced, not sufficiently educated.

These were by no means problems peculiar to Algeria. However, the circumstances of the Algerian situation combined to stop women from breaking through the strength of male resistance. Politically, the enforcement of segregation after independence of male/female cells prevented the women from confronting the men at a local level. Moreover, the revolutionary government did not introduce laws which changed the laws relating to marriage and the family. Men could still divorce their wives by simple repudiation. The resulting insecurity meant that women were very afraid of resisting their husbands' will. The internalization of women in the household was particularly strong and male suspicion of female emergence consequently very potent. The saying: 'La femme fasse le couscous et nous la politique' ('Women make food and we make politics') carried a real force. This combined with the determination of the men to recover the power colonization had taken from them.

Muslim religion reinforced the subordination of women. Just as seventeenth-century puritans turned to the Bible for arguments about Adam's rib and the inspiration of Deborah and Jael, Algerians in the 1960s quoted texts from the Koran. Though Mohammed's teaching was relatively enlightened in the context of the seventh century – he exhorted his followers to treat their wives better than their cattle – it leaves much to be desired for women who had just emerged from fighting the French. But Hachemi Tidjani, president of an association called The Brave, was declaring in June 1964 that there had never been a prophetess – thus proving conclusively the inferiority of women and topping his argument with the fact that women's brains were biologically below men's.[49]

Most important though is the general political situation of the Algerian Revolution which meant that it was impossible to try to overcome these in a decisive manner. Ben Bella's attempt to find a middle road to socialism, avoiding both the capitalist and communist camps, immediately involved him in financial trading contradictions and in considerable ambiguities when he tried to carry through domestic reforms. After his fall Algeria moved farther to the right. Not only did the oppression of women continue openly and blatantly but there was barely even a rhetorical protest against it. Criticism of the regime in general became more and more difficult. Polygamy continued in the countryside and if anything was on the increase. A peasant could murder his wife in 1967 and feel quite within his rights if he claimed she was unfaithful.

Paranoia mounted against 'Bolshevik atheism' and 'European and Jewish materialism'. Fanon's books became suspect. Instead 'revolutionary Islamic humanism' became the lofty title for distrust of foreigners and foreign influences and an excuse for reverting to the most reactionary measures in relation to sex and the family. It became fashionable to make a distinction between 'traditional traditionalism and colonial traditionalism'.[50] If anything, from the women's point of view the second was rather more favourable to liberation than the first. Women could not use the ideology of the revolution to argue their case, because unlike Marxism, Islamic nationalism is an exclusive theory which distinguishes from rather than extends towards. Boumedienne expressed clearly the difference between the future which Algerian society holds for girls and boys in a speech at a lycée prize-giving in Algiers in 1969. The girls' role is as mothers and upholders of Islamic-Arab morality; the boys' is to assume political responsibility for the state. The daily paper *El Moudjahid* repeats this: 'The woman is the guardian of the traditions of the vertebral column of the family, the cell of the basis of society. And all morality or depravity in the family or in society is determined primarily by the behaviour of the woman. Her role is all-important.'[51]

In the countryside the women live as they have lived for centuries. The little girls go out to look after the flocks; they accept the husband their father has chosen for them. In the small towns they are similarly confined. In Algiers young women students, secretaries, professionals, enjoy a certain independence personally, but they are quite separate from most of the women. They constitute the tiny minority of women elected to the assemblies of government. But even this measure of privileged emancipation goes when they marry and have children. Apart from the urban middle-class women the only others with economic independence are women in industry.

But these are numerically insignificant and are exclusively in textiles and clothing. Domestic service or work in agriculture is much more common. There was an initial impetus to involve women in production and the need is still recognized by some of the men in the party, but this would undoubtedly shatter the hold of the men over their women, and the separate but different line of development is more popular. In tones reminiscent of Victorian England the writer of a letter to *El Moudjahid* in March 1967 asserted that 'the man must see in his wife ... a pleasant companion, one who after a long day working consoles him in his troubles and relieves his tiredness.'[52]

The young Algerian girl faces many contradictions. At one level there are practical restrictions: she is forced to leave school, she is watched by her brother when she is out with friends. She has to guard her virginity or be socially disgraced. But meanwhile another world communicates itself on the media. It is apparent to her that men are preoccupied with the sexual western images they condemn, and that prostitution and women abandoned by men divorcing them are increasing. She oscillates between individual submission and defiant rebellion. But there is no way out – whatever she does is completely dependent on men and determined by them.

She is not yet free, and whatever she does she continues to place herself to act, to judge in relation to man. He remains for her the measure of everything: she fears him or defies him, respects him or provokes him, she never neglects him ... he never stops looking at her, she never stops seeing him, she says she's free, she feels she is guilty.[53]

The cultural emergence of women is quite inseparable from the general development of Algerian society. It is impossible for women to break with their own specific colonization and oppression when the old colonizers are simply replaced by new ones.

There are, however, several factors which although inadequate as a basis of genuine emancipation may well heighten the contradiction between the attempt to bind women in Islamic-Arab tradition and the economic development of Algeria. There is the likelihood that industrialization will bring more women into the labour force in the factories; eighty per cent of the women are now literate. Both these serve to make women dissatisfied with the lives their mothers had to lead. Since 1966 family planning has started in an experimental way in the large towns. Nor are all women completely passive in accepting their fate. The National Union of Algerian Women (U.N.F.A.) for example continues to maintain that it is necessary to struggle 'against certain negative traditions which have no reason for existing'. These are held to be the family code and legal position of women, polygamy, divorce by male repudiation, and the right of 'djebr', which allows the father to marry his children as he pleases. Young girls have stumbled into consciousness despite so many obstacles and the defensive postures which are a result of the hegemony of Arab-Islamic tradition as official ideology. A girl wrote to a magazine: 'Woman should be free. She must not imitate men stupidly. She's equal to men and she should not lower herself depending on the attitude of her husband. She must be independent.'[54]

This is still a moral feminism which asserts the individual woman's equal rights but in the Algerian context it is radical indeed. But alone it will be powerless to transform the situation of women. Algerian women await liberation. Their fate is a warning against too great a hope. The failure of the Algerian Revolution serves to bring a perspective to other revolutions in developing countries.

Now in 1971 in France the daughters of Algerian immigrants protest, not like Nefissa against foreign colonialism, but as women who do not want to share the bed of a man they don't desire. Their weapon is the time-honoured one of women in similar circumstances – suicide. We can retreat even as we advance. In isolation we can destroy one another.

Patronage takes several shapes. Sometimes it is the assumption that everyone must naturally want to be what you are or what you hope to be. Sometimes it is quite the opposite, the assumption that other human beings are a different order of creature from yourself and therefore would never share your aspirations. The disinherited are sensitive about such attitudes. As a woman I am aware of patronage. As a white middle-class woman from one of the metropolitan countries I am also deeply implicated in the arrogance of the possessors. As a Marxist and as a feminist I cherish the elements in bourgeois humanism which Marx incorporated and transformed in his thinking. I do not want the revolutionary movement to push them aside. But at the same time I am conscious of the difficulty which western Marxists have in distinguishing between our own cultural heritage of assumed superiority and the importance of insisting that communism is the kingdom of freedom not necessity. Because so far all revolutionary movements have had to settle for something less, because they have to solve such material and fundamental problems and because the experience of the Soviet Union provides no clear alternative, it is often difficult to maintain the tension between solidarity and honesty. I *am* doubtful of asceticism, I *am* puzzled about the exact experience of polygamy, I *am* confused about the relevance of fashion, clothes and make-up. I *don't* know what it is like to be Vietnamese, or Cuban, or Algerian. I have many ignorances and much hesitancy, which can't be cleared just by thinking about them. We will learn more from what we do. The emergence of women's consciousness, very recently, for example, in such diverse colonial situations as Mozambique, Palestine and Northern Ireland, will help further to define the nature of oppression and the possibility of liberation.

In all the discussions about the nature of the revolutions in the twentieth century, there have been relatively few attempts to describe the experience of women. The generation which became active in left politics in the sixties inherited silence and ambiguity. A legacy of cold war propaganda about the family, pressure from an expanding market for the beauty industry and consumer durables, stifled any questioning of the woman's role in advanced capitalism. Meanwhile the Soviet Union, so long important as the model of a revolutionary alternative, had retreated from the creative experiments of the twenties. The tragic and faltering earlier attempts, specifically to connect female aspirations with revolution, and the uncertainty and tension these produced, have been obscured by their own failure and by the failure of the working class in western capitalism yet to create socialism. The return to our past through the women's liberation movement is at once circular and proximate. Circular, because the movement which has developed recently has consisted mainly of women in a much more advantageous position than the women who stormed bakers' shops in the nineteenth century or joined national liberation movements in the twentieth. Proximate, because the consciousness of people in the most diverse circumstances of resistance is capable of curiously intimate encounters.

The liberation of women has never fully been realized, and the revolution within the revolution remains unresolved. The connection between feminism, the assertion of the claims of women as a group, and revolutionary socialism is still awkward. Their synthesis cannot merely be intellectual, but will come out of the ideas we make practical, dissolving, preserving and exploding our present conceptions of both.

This is a book in which feminism and Marxism come home to roost. They cohabit in the same space somewhat uneasily. Each sits snorting at the other and using words which are strange and foreign to the other. Each is huffy and jealous about its own autonomy. They are at once incompatible and in real need of one another. As a feminist and a Marxist I carry their contradictions within me and it is tempting to opt for one or the other in an effort to produce a tidy resolution of the commotion generated by the antagonism between them. But to do that would mean evading the social reality which gives rise to the antagonism. It would mean relying on pre-packaged formulas which come slickly off the tongue and then melt as soon as they are exposed to the light of day.

Marxism was developed as a means of understanding the way in which capitalist society functioned and how it could thus be changed. However, it retained a certain ambiguity about the liberation of women. Capitalism has itself got older and more sophisticated in its operation, while, at the same time, the political organization of all people throughout the world who have been excluded from the privileges of capitalism has greatly enlarged and extended what we can do. Marxism has to grow towards and through these developments before it can adequately explain modern capitalism. Marxists have in general assumed that the overthrow of capitalist society will necessitate a fundamental transformation in the organization and control of production and the social relations which come from the capitalist mode of production. Women's liberation implies that if the revolutionary movement is to involve women, not as supporters or attendants only, but as equals, then the scope of production must be seen in a wider sense and cover also the production undertaken by women in the family and the production of self through sexuality. That is, in fact, a reassertion of Marx's concern to study how human beings reproduce their lives in a total way. It is also a crucial part of any strategy to be employed against advanced capitalism.

Many women in women's liberation are not revolutionaries. But the demands they make for their own improvement require such a fundamental change in society that they are completely inconceivable without revolution. An understanding is coming out of women's liberation of the way in which the present organization of the family holds women down, together with the recognition of the need to alter dramatically the system by which work is divided between the sexes. Such a change immediately raises the need to transform the whole cultural conditioning of women and, hence, of men, as well as the upbringing of children, the shape of the places we live in, the legal structure of our society, our sexuality and the very nature of work for the accumulation of private profit rather than for the benefit of human beings in general. This is an emerging idea and the means by which it will be realized and the shape it will assume are still not worked out. But the crucial feature of this new feminism as an organizing idea is that these changes will not follow a socialist revolution automatically but will have to be made explicit in a distinct movement now, as a precondition of revolution, not as its aftermath. This is obviously different from the emphases of the orthodox Marxist tradition. The fact that no socialist revolution has occurred in the countries of advanced capitalism inevitably leaves us only with an imponderable dilemma. Similarly the general problems of all societies in which there have been revolutions have become so completely intertwined with the specific problems of women that it is difficult to disentangle cause from effect.

The connection between the oppression of women and the central discovery of Marxism, the class exploitation of the worker in capitalism, is still forced. It is still coming out of the heads of women like me as an idea. It is still predominantly just a notion in the world. I believe the only way in which their combination will become living and evident is through a movement of working-class women, in conscious resistance to both, alongside black, yellow and brown women struggling against racialism and imperialism. We are far from such a movement now. But when the connection between class, colonial and sexual oppression becomes commonplace we will understand it, not as an abstract imposed concept, but as something coming out of the experience of particular women.

Some of the pamphlets and journals referred to in the text are not generally available in most commercial bookshops or in libraries. Although some may be out of print here are the publication addresses:

*Comment* Communist Party, 16 King Street, London.

*International Socialism* and A. Kollontai, *Communism and the Family* Pluto Press *International Socialism*, 6 Cottons Gardens, London E2.

*The Irrational in Politics* Solidarity Pamphlet no. 33, c/o H. Russell, 53A Westminster Road, Bromley, Kent.

A. Kollontai, *Women Workers' Struggle for their Rights* Falling Wall Press, 79 Richmond Road, Montpelier, Bristol, BS6 5EP.

*Leviathan* 968 Valencia Street, San Francisco, California 9410, U.S.A.

*Monthly Review* 116 West 14th Street, New York 10011, U.S.A.

Publications for the Society for Anglo-Chinese Understanding, and general material about China Society for Anglo-Chinese Understanding, 24 Warren Street, London.

*Shrew* Women's Liberation Workshop, 3 Shavers Place, Haymarket, London SW1.

*Socialist Woman* and Fidel Castro, *Women's Liberation, The Revolution Within the Revolution* Merit Pamphlets, New York, 1970. Red Books, 182 Pentonville Road, London N1.

*Stand* 58 Queen's Road, Jesmond, Newcastle upon Tyne 2.

*Women, A Journal of Liberation* 3028 Greenmount Avenue, Baltimore, MD21218, U.S.A.

Some of these are also obtainable from Collets, Charing Cross Road, and from Agit Prop, 248 Bethnal Green Road, London E2.

For a bibliography of the books mentioned in the text see amongst others Sheila Rowbotham, *Women's Liberation and Revolution*, a bibliography, obtainable from Falling Wall Press.

# Bibliography

This bibliography is part of an extensive descriptive bibliography compiled by Sheila Rowbotham entitled *Women's Liberation and Revolution* which was first published in March 1972 by the Falling Wall Press, 79 Richmond Road, Montpelier, Bristol.
Those books marked with an asterisk are particularly useful.
Paperback editions are indicated by (p).

## Some general books on women's liberation

BEAUVOIR, Simone de, *The Second Sex*, London, Cape, 1968, Four Square (p), 1969; and *The Nature of the Second Sex*, London, Four Square (p), 1968.

FIGES, Eva, *Patriarchal Attitudes*, London, Faber, 1970.

FIRESTONE, Shulamith, *The Dialectic of Sex: The Case for Feminist Revolution*, London, Cape, 1971.

FRIEDAN, Betty, *The Feminine Mystique*, London, Penguin (p), 1968.

GREER, Germaine, *The Female Eunuch*, London, MacGibbon & Kee, 1970, Paladin (p), 1971.

MILLETT, Kate, *Sexual Politics*, London, Hart-Davis, 1971.

MITCHELL, Juliet, *Woman's Estate*, London, Penguin (p), 1971.

MORGAN, Robin (ed.), *Sisterhood is Powerful: An Anthology of Writings from the Women's Liberation Movement*, New York, Vintage Trade Books (p), Random House, 1970.

TANNER, Leslie B. (ed.), *Voices from Women's Liberation*, New York, Signet (p), 1971.

## General histories of feminism

ABENSOUR, Léon, *Histoire Génerale du Feminisme*, Paris, 1921.

BLEASE, W. Lyon, *The Emancipation of English Women*, London, 1910.

*COWLEY, Joyce, *Pioneers of Women's Liberation*, Merit pamphlet.

*DANGERFIELD, George, *The Strange Death of Liberal England*, London, MacGibbon & Kee, 1966, Paladin (p), 1970.

Bibliography

*FLEXNER, E., *Century of Struggle: The Woman's Rights Movement in the U.S.*, Atheneum (p), 1968.
*GORDON, Ann D., BUHLE, Mari-Jo and SCHROM, Nancy F., 'Women in American Society', in *Radical America*, vol. V, no. 4.
HAYS, H. R., *The Dangerous Sex: The Myth of Feminine Evil*, London, Methuen, 1966.
*IRELAND, Waitrand, 'You don't need the Vote to Raise Hell. The rise and fall of the Suffrage Movement', in *Leviathan*, vol. 2, no. 1, May 1970.
KRADITOR, Aileen, *The Ideas of the Woman Suffrage Movement*, New York, Columbia University Press, 1965.
KRADITOR, Aileen, *Up from the Pedestal: Selected Writings in the History of American Feminism*, Chicago, Quadrangle, 1968.
O'NEILL, William, *The Woman Movement: Feminism in the United States and England*, London, Allen & Unwin (p), 1969.
O'NEILL, William, *Everyone was Brave: The Rise and Fall of Feminism in America*, Chicago, Quadrangle, 1969.
RAMELSON, Marion, *Petticoat Rebellion*, London, Lawrence & Wishart, 1967.
TANNER, Leslie B. (ed.), *Voices from Women's Liberation*, New York, Signet (p), 1971.
'Women in History: a Re-creation of Our Past', in *Women: a Journal of Liberation*, spring 1970.
'Women in Revolution', in *Women: a Journal of Liberation*, summer 1970.

## Women and the Puritan Revolution in England and America

ADAMS, C. F., *Antinomianism in the Colony of Massachusetts Bay, 1636–38*, Boston, 1894 (reprinted, Burt Franklin, 1966).
BROCKBANK, E. E., *Richard Hubberthorne of Yealand*, London, 1929.
*CLARK, Alice, *The Working Life of Women in the Seventeenth Century*, London, 1919 (reprinted, F. Cass, 1968).
COHN, Norman, *The Pursuit of the Millennium*, London, 1959, Paladin (p), 1970.
GARDINER, Dorothy, *English Girlhood at School*, London, 1929.
GUILLET, Edwin C., *The Pioneer Farmer and Backwoodsman*, Toronto, Toronto University Press, 1963.
*HILL, Christopher, *Society and Puritanism in Pre-Revolutionary England*, London, Secker & Warburg, 1964, Panther (p), 1969.
HILL, Christopher, *Puritanism and Revolution*, London, Panther (p), 1968.

KETTLE, Arnold, *An Introduction to the English Novel*, London, Hutchinson (p), 1967.

MACARTHUR, Ellen, 'Women Petitioners and the Long Parliament', in *English Historical Review*, vol. XXIV, 1909.

PINCHBECK, Ivy, and HEWITT, Margaret, *Children in English Society*, London, Routledge, 1969.

*THOMAS, Keith, 'Women in the Civil War Sects', in *Past and Present*, no. 13, 1958.

UNDERWOOD, Dale, *Etherege and the Seventeenth-Century Comedy*, Yale University Press, 1957.

WALZER, Michael, *The Revolution of Society*, London, Weidenfeld & Nicolson, 1966.

WRIGHT, Louis B., *Middle-Class Culture in Elizabethan England*, Cornell University Press, 1958.

## The eighteenth century and the French Revolution: France and England

ABENSOUR, Léon, *La Femme et le Feminisme avant la Révolution*, Paris, 1928.

CHEVALIER, Louis, *Classe Laborieuse et Classes Dangereuses*, Paris, 1958.

COBB, Richard, *A Second Identity: Essays on France and French History*, London, Oxford University Press, 1969.

GOLDSMITH, Margaret, *Seven Women against the World*, London, 1935.

*RACZ, Elizabeth, 'The Women's Rights Movement in the French Revolution', in *Women: A Journal of Liberation*, summer 1970.

RUDÉ, George, *The Crowd in the French Revolution*, London, Oxford University Press, 1959, (p) 1968.

*RUDÉ, George, *The Crowd in History: a Study of Popular Disturbances in France and England, 1730–1848,* New York, Wiley (p), 1964.

STORR, M. S., *Mary Wollstonecraft et le Mouvement Féminist dans la Littérature Anglaise*, Paris, 1932.

UTTER, R. P. and NEEDHAM, G. B., *Pamela's Daughters*, London, 1937.

VILLIERS, Baron Marc de, *Histoire des Clubs des Femmes et des Légions d'Amazone 1793–1848*, Paris 1871.

*WOLLSTONECRAFT, Mary, *Vindication of the Rights of Women*, London, 1792 and *Posthumous Works*, London, 1798.

Bibliography

Feminism and the early radical and socialist movements: France, America, England, Russia

ABENSOUR, Léon, *Le Féminisme sous la Règne de Louis Philippe et en 1848*, Paris, 1913.

BESTOR, Arthur E. jnr, *Backwoods Utopia*, University of Philadelphia, 1950.

*BRAILSFORD, H. N., *Shelley, Godwin and their Circle*, London, 1951.

*COLE, G. D. H., *A History of Socialist Thought*, London, Macmillan, 1953.

DEMAR, Clair, *Ma Loi d'Avenir et l'Appel d'une Femme du Peuple sur l'Affranchissement de la Femme*, Paris, 1833.

DEPVIN, Jeanne, *Cours de Droit Social pour les Femmes*, Paris, 1848.

DOLLÉANS, Edouard, *Feminisme et Mouvement Ouvrier*, Paris, 1951.

FOURIER, C., *Théorie des Quatre Mouvements* in *Oeuvres Complètes*, Paris, 1841-5.

*FRYER, Peter, *The Birth Controllers*, London, Corgi (p), 1967.

GATTEY, Charles Nelson, *Gauguin's Astonishing Grandmother: Flora Tristan*, London, Femina, 1970.

GRAY, John, *A Lecture on Human Happiness*, London, 1825.

GREPON, Marguerite, *Une Croisade pour un Meilleur Amour*, Paris, 1967.

HARRISON, J. F. C., *Robert Owen and the Owenites in Britain and America: the Quest for the New World*, London, Routledge, 1969.

*KILLHAM, John, *Tennyson and 'The Princess': Reflections of an Age*, London, Athlone, 1958.

LUBAC, Henri de, *The Unmarxian Socialist: A Study of Proudhon*, London, 1948.

MILLER, Percy (ed.), *Margaret Fuller, American Romantic*, New York, 1963.

*PANKHURST, Richard K., *William Thompson, 1775-1853*, London, 1954.

PANKHURST, Richard K., 'Fourierism in Britain', in *International Review of Social History*, vol. I, 1956.

SHELLEY, P. B., Notes on 'Queen Mab' in his *Poetical Notes*, London, 1947.

SMITH, W. Anderson, *Shepherd Smith the Universalist*, London, 1892.

SULLEROT, Evelyne, 'Journaux Féminins et Lutte Ouvrière' in *La Presse Ouvrière*, Paris, Jacques Godechot, 1966.

THOMAS, Clara, *Love and Work Enough: The Life of Anna Jameson*, London, Macdonald, 1967.

*THOMAS, Edith, *Les Femmes de 1848*, Paris, 1948.

THOMPSON, Dorothy (ed.), *The Early Chartists*, London, Macmillan (p), 1971.

*THOMPSON, William, *Appeal of one half of the Human Race, Women, against the pretentions of the other half, Men, to retain them in political and thence in Civil and Domestic Slavery*, London, 1825.

ZELDIN, David, *The Educational Ideas of Charles Fourier, 1772–1837*, London, Cass, 1967.

## Marx and Engels on women's liberation[1]

COLLINS, H. and ABRAMSKY, C., *Karl Marx and the British Labour Movement*, London, 1965.

*DRAPER, Hal, 'Marx and Engels on Women's Liberation', in *International Socialism*, July/August 1970.

ENGELS, Friedrich, *The Condition of the Working Class in England*.

*ENGELS, Friedrich, *Origin of the Family*.

GEIGER, H. Kent, *The Family in Soviet Russia*, Harvard University Press, 1968.

HODGKIN, Thomas, *Love and the Revolutionaries*, Millicent Fawcett Lecture, Bedford College, University of London, sections printed in *Oxford Left*, 1968.

MARX, Karl, *Economic and Philosophic Manuscripts*.

MARX, Karl, *Capital*.

MARX, Karl (edited by E. J. Hobsbawm), *Pre-capitalist Economic Formations*, London, Lawrence & Wishart, 1964.

MARX, Karl (edited by David McLellan), *Marx's Grundisse*, London, Macmillan, 1971.

MARX, Karl and ENGELS, Friedrich, *The Communist Manifesto*.

MARX, Karl and ENGELS, Friedrich, *The Holy Family*.

MARX, Karl and ENGELS, Friedrich, *The German Ideology*.

**Marxism and the Liberation of Women: Quotations from Marx, Engels, Lenin, Stalin, Mao Tse-tung, Union of Women for Liberation*.

## The family and the position of women in the nineteenth century: France, U.S., Britain

*BANKS, J. A. and Olive, *Feminism and Family Planning*, Liverpool University Press, 1964.

DAUBIE, J., *La Femme Pauvre aux XIX Siècle*, Paris, 1866.

FONER, Philip, *The History of the Labour Movement in the United States*, New York, International Publishers Co., 1947–65.

[1] Publication details are not generally included for works by Marx and Engels because they are published, in full or in selection, in so many editions.

Bibliography

*HENRY, Alice, *The Trade Union Woman*, New York, 1915.

HEWITT, Margaret, *Wives and Mothers in Victorian Industry*, London, Barrie & Rockliff, 1958.

*HOUGHTON, W. E., *The Victorian Frame of Mind, 1830–1870*, Yale University Press, 1957 (p).

LLOYD, A. L., *Folk Song in England*, London, Lawrence & Wishart, 1967.

*PINCHBECK, Ivy, *Women Workers and the Industrial Revolution, 1750–1850*, London, 1930 (reprinted F. Cass, 1969).

MARCUS, Steven, *The Other Victorians: A Study of Sexuality and Pornography in Mid-Nineteenth Century England*, London, Weidenfeld & Nicolson, 1969, Corgi (p), 1969.

NEFF, W. F., *Victorian Working Women*, New York, A.M.S. Press, 1929.

*THOMPSON, Dorothy, *The British People, 1760–1902*, London, Heinemann Educational, 1969.

THOMPSON, E. P., *The Making of the English Working Class*, London, 1963, Penguin (p), 1970.

Feminism and socialist and anarchist movements in the late nineteenth and early twentieth centuries: Germany, Russia, U.S., Britain, France, Italy

BALABANOFF, Angelica, *My Life as a Rebel*, London, 1938.

BAX, E. Belfort, *Essays in Socialism*, London, 1907.

*BEBEL, A., *Woman in the Past, Present and Future*, London, 1885.

BONDFIELD, Margaret G. and OLIVER, Kathlyn, *Shop Workers and the Vote, Domestic Servants and Citizenship*, People's Suffrage Federation (no date).

CARPENTER, Edward, *My Days and Dreams*, London, 1918.

CARPENTER, Edward, *Love's Coming of Age*, Manchester, 1896.

CHERNYSHEVSKY, N. G., *A Vital Question; or, What is to be Done?*, New York, 1886; Vintage Books (p), 1961.

CONLON, Lil, *Cumann na mBan and the Women of Ireland, 1913–25*, Kilkenny, 1969.

CRONWRIGHT-SCHREINER, S. C. (ed.), *Letters of Olive Schreiner*, London, 1924.

DRINNON, Richard, *Rebel in Paradise: A Biography of Emma Goldman*, University of Chicago Press, 1961, Beacon Press (p), 1970.

FIGNER, Vera, *Memoirs of a Revolutionist*, London, 1929.

GOLDMAN, Emma, *Anarchism and Other Essays*, New York, 1910 (partly reprinted in *Anarchy*, October 1965 as Emma Goldman, 'It's a man's world').

# Bibliography

GOLDMAN, Emma, *Living My Life*, New York, 1931; Dover (p), 1970.

GREIG, Teresa Billington and BONDFIELD, Margaret, *Verbatim Report of Debate on December 3rd 1907: Sex Equality versus Adult Suffrage*, Adult Suffrage Society, 1907.

HOBMAN, D. L., *Olive Schreiner: Her Friends and Times*, London, Pemberton, 1955.

KENDALL, Walter, *The Revolutionary Movement in Britain, 1900–21*, London, Weidenfeld & Nicolson, 1969.

LAMPERT, E., *Sons against Fathers*, London, Oxford University Press, 1964.

MCMILLAN, Margaret, *The Life of Rachel McMillan*, London, 1927.

MARX, Eleanor and AVELING, E., 'The Woman Question', in *Westminster Review*, 1885. Reprinted in *Marxism Today*, vol. XVI, no. 3, March 1972.

MEIZER, J. M., *Knowledge and Revolution: The Russian Colony in Zurich, 1870–1873*, New York, Fernhill, 1965.

*MITCHELL, David, *Women on the Warpath*, London, Cape, 1966.

MITCHELL, Geoffrey (ed.), *The Hard Way Up: The Autobiography of Hannah Mitchell, Suffragette and Rebel*, London, Faber & Faber, 1968.

MONTEFIORE, Dora, *From a Victorian to a Modern*, London, 1927.

MONTEFIORE, Dora, *Singings through the Dark*, London, 1898.

PANKHURST, E. Sylvia, *The Suffragette Movement: An Intimate Account of Persons and Ideals*, London, 1931.

PANKHURST, E. Sylvia, *The Suffragette: The History of the Women's Militant Suffrage Movement, 1905–1910*, New York, 1911.

PANKHURST, E. Sylvia, *The Life of Emmeline Pankhurst*, London, 1935.

PANKHURST, E. Sylvia, *Writ on Cold Slate*, London, 1922.

SCHREINER, Olive, *Story of an African Farm*, London, 1883, Penguin (p), 1970.

SCHREINER, Olive, *Woman and Labour*, London, 1911.

SHAW, Bernard, *The Quintessence of Ibsenism*, London, 1891.

STEINBERG, I., *Spiridonova: Revolutionary Terrorist*, London, 1933.

STEPNIAK [pseudonym], *Underground Russia: Revolutionary Profiles and Sketches from Life*, London, 1883.

*THOMAS, Edith, *The Women Incendiaries*, London, Secker & Warburg, 1967.

TSUZUKI, C., *H. M. Hyndman and British Socialism*, London, Oxford University Press, 1961.

TSUZUKI, C., *The Life of Eleanor Marx, 1855–98: A Socialist Tragedy*, London, Oxford University Press, 1967.

Bibliography

TSUZUKI, C., 'The Impossibilist Revolt in Britain', *International Review of Social History*, vol. I, 1956.

WILKINSON, Lily Gair, *Revolutionary Socialism and the Women's Movement*, Edinburgh, Socialist Labour Party (no date; *c.* 1910).

*Women's* [later *Workers'*] *Dreadnought*.

WOODROOFE, Debby, 'American Feminism 1848–1920', in *Women in Revolt, International Socialist Review*, March 1971.

## Russian Revolution

ALBERT, Valerie, 'It's the Women who have saved Russia from collapse', in *Pulse*, 30 December 1967.

BERNSTEIN, Marcelle, 'The Hard Hat Girls', in *Observer Colour Supplement*, 31 January 1971.

BRYANT, Louise, *Mirrors of Moscow*, New York, 1921.

BRYANT, Louise, *Six Red Months in Russia*, London, 1919.

DEUTSCHER, Isaac, *Stalin*, London, Penguin (p), 1966.

DIDSUSENKO, A., *Soviet Children*, Moscow, 1967

*DUNN, Erica and KLEIN, Judy, 'Women in the Russian Revolution', in *Women: a Journal of Liberation*, summer 1970.

FRY, John, 'The Soviet Health Service', in *Guardian*, 19 July 1967.

*GEIGER, H. Kent, *The Family in Soviet Russia*, Harvard University Press, 1968.

GOULD, Donald, 'Russia's Health Service', in *New Statesman*, 9 June 1967.

*HALLE, Fannina W., *Woman in Soviet Russia*, London, 1933.

HALLE, Fannina W., *Woman in the Soviet East*, London, 1938.

*KOLLONTAI, Alexandra, *Communism and the Family*, London, Pluto Press (p), 1971.

*KOLLONTAI, Alexandra, *Free Love*, London, 1932.

*KOLLONTAI, Alexandra, *Women Workers' Struggle for their Rights*, Bristol, Falling Wall Press (p), 1971.

KOLLONTAI, Alexandra, *The Workers' Opposition*, Reading, Solidarity pamphlet, 1962.

KOLLONTAI, Alexandra, *The Autobiography of a Sexually Emancipated Woman*, with an Introduction by Germaine Greer, London, Orbach & Chambers (p), 1972.

KRUPSKAYA, N., *Memories of Lenin*, London, 1930.

*LENIN, V. I., *On the Emancipation of Women*.

LENIN, V. I., *On the National Question*.

LENIN, V. I., *The Development of Capitalism in Russia*.

MACE, David and Vera, *The Soviet Family*, London, 1964.

MAYAKOVSKY, V. V. (edited by Patricia Blake), *The Bedbug and Selected Poetry*, London, 1961.

*PALENCIA, Isabel de, *Alexandra Kollontay*, New York, 1947.

PAVLOVA, Ludmilla, *Women in my Country*, Novosti Press Agency (no date).

POPOVA, N. V., *The Part Played by Women in Socialist Society*, Moscow, 1967.

*REICH, W., *The Sexual Revolution*, New York, Noonday (p), 1963; London, Vision Press, 1969.

*ROWBOTHAM, Sheila, 'Alexandra Kollontai: Women's Liberation and Revolutionary Love', in *The Spokesman*, June and July 1970.

*SCHLESINGER, R. A. J., *Changing Attitudes in Soviet Russia: The Family*, London, 1949.

*SMITH, Jessica, *Woman in Soviet Russia*, New York, 1928.

STALIN, J., excerpts in *Marxism and the Liberation of Women*, Union of Women for Liberation.

SULLEROT, Evelyne, *Histoire et Sociologie du Travail Féminin*, Paris, 1958.

TIDMARSH, Kyril, 'Russia Plans More Shopping Centres', in *The Times*, 14 September 1967.

*TROTSKY, Leon, *Problems of Life*, London, 1924.

TROTSKY, Leon, *History of the Russian Revolution*, London, Penguin (p), 1969.

TROTSKY, Leon, *The Revolution Betrayed*, New York, 1937.

## China

ANDERSON, Dick, *Grass Roots Self-Government*, Society for Anglo-Chinese Understanding (S.A.C.U.), 1969.

*BEAUVOIR, Simone de, *The Long March*, 1958, Deutsch and Weidenfeld & Nicolson, 1958.

BERGER, Roland, *The Cultural Revolution and the Family*, S.A.C.U., February 1969.

BLACKBURN, Fei-Ling (née DAVIES), *The Role and Organisation of Chinese Secret Societies in the Late Ch'ing*, M.Phil. thesis, London, 1968.

*BUNCH-WEEKS, Charlotte, 'Asian Women in Revolt', *Women: a Journal of Liberation*, summer 1970.

CHIN P'ING MEI, *The Adventurous History of Hsi Men and His Six Wives*, London, 1959.

*GREENE, Felix, *A Divorce Trial in China*, New England Free Press.

GREENE, Felix, *Visit to a Rural Commune*, Radical Educational Project.

Bibliography

*HINTON, William, *Fanshen: A Documentary of Revolt in a Chinese Village*, Random House, Vintage Trade Books (p), 1968.

*HORN, Joshua S., *Away with All Pests*, London, Hamlyn, 1969.

*LANDY, L., *Women in the Chinese Revolution*, International Socialism pamphlet.

LEVY, Marion J., *The Family Revolution in Modern China*, New York, Octagon, 1963, Atheneum (p), 1968.

*LU HSUN (translated by Yang Hsien-Yi and Gladys Yang), *Selected Works*, Peking, 1960.

MAO TSE-TUNG, excerpts in *Marxism and the Liberation of Women*, Union of Women for Liberation.

MAO TSE-TUNG, 'Report on an Investigation of the Peasant Movement in Hunan', in *Selected Works of Mao Tse-tung*, London, Lawrence & Wishart, 1954.

MUTUTANTRI, Barbara, 'Women in China', in *Eastern Horizon*, September–October 1968.

*MYRDAL, Jan, *Report from a Chinese Village*, London, Penguin (p), 1967.

O'BRIEN, Jo, Review of *Birdless Summer*, in *Socialist Woman*, July–August 1969.

ORLEANS, Leo A., 'Evidence from Chinese Medical Journals on Current Population Policy', in *China Quarterly*, no. 40, October–December 1969.

PEI-KU HUNG, 'A Girl's Herding Team', in *China Reconstructs*, vol. 18, no. 9, September 1969.

RUSSELL, Maud, 'Urban People's Communes in China', New York, *Far East Reporter*.

SALAF, Judith Weitner and MERKK, Judith, 'Women in Revolution', in *Berkeley Journal of Sociology*, 1970.

*SNOW, Helen Foster, *Women in Modern China*, The Netherlands, 1967.

STRONG, Anna Louise, *The Rise of the Chinese People's Communes*, Peking, 1964.

'Throw the Buying and Selling Type of Matrimony into the Rubbish Dump of History', *China in the News*, 11 January 1971, China Reprints, S.A.C.U.

WITKE, Roxanne, 'Mao Tse-tung, Women and Suicide in the May Fourth Era', *China Quarterly*, July–September 1967.

'The Women of China', *Red Papers*, no. 3.

YANG YUN YU, *Report of the Struggle between Two Lines at the Moscow World Congress of Women*, Peking, 1963.

ZELL, Ann, *Early Beginnings of the Development of Working Class Institutions in China*, M.Phil. thesis, University of London, 1970.

# Imperialism and women's liberation as part of national liberation

## General

BOSERUP, Esther, *Women's Role in Economic Development*, London, Allen & Unwin, 1970.

FANON, Frantz, *Black Skin, White Masks*, London, MacGibbon & Kee, 1968, Paladin (p), 1970.

KELLY, Mary, 'National Liberation Movements and Women's Liberation', *Shrew*, December 1970.

## Algeria

FANON, Frantz, *A Dying Colonialism*, London, Penguin (p), 1970.

FANON, Frantz, *The Wretched of the Earth*, London, MacGibbon & Kee, 1965; Penguin (p), 1970.

FYTTON, Francis, 'Manifestation', *Strand*, vol. 6, no. 3.

RABET, Fadela m', *La Femme Algérienne*, Paris, 1968.

RABET, Fadela m', *Les Algériennes*, Paris, 1969.

VANDVELDE, Hélène, 'Condition Feminine: L'Emancipation est Freinée par le Conformisme Social', in *Le Monde*, 24–5 January 1971.

## Cuba

*BERMAN, Joan, 'Women in Cuba', in *Women: a Journal of Liberation*, summer 1970.

*CAMARANO, Chris, 'Cuban Women', in *Leviathan*, May 1970.

CASTRO, Fidel, *Women's Liberation: The Revolution within the Revolution*, The Santa Clara Speech, 9 December 1966, New York, Merit pamphlet, 1970.

GUEVARA, Che, *Reminiscences of the Cuban Revolutionary War*, London, Allen & Unwin, 1968, Penguin (p), 1969.

KENNEDY, Mary, 'Cuban Women', in *Shrew*, December 1970.

LEIGH, Bessie, 'Woman's Place in Cuba', in *Comment*, vol. 7, no. 47, 22 November 1969.

LOCKWOOD, Lee, *Castro's Cuba, Cuba's Fidel*, New York, Macmillan, 1967; Random House, Vintage Trade Books (p), 1969.

*SUTHERLAND, Elizabeth, *The Youngest Revolution*, London, Pitman, 1970.

## Vietnam

*DAVIN, Anna, 'Women in Vietnam', in *Shrew*, December 1970.

GELLHORN, Martha, 'The Vietcong's Peacemaker', in *The Times*, 27 January 1969.

# Bibliography

HO CHI MINH, *Selected Articles and Speeches*, London, Lawrence & Wishart, 1969.

*\*Vietnamese Women*, Vietnamese Studies, Hanoi, 1966.

*WEEKS, Charlotte Bunch, 'Asian Women in Revolt,' in *Women: a Journal of Liberation*, summer 1970.

# Notes

## Chapter 1

1. C. F. Adams (ed.), *Antinomianism in the Colony of Massachusetts Bay*, 1636–8, Boston, 1894, p. 329.
2. E. E. Brockbank, *Richard Hubberthorne*, London, 1929, pp. 90–91.
3. W. Butler Bowden (ed.), *The Book of Margery Kempe*, Everyman, London, 1954, pp. 15–16.
4. Ivy Pinchbeck and Margaret Hewitt, *Children in English Society*, London, 1969, p. 200.
5. Quoted in Louis B. Wright, *Middle-Class Culture in Elizabethan England*, University of North Carolina, p. 435.
6. Quoted in Keith Thomas, 'Women in the Civil War Sects', *Past and Present*, no. 13, 1958, p. 48.
7. ibid., p. 52.
8. Quoted in Wright, *Middle-Class Culture in Elizabethan England*, p. 503. For an example of anti-feminist propaganda see *The Women's Fegaries*, c. 1675.
9. Quoted in Ellen MacArthur, 'Women Petitioners and the Long Parliament', *E.H.R.*, vol. XXIV, 1909, p. 700.
10. Alice Clark, *The Working Life of Women in the Seventeenth Century*, London, 1919, p. 271.
11. Roger l'Estrange, *The Woman as good as the Man or the equality of both sexes*, 1677.
12. Quoted in R. P. Utter and G. B. Needham, *Pamela's Daughter*, London, p. 31.
13. Mary Astell's *A Serious Proposal*, quoted in M. S. Storr, *Mary Wollstonecraft et le mouvement feminist dans la littérature anglaise*, Paris, 1932, p. 26.
14. Hannah Wooley, quoted in Storr, *Mary Wollstonecraft*, p. 22.
15. Mary Astell, quoted ibid., p. 31.
16. Sophia, quoted ibid., p. 43.
17. Quoted in Christopher Hill, 'Clarissa Harlowe and her Times', in *Puritanism and Revolution*, London, 1962, p. 389. This section is

based on Christopher Hill's essay and on the discussion of *Clarissa* in Arnold Kettle, *An Introduction to the English Novel*, London, 1962, pp. 69–76.
18. W. Lyon Blease, *The Emancipation of English Women*, London, 1921, p. 50.
19. 'The Jovial Cutlers', quoted in E. P. Thompson, 'Time, Work-Discipline and Industrial Capitalism', *Past and Present*, no. 38, p. 73.

## Chapter 2

1. Léon Abensour, *La Femme et le Féminisme avant la Révolution*, Paris, 1928, p. 430.
2. Mary Wollstonecraft, *Posthumous Works*, vol. 3, London, 1798, p. 30.
3. Quoted in Storr, *Mary Wollstonecraft*, p. 158.
4. Wollstonecraft, *Posthumous Works*, vol. 3, p. 65.
5. ibid., p. 48.
6. Mary Wollstonecraft, *Vindication of the Rights of Women*, London, 1792, p. 70.
7. ibid., p. 135.
8. ibid., p. 50.
9. Wollstonecraft, *Posthumous Works*, p. 78.
10. Wollstonecraft, *Vindication*, pp. 3–4.
11. ibid., p. 33.
12. ibid., pp. 51–2.
13 ibid , p. 87.
14. ibid., p. 40.
15. Quoted in Storr, *Mary Wollstonecraft*, p. 153.
16. Wollstonecraft, *Vindication*, pp. 155–6.
17. ibid., p. 342.
18. Quoted in Storr, *Mary Wollstonecraft*, p. 403.
19. Quoted in H. N. Brailsford, *Shelley, Godwin and their Circle*, London, 1951, pp. 170–72.
20. W. Blake, 'Jerusalem', *Complete Writings*, Oxford, 1966, p. 708.
21. P. B. Shelley, 'Notes on *Queen Mab*', from *Shelley's Poetical Works*, London, 1947, pp. 806–7.
22. Quoted in Peter Fryer, *The Birth Controllers*, Corgi Books, London, 1967, p. 84.
23. Richard K. Pankhurst, *William Thompson*, London, 1954, p. 52.
24. ibid., p. 59.

25. William Thompson, *Appeal of one half the Human Race, Women, against the pretentions of the other Half, Men, to retain them in Civil and Domestic Slavery*, London, 1825, p. 2.
26. ibid., p. 151.
27. ibid., p. 165.
28. ibid.
29. ibid., p. 85.
30. ibid., p. 79.
31. ibid., p. 189.
32. ibid., p. 42.
33. ibid., p. 196.
34. C. Fourier, 'Théories des Quatre Mouvements', *Oeuvres Complètes*, Paris, 1841–5, p. 43.
35. ibid., p. 222.
36. Edith Thomas, *Les Femmes de 1848*, Paris, 1948, p. 47.
37. Clair Demar, *Ma Loi d'Avenir*, and *L'Appel d'une femme au peuple sur l'affranchissement de la femme*, Paris, 1833, p. 74.
38. Jeanne Deroin, 'Cours de droit social pour les femmes', 1848, p. 6.
39. Flora Tristan, *L'Union Ouvrière*, quoted in Charles Neilson Gattey, *Gaugin's Astonishing Grandmother*, London, 1970, p. 180.
40. G. D. H. Cole, 'Socialist Thought. The Forerunners', *A History of Socialist Thought*, vol. I, London, 1953, p. 186.
41. Gattey, *Gaugin's Astonishing Grandmother*, p. 173.
42. Thomas, *Les Femmes de 1848*, p. 29.
43. Margaret Fuller, *Woman in the Nineteenth Century*, quoted in Perry Miller, *Margaret Fuller, American Romantic*, New York, 1963, p. 188.
44. ibid., p. 148.
45. ibid., p. 149.
46. ibid., p. 143.
47. ibid., p. 146.

*Chapter 3*

1. K. Marx, *Economic and Philosophic Manuscripts*; T. B. Bottomore (ed.), *Karl Marx – Early Writings*, London, p. 154.
2. F. Engels, *Principles of Communism*, quoted in H. Kent Geiger, *The Family in Soviet Russia*, Cambridge, Mass., 1968, p. 21.
3. K. Marx, F. Engels, *The Communist Manifesto*, in *Selected Works of Marx and Engels*, London and Moscow, 1968, p. 50.

Notes

4. K. Marx, F. Engels, *The Holy Family* (1845), Moscow, 1956, p. 258.

5. ibid., p. 232.

6. F. Engels, *The Origin of the Family*, London, 1960, pp. 89–90.

7. K. Marx, F. Engels, *The German Ideology*, Moscow, 1965, p. 42.

8. ibid., p. 43.

9. ibid., p. 41.

10. Engels, *The Origin of the Family*, p. 1.

11. ibid., p. 2. See 'The Irrational in Politics', *Solidarity* pamphlet, no. 33, June 1970, pp. 10–18, for a general discussion of *The Origin of the Family*.

12. P. J. Richardson, *The Rights of Women*, quoted in Dorothy Thompson, *The Early Chartists*, London, 1971, pp. 122–3.

13. F. Engels, *The Condition of the Working Class*, in *Marx and Engels on Britain*, Moscow, 1962, pp. 178–9.

14. K. Marx, *Capital*, translated from the third German edition by Samuel Moore and Edward Aveling, vol. I, ed. Dona Torr, London, 1957, p. 495.

15. ibid., p. 496.

16. ibid., p. 496.

17. Marx, *The Holy Family*, p. 31.

18. Marx, 'Peuchet on Suicide', quoted in Hal Draper, 'Marx and Engels on Women's Liberation', *International Socialism*, July/August 1970, p. 22.

19. Engels, *Principles of Communism* (1847, p. 18), quoted in Geiger, *The Family in Soviet Russia*, p. 21.

20. Engels, *The Origin of the Family*, pp. 89–90.

21. The study of the specific position of women in advanced capitalism is coming out of the movement for liberation. Indirectly the analysis Marx has left us of the male worker in capitalist commodity production and his writing on precapitalist economic formations are as relevant as his writing directly on the position of women. See, for example:

    Margaret Benston, 'Political Economy of Women's Liberation', *Monthly Review*, vol. 21, 4 September 1969.

    Linda Gordon, 'Families', *Bread and Roses*, New England Free Press.

    Kathy McAfee and Myrna Wood, 'Bread and Roses', *New England Free Press* and *Agit-Prop*.

    Juliet Mitchell, *Woman's Estate*, Penguin, London, 1971.

    Peggy Morton, 'A Woman's Work is Never Done. Notes on the Family under Capitalism', *Leviathan*, May 1970.

Sue Sharpe, 'The role of the nuclear family in the oppression of women', *New Edinburgh Review*, no. 18, summer 1972.


*Chapter 4*

1. A. Popp, *Autobiography of a Working Woman*, London, 1912, p. 93.
2. A. Bebel, *Women in the Past, Present and Future*, London, 1885, p. 1.
3. ibid., p. 72.
4. ibid., p. 113.
5. ibid., p. 1.
6. ibid., p. 220.
7. E. Marx and E. Aveling, 'The Woman Question, A Socialist Point of View', *Westminster Review*, 1885, vol. VI, no. 25, p. 211. Also published as a pamphlet, 'The Woman Question', London, 1886.
8. ibid., p. 222.
9. William Morris, 'The Society of the Future', quoted in E. P. Thompson, *William Morris, Romantic to Revolutionary*, London, 1955, p. 815.
10. E. Carpenter, *Love's Coming of Age*, p. 113.
11. ibid., p. 61.
12. ibid., p. 63.
13. Edith A. Macduff to Edward Carpenter, 12 May 1894, Carpenter Collection, Sheffield.
14. Louise Bryant, *Six Red Months in Russia*, London, 1919, p. 168.
15. Edward Carpenter, *My Days and Dreams*, London, 1918, p. 229.
16. ibid., p. 231.
17. Olive Schreiner to Havelock Ellis, 23 March 1885, in S. C. Cronwright-Schreiner, *Letters of Olive Schreiner*, London, 1925, p. 65.
18. Quoted in D. L. Hobman, *Olive Schreiner, Her Friends and Times*, London, 1955, p. 85.
19. Cronwright-Schreiner, *Letters of Olive Schreiner*, p. 142.
20. ibid., p. 280.
21. Olive Schreiner, *Woman and Labour*, London, 1911, pp. 201–3.
22. ibid.
23. Quoted in Richard Drinnon, *Rebel in Paradise*, Chicago, 1961, p. 29.
24. Emma Goldman, *Anarchism and Other Essays*, New York, 1910, p. 223.

# Notes

25. ibid., p. 220.
26. ibid., p. 225.
27. ibid., p. 227.
28. ibid., p. 217.
29. See for example Alexandra Kollontai, *Women Workers' Struggle for their Rights*, translated by Celia Britton, The Falling Wall Press, Bristol, 1971.
30. ibid., p. 230.

## Chapter 5

1. A. L. Lloyd, *Folk Song in England*, London, 1967, pp. 190–93.
2. 'The Lass of Islington', V. de Sola Pinto and A. E. Rodway, *The Common Muse*, Penguin edition, London, 1965, p. 569.
3. Lloyd, *Folk Song in England*, p. 226.
4. Nottingham Date Book, quoted by Jo O'Brien, 'Women and Children in Working-Class Life in the Nineteenth Century', unpublished paper given at Women's Liberation Conference, Oxford, February 1970.
5. Quoted in Edith Thomas, *The Women Incendiaries*, London, 1967, p. 31.
6. ibid.
7. ibid., p. 45.
8. ibid., p. 121.
9. ibid.
10. ibid., pp. xi–xii.
11. ibid., pp. 151–2.
12. ibid.
13. Quoted in Aileen S. Kraditor (ed.), *Up From the Pedestal*, Chicago, 1968, pp. 50–52.
14. Quoted in 'Women in History: A Recreation of Our Past', from *Woman, A Journal of Liberation*, spring 1970, p. 16.
15. ibid.
16. Alice Henry, *The Trade Union Woman*, New York, 1915, p. 5.
17. Quoted by O'Brien, 'Women and Children in Working-Class Life in the Nineteenth Century'.
18. Quoted in J. Ramsay MacDonald, *Women in the Printing Trades*, London, 1904, p. 33.
19. Quoted in Ivy Pinchbeck, *Women Workers and the Industrial Revolution, 1750–1850*, London, 1930, p. 199.
20. Quoted in Henry, *The Trade Union Woman*, p. 24.

21. *La Voix des Femmes*, 20 March 1841.
22. ibid., 3 April 1848.
23. ibid., 31 March 1848.
24. Thomas, *The Women Incendiaries*, pp. 79–80.
25. Quoted in Evelyne Sullerot, 'Journaux Feminins et Lutte Ouvrière', in Jacques Godechot (ed.), *La Presse Ouvrière*, 1966, p. 106.
26. Stepniak, *Underground Russia*, London, 1883, p. 23.
27. Quoted in Fannina Halle, *Woman in Soviet Russia*, London, 1933, pp. 42–3.
28. Quoted in I. Steinberg, *Spiridonova – Revolutionary Terrorist*, London, 1935, p. 95.
29. ibid., p. 98.
30. Popp, *Autobiography of a Working Woman*, London, 1912, p. 107.
31. ibid., p. 133.
32. Dora Montefiore, *From a Victorian to a Modern*, p. 65.
33. Georgia Pearce, 'A Russian Exile – Alexandra Kollontai and the Russian Woman Worker', *The Woman Worker*, 19 May 1909, p. 469.
34. Quoted in *McClure's*, October 1910, in Harvey Swados (ed.), *Years of Conscience – The Muckrakers*, New York, 1962.
35. Council of East London Federation, Minute Book, 28 February 1914, Sylvia Pankhurst papers, Amsterdam Institute of Social History.
36. ibid., 27 January 1914.
37. *La Voix des Femmes*, 23 and 28 March 1848.

## Chapter 6

1. L. Trotsky, *Problems of Life*, London, 1924, p. 99.
2. Jessica Smith, *Women in Soviet Russia*, New York, 1928, p. 6.
3. Quoted in R. A. J. Schlesinger, *Changing Attitudes in Soviet Russia: The Family*, London, 1949, p. 328.
4. Smith, *Women in Soviet Russia*, p. 16.
5. ibid., p. 16.
6. ibid., pp. 53–4.
7. ibid., p. 57.
8. Louise Bryant, *Mirrors of Moscow*, New York, 1923, pp. 120–21.
9. Fannina Halle, *Woman in the Soviet East*, London, 1938, p. 181.
10. Schlesinger, *Changing Attitudes in Soviet Russia: The Family*, p. 91.
11. V. I. Lenin, *On the Emancipation of Women*, Moscow, 1967, p. 79.

Notes

12. A. Kollontai, *Communism and the Family*, Plato Press, London, 1971, p. 15.
13. L. Trotsky, *Problems of Life*, London, 1924, p. 48.
14. ibid., pp. 59–60.
15. ibid., p. 68.
16. ibid., p. 94.
17. Quoted in Halle, *Woman in Soviet Russia*, pp. 376–7.
18. See W. Reich, *The Sexual Revolution*, Part II, New York, 1967, pp. 153–269.
19. A. Kollontai, *Free Love*, London, 1932, p. 124.
20. Halle, *Woman in Soviet Russia*, p. 372.
21. Smith, *Woman in Soviet Russia*, p. 1.
22. ibid., p. 56.
23. Trotsky, *Problems of Life*, p. 90.
24. Smith, *Woman in Soviet Russia*, p. 170.
25. Reich, *The Sexual Revolution*, p. 214.
26. Quoted in Geiger, *The Family in Soviet Russia*, p. 59.
27. ibid., p. 59.
28. Quoted in Schlesinger, *Changing Attitudes in Soviet Russia: The Family*, p. 140.
29. ibid., pp. 99–100.
30. Trotsky, *Problems of Life*, p. 45.
31. David and Vera Mace, *The Soviet Family*, London, 1964, p. 68.
32. Reich, *The Sexual Revolution*, p. 173.
33. ibid.
34. Quoted in Geiger, *The Family in Soviet Russia*, p. 66.
35. Lenin, *On the Emancipation of Women*, pp. 105–8.
36. Quoted in Geiger, *The Family in Soviet Russia*, p. 63.
37. Isabel de Palencia, *A. Kollontai*, New York, 1947, p. 146.
38. ibid., p. 142–3.
    The following description of Kollontai's novels originally appeared in 'Alexandra Kollontai: Women's Liberation and Revolutionary Love', by Sheila Rowbotham, *The Spokesman*, summer 1970.
39. Kollontai, *Free Love*, p. 237.
40. ibid., p. 243.
41. De Palencia, *Alexandra Kollontai*, p. 137.
42. Kollontai, *The Revolution of Life and Morals*, in Schlesinger, p. 59.
43. Kollontai, excerpts from *Love of Three Generations*, in Schlesinger, pp. 73–4.
44. De Palencia, *Alexandra Kollontai*, pp. 137, 132, 160–66.
45. Kollontai, *The New Morality and the Working Class*, quoted in Reich, p. 170.

46. Quoted in Geiger, *The Family in Soviet Russia*, p. 86.

47. Schlesinger, *Changing Attitudes in Soviet Russia: The Family*, pp. 186–7.

48. Quoted in Erica Dunn and Judy Klein, 'Women in the Russian Revolution', in *Women: A Journal of Liberation*, summer 1970, pp. 25–6.

49. L. Trotsky, *The Revolution Betrayed*, New York, 1937, pp. 151–2.

50. David and Vera Mace, *The Soviet Family*, p. 101.

51. ibid., p. 90.

52. Geiger, *The Family in Soviet Russia*, p. 130.

53. Isaac Deutscher, *Stalin*, Penguin Books, London, 1966, p. 333.

54. Quoted in Geiger, *The Family in Soviet Russia*, p. 304.

55. *The Times*, 18 December 1966.

56. These statements are based on:
    Geiger, *The Family in Soviet Russia*, pp. 187–93.
    Evelyne Sullerot, *Histoire et Sociologie du Travail Féminin*, Paris, 1958, p. 208.
    N. V. Popova, *The Part Played by Women in Socialist Society*, Moscow, 1967, pp. 28–36.
    A. Didsusenko, *Soviet Children*, Moscow, 1967.
    Ludmilla Pavlova, *Women in My Country*, Novosti Press Agency Publishing House, Moscow.
    Agnes Shackleton, 'Life in Russia Today', in *Peace and Freedom*, November–December 1964.
    Dr John Fry, 'Soviet Health Service', *Guardian*, 19 July 1967.
    Donald Gould, 'Russia's Health Service', *New Statesman*, 9 June 1967.
    Kyril Tidmarsh, 'Russia Plans More Shopping Centres', *The Times*, 14 September 1967.
    Alexander Werth, 'Fifty Years After', *New Statesman*, 29 September 1967.

57. N. V. Popova, op. cit., pp. 11–17.

58. L. Pavlova, *Women in My Country*.

59. Valerie Albert, 'It's the Women who have Saved Russia from Collapse', in *Pulse*, 30 December 1967.

60. Mace, *The Soviet Family*, p. 104.

61. Quoted in Geiger, *The Family in Soviet Russia*, p. 226.

62. Trotsky, *The Revolution Betrayed*, p. 157.

63. Geiger, *The Family in Soviet Russia*, p. 185.

64. Marcelle Bernstein, 'The Hard Hat Girls', *Observer Colour Supplement*, 31 January 1971.

Notes

65. Quoted in Albert, 'It's the Women who have Saved Russia from Collapse'.

*Chapter 7*

1. Helen Foster Snow, *Women in Modern China*, The Netherlands, 1967, p. 46.
2. See Marion J. Levy, *The Family Revolution in Modern China*, Harvard, 1949, pp. 290–338.
3. Fei-ling Davies, 'The Role and Organization of Chinese Secret Societies in the Late Ch'ing', M.Phil. Thesis, London, 1968, pp. 198–200.
4. Ann Zell, 'Early Beginnings of the Development of Working-Class Institutions in China', M.Phil. Thesis, London, 1970, p. 30.
5. Roxane Witke, 'Mao Tse-tung, Women and Suicide in the May Fourth Era', in *China Quarterly*, July–September 1967.
6. ibid., p. 136.
7. ibid., p. 142.
8. ibid., p. 140.
9. Charlotte Bunch-Weeks, 'Asian Women in Revolution', in *Women: A Journal of Liberation*, summer 1970, p. 3.
10. Foster Snow, *Women in Modern China*, p. 203.
11. ibid., p. 216.
12. ibid., p. 205.
13. Quoted in Jo O'Brien, 'On Reading *Birdless Summer*', in *Socialist Woman*, July–August 1969.
    N.B. This section on Han Suyin is based on Jo O'Brien's review.
14. Witke, *Mao Tse-tung, Women and Suicide*, p. 138.
15. Mao Tse-tung, 'Report on an Investigation of the Peasant Movement in Hunan', in *Quotations from Mao Tse-tung*, London, 1967, p. 169.
16. William Hinton, *Fanshen*, New York, 1968, p. 397.
17. ibid., pp. 157–8.
18. Anna Louise Strong, *The Rise of the Chinese People's Communes*, Peking, 1964, p. 64.
19. Jan Myrdal, *Report from a Chinese Village*, London, 1965, pp. 220–22.
20. Leo A. Orleans, 'Evidence from Chinese Medical Journals on Current Population Policy', in *China Quarterly*, no. 40, October–December 1969, p. 142.
21. Myrdal, *Report from a Chinese Village*, pp. 226–7.

22. Joshua Horn, *Away With All Pests*, London, 1969, p. 141.
23. Maud Russell, 'Urban People's Communes in China', *New York Far East Reporter*, pp. 8–9.
24. Simone de Beauvoir, *The Long March*, London, 1958, p. 153.
25. Myrdal, *Report from a Chinese Village*, p. 22.
26. Yang Yun-yu, *Report of the Struggle Between Two Lines at the Moscow World Congress of Women*, Peking, 1963, p. 37.
27. Barbara Mututantri, 'Women in China', in *Eastern Horizon*, vol. 7, no. 7, September–October 1968, p. 50.
28. ibid., p. 46.
29. Dick Anderson, 'Grass Roots Self-Government', *S.A.C.U. News*, (Society for Anglo-Chinese Understanding), March 1969.
30. Roland Berger, 'The Cultural Revolution and the Family', *S.A.C.U. News*, February 1969.
31. Anna Louise Strong, *Letter from China*, no. 46, 29 January 1967.
32. Pei-ku Hung, 'A Girls' Herding Team', in *China Reconstructs*, vol. 18, no. 9, September 1969.
33. 'Throw the Buying-and-Selling Type of Matrimony into the Rubbish Dump of History', in *China in the News*, 11 January 1971, China Reprints 1, S.A.C.U.
34. Quoted by Jo O'Brien, in 'On Reading *Birdless Summer*', *Socialist Woman*, July–August 1969.

## Chapter 8

1. Caliban in *The Tempest*; quoted by O. Mannoni, *Prospero and Caliban*, New York, 1964, p. 76.
2. Esther Boserup, *Woman's Role in Economic Development*, London, 1970, p. 147.
3. Cora Ureede de Stuer, *The Indonesian Woman*, The Hague, 1960, pp. 84–5.
4. Quoted in 'Vietnamese Women', *Vietnamese Studies*, 10, Hanoi, 1966, pp. 8–9.
5. ibid., pp. 17–18.
6. ibid., p. 31.
7. ibid., p. 33.
8. ibid., p. 35.
9. Martha Gellhorn, 'The Vietcong's Peacemaker', *The Times*, 27 January 1969.
10. ibid.,
11. 'Vietnamese Women', *Vietnamese Studies*, p. 40.

12. See Anna Davin, 'Women in Vietnam', *Shrew*, December 1970, pp. 5–8, for an account of this interview. The information which is not in this article comes from notes taken at the meeting.
13. Davin, *Women in Vietnam*, p. 7.
14. ibid.
15. Charlotte Bunch-Weeks, 'Asian Women in Revolution', in *Women, A Journal of Liberation*, summer 1970, p. 9. See also *Off Our Backs*, 26 June 1970.
16. 'Vietnamese Women', p. 53.
17. ibid., p. 54.
18. Jack Woddis, *Ho Chi Minh – Selected Articles and Speeches, 1920–1967*, London, 1969, pp. 129–30.
19. Gellhorn, 'The Vietcong's Peacemaker', *The Times*, 27 January 1969.
20. Alice Wolfson, 'Budapest Journal', in *Off Our Backs*, 14 December 1970, p. 2.
21. ibid.
22. ibid.
23. Bunch-Weeks, 'Asian Women in Revolution', p. 9.
24. Wolfson, 'Budapest Journal', p. 2.
25. ibid.
26. Fidel Castro, 'Women's Liberation: The Revolution within the Revolution', from *The Santa Clara Speech*, 1966, Merit Pamphlet, New York, 1970.
27. Quoted in Chris Camarano, 'Cuban Woman', *Leviathan*, vol. 2, no. 1, May 1970, p. 42.
28. Che Guevara, *Reminiscences of the Cuban Revolutionary War*, London, 1968, pp. 147–8.
29. From notes of the tape recording. For a short account of this meeting see Mary Kennedy, 'Cuban Women', *Shrew*, December 1970, pp. 8–10.
30. Bessie Leigh, 'Woman's Place in Cuba', *Comment*, 22 November 1969, p. 751.
31. Elizabeth Sutherland, *The Youngest Revolution*, London, 1970, p. 175.
32. Castro, 'The Revolution within the Revolution', *Santa Clara Speech*, 1966.
33. Quoted in Leigh, 'Woman's Place in Cuba', p. 750.
34. Sutherland, *The Youngest Revolution*, p. 171.
35. Lee Lockwood, *Castro's Cuba, Cuba's Fidel*, New York, 1965, p. 106.
36. See Sutherland, *The Youngest Revolution*, 'Colony Within the

Colony', and 'Two Weeks on the Isle of Youth', pp. 138–68, and pp. 211–77.

37. ibid., p. 184.
38. Lockwood, *Castro's Cuba, Cuba's Fidel*, p. 107. On the attitude to male homosexuality and its connection to *machismo*, see Tony Harrison, 'Shango the Shaky Fairy', *London Magazine*, April 1970, pp. 5–27.
39. Sutherland, *The Youngest Revolution*, p. 179.
40. ibid., p. 183.
41. Joan Berman, 'Women in Cuba', in *Women: A Journal of Liberation*, vol. 1, no. 4, p. 12.
42. Sutherland, *The Youngest Revolution*, p. 183.
43. ibid., pp. 187–8.
44. ibid.
Since writing this, an article has been translated into English from the March–June 1971 issue of *Casa de las Americas*, a Culson Journal, with the title 'Towards a Science of Liberation'. It shows a concern to work out the theoretical connection between Marxism as a means of understanding capitalist societies and women's liberation.
45. Frantz Fanon, *A Dying Colonialism*, Penguin Books, London, 1970, p. 25.
46. ibid., p. 28.
47. ibid., p. 44.
48. Frantz Fanon, *The Wretched of the Earth*, Penguin Books, London, 1970, pp. 206–7.
49. Fadela m'Rabet, *La Femme Algérienne*, Paris, 1968, p. 15.
50. Fadela m'Rabet, *Les Algériennes*, Paris, 1969, p. 101.
51. Hélène Vandvelde, 'Condition Féminine: L'Emancipation est Freinée par le Conformisme Social', *Le Monde*, 24–5 January 1971.
52. m'Rabet, *Les Algériennes*, p. 106.
53. m'Rabet, *La Femme Algérienne*, p. 61.
54. ibid., p. 70.

# Index

# Index

# Index

# Index

# Index

ative movement; Rousseau; Wollstonecraft

vaginal sponge, 46
Venceremos brigade (Cuba), 226
venereal disease, 33, 65, 191
Verdure, Maria, 118
Versailles, women's march to (1871) 103, 104
Vesuviennes, 123–4
Victorian era, 192; bourgeois *v.* working-class family in, 70–73
Vietnam, 206–20
Vietnamese Women's Union, North: 216, 217; South, *see* Union of Women for Liberation of South Vietnam
Vietnamese Workers' Party, 209, 213, 215–16, 217
*Vindication* (Wollstonecraft), 40–45, 50, 87
Voilquin, Susanne, 53, 54, 120
*La Voix des Femmes*, 117, 119, 120, 121, 122, 130
Voroshilov, K. I., 162

wages (for women workers), 113–114, 115, 116, 117, 121, 130, 147, 149, 165; *see also* industry
Wang Jui-jin, 194
War Communism (U.S.S.R.), 147, 148
West Indies, 200, 202
*The Westminster Review*, 86–7
*What is to be Done?* (Chernychevsky), 79, 124
Wheeler, Anna, 48, 55
'White-Haired Girl' (China), 194–5
Whitehead, Rev. Edward, 16
Whitman, Walt, 89
widows, 19, 176, 178

wife-beating, 25
wife-selling, 173, 197–8
Wild, Hortense, 120
Wobblies (U.S A.), 110
Wolff, Maria, 106
Wolfson, Alice, 219–20
Wollstonecraft, Mary, 40–45, 47, 48, 57, 81
*Woman and Labour* (Schreiner), 95
*Woman and Socialism* (Bebel), 80–84
*Woman in the Nineteenth Century* (Fuller), 56–7
*The Woman Worker*, 128
*Woman's Estate* (Mitchell), 76
*Women in Modern China* (Snow), 174
*Women's Bell*, 179
Women's Day (Russia), 134, 138
women's clubs, 103, 120–23, 143
women's congresses, Soviet, 140, 142, 143
Women's International Democratic Federation, 207; Budapest Conference (1970), 218–19
women's petitions (in seventeenth century), 15–16, 24–5
Women's Rights Convention, Ohio, U.S.A. (1851), 100
'The Women's sharpe revenge' (pamphlet, 1640), 24
Women's Social and Political Union (Britain), 130–31
*Women's Voice* (China), 180
Woodhull, Victoria, 79
Wooler, T. J., 46
Wordsworth, William, 41
Workers' International, Flora Tristan's concept of, 54, 55
Workers' Opposition (Russia), 128

# Index

p. 82.   Possible adapt to "as philosophers" seeing
everyone else's oppression but that of the ♀
among us.

　　　　Conferences on sex discrimination in
　　　　philosophy texts + teaching (content + style)
　　　　　　Statewide.

　　　　Committee pamphlets on sex discrimination.
　　　　　　Sexism + professionalism.

　　　　Conferences on alternatives
　　　　　　preferential hiring
　　　　　　men just to come off it.

Other committees already know something about surveys —
how + how not.

Get the committee going first with some things it <u>can do</u>. — At
least mix in some fairly tangible successable things.